Multihull
Voyaging

By the same author
LOW-RESISTANCE BOATS

Multihull
Voyaging

THOMAS FIRTH JONES

S

SHERIDAN
HOUSE

First published 1994 by
Sheridan House Inc.
145 Palisade Street
Dobbs Ferry, NY 10522

The publisher takes no responsibility for the use of any of the materials or methods described in the book, nor for the products thereof.

Library of Congress Cataloging-in-Publication Data

Jones, Thomas Firth, 1934–
    Multihull voyaging / Thomas Firth Jones.
        p. cm.
    Includes index.
    ISBN 0-924486-56-2 : $27.50
    1. Multihull sailboats. 2. Sailing. I. Title.
GV811.55.J66   1994
796.1′24 — dc20   94-5801
                                                                   CIP

Drawings by the author
Photographs by the author unless otherwise credited

Design by Jeremiah B. Lighter

Printed in the United States of America

ISBN 0-924486-56-2

For Ruth Wharram
and João Carlos Fraga

ACKNOWLEDGEMENT

My thanks to Derek Kelsall who read the manuscript for errors of fact, not opinion. To James Wharram and Vance Buhler for all they have taught me about multihulls. To Lock Crowther who has regrettably died since this book was written. To Tom LaMers, and Tony Smith. To Lothar Simon of Sheridan House for helping me to remember what a book should be. To my wife Carol for help with every phase of this project, from outlining to spelling.

Parts of this book originally appeared in different form in *Multihulls* magazine.

Contents

Introduction

ONE PRETTY MORNING we were sailing our 28-foot trimaran out through the jetties of Cuttyhunk Pond. I was at the tiller, and my wife Carol was up forward, tidying lines. Very gradually we were overtaking a larger monohull motoring out ahead of us. "Why don't we sail?" Carol overheard the wife ask.

"There isn't any wind," her husband said from behind his destroyer wheel.

"That trimaran is sailing," the wife persisted.

"Yeah, but if there was any wind, that trimaran would take off like a bat out of hell."

I'm not sure he was right, but we were tickled to have him think so. All sailboats are slow compared to bats or even to bicycles, because water is so dense and so hard to push through, compared to air. The extra speed that a multihull does get comes from pushing aside less water than a fat, heavy monohull. This extra speed is responsible for the second great wave of popularity that multihulls are now enjoying. It all happened in one week, when millions of televisions showed *Stars and Stripes* in the 1988 America's Cup, walking away from a monohull twice her length. The best joke is this: The defenders of that cup, the real-estate speculators and other entrepreneurs who *had* to keep that cup in San Diego, were the very people who had been lambasting multihulls for so many years.

The first wave rose up 40 years ago, when young men recently home from war in the South Pacific began to build imitations of the native craft they had seen. It was immediately clear that these boats were cheaper, quicker, and more comfortable than conventional single-hulled sailboats. Naturally enough, the people who designed, sold, or owned monohulls did not take kindly to them, and safety was the stick they used to beat the multihull dog. Their arguments never had the least merit, but they were repeated so often and so shrilly that my publisher insists I reply. This I do, grudgingly, in the first chapter.

The rest of the book is devoted to the boats as they are today, and to the voyaging. Glossy photos and advertising blurbs are available from salesmen, so I have not burdened the book with them. Rather, I have tried to show, with my own words and drawings, the various types of multihulls now sailing, and to explain their differences and the thinking that went into designing them. With a few exceptions, the examples discussed are under 35 feet long, because boats bigger than that are usually only suitable for commercial purposes, such as chartering, racing, and corporate entertaining; and because concepts are easier to understand when the examples are smaller and simpler. In discussing the voyaging, I have, whenever possible, relied on our own and our friends' experiences, rather than on accounts published elsewhere. Carol and I have voyaged some 40,000 miles in multihulls, including six Atlantic crossings and hundreds of shorter coastal passages. In port, we have always sought out other multihull sailors, and learned what we could from them.

John Kettlewell, who used to clerk in a nautical bookstore, likes to tell how Walter Greene, stopping in to buy a few books for the slack hours of a long-distance race, would heft them judiciously, assessing their weight as much as their contents. The safety as well as the speed of any boat is compromised by overloading, but on multihulls that happens much quicker. Because they have a small waterplane (a small footprint on the water), adding weight depresses them rapidly. Compared to a monohull, a catamaran is a poor load carrier, and a trimaran is even worse.

If they can be kept light, multihulls are wonderful boats. They can be driven by surprisingly small rigs, and the large deck and the easy motion make handling the rig easier and safer. Voyaging in any boat smaller than an ocean liner is never as comfortable as staying at home; but on a multihull, you can at least eat, sleep, and work the boat from a level platform that pitches little, and rolls even less. Women especially like them: Carol is, if anything, more adamant than I am that a boat with two hulls is the minimum for going to sea. In this book, I hope to show you the security and pleasures of multihull voyaging.

PART

ONE

THE BOATS

1

Safety First

THE NOVICE GRASPS the multihull concept readily. My father-in-law expressed alarm when he learned that Carol and I were about to sail to New England on a 23-foot boat. But when we told him it was a catamaran, he was relieved. "Oh, well . . ." he said, and he held out his two hands as if they were a balance scale. It would be easy enough to demonstrate, mathematically or diagrammatically, what he grasped intuitively: Two or three hulls are three or four times more stable than one hull. Statistically, it is equally easy to show that multihulls are knocked down or turned over very much less often than monohulls. Therefore, if you do not want to be knocked down or rolled over, you should not consider a boat with one hull. It's as simple as that.

Yes, say the monohull sailors, but after you're knocked down or turned over, isn't it better to be in a monohull? It might come back up, they argue (these people are always arguing), if the keel doesn't come off or the cabin isn't stove in, or the hull doesn't fill with water. So it might, but very often one of those three things does happen. At other times, the mast (commonly broken in a knock-down) will bash a hole in the boat, and the ballast will then sink her. I have no experience with turning sailboats over to see what happens next, and little interest in arguing which would be the best boat for such experiments. People who want to go voyaging should get themselves safe boats, and learn how to plan their voyages and handle their boats so that they don't turn over.

For many years, the Coast Guard has required safety inspections for vessels carrying more than six passengers for hire. The rules have never specified how many hulls the vessel may have. This might be oversight or ignorance, but I doubt it. What the rules do require is that the vessel pass a stability test, and if she has sails, her rig must be proportioned to her stability. Also lifejackets and liferafts, fire extinguishers, and quite a list of other gear—though not a motor—are required. (A motor is considered a fire hazard, not a safety feature.) A certain quality of construction is expected, and the vessel is inspected regularly for deterioration.

To my mind, watertight bulkheads are one of the most important Coast Guard requirements for passenger vessels. I can't see why they're less important for yachts. A yacht as stable as a multihull, well sailed on well-planned voyages, is so unlikely to capsize that I'd rather not waste time discussing it. However, any yacht that is sailed far enough is certain to hit debris in the ocean, and perhaps hard enough to hole the hull. Multihulls, which are usually more lightly built, are especially vulnerable; but even tank-like monohulls often spring leaks bigger than bilge pumps can handle. What with whale attacks and other mysteries of the deep, no boat should go far from shore without at least a collision bulkhead forward.

Two half-measures are possible: Some boats have bunks forward, and under the bunks is a sealed compartment, perhaps filled with foam. That's pretty good collision insurance, but won't help much if the boat is holed or springs a leak aft of the bunk. And multihulls are compartmented anyway, especially trimarans; you can take the whole bottom out of the main hull and still sail (though sluggishly) on the buoyancy of the floats. Nevertheless, for greatest safety, all yachts should have watertight bulkheads. They make that forward space less accessible for accommodation, but it's the worst space in the boat, with the most noise and motion in a seaway.

There are honest differences of opinion about the smallest safe size for a voyaging multihull. As waves are the same size and winds the same strength, no matter what size the boat, in theory it seems that the larger boat must be safer. In practice, it isn't so, because the gear gets bigger and harder to handle, and if repairs or other improvisation are required, they may be formidable. Carol and I survived a hurricane, 30 miles from the eye and 300 miles from land, in a catamaran with a 19-foot 3-inch waterline. Her hulls were 1/4-inch plywood, and her beams were two 2x4s each, glued together. If we were to choose a boat to reenact that experience, we'd choose that boat. It's the experience we wouldn't choose again.

The best argument for a big boat is that, so long as the gear can be handled and nothing needs fixing, she will be kinder on her crew than a small boat. The crew will therefore be in better shape—less wet, bruised, and dazed—and therefore better able to keep the boat upright and moving. The counter-argument is that, like a well-corked bottle, a small boat can be tumbled around and survive longer. An ant can be dropped from a 20-foot tower and walk away from it. A cow takes it less well. My own feeling is for the corked bottle, but I'm not adamant about it. It's certainly true that a smaller boat will take longer to complete any given voyage, and therefore is more likely to meet bad weather.

For voyaging safety, multihulls must be longer than monohulls, because they carry weight less well, and the crew and their minimal gear and provisions weigh the same in boats of all configurations. That little catamaran was near minimum size, I'd say, for two people coming home from Bermuda to the East Coast. We had a third person aboard on the way down, but he chose not to return with us, and if he had, the extra weight might have been fatal. A tri, carrying weight less well than a cat, might need to be at least 22 feet on the water to do the same job. James Wharram, who designed our cat, now has an even smaller model with some pretense to accommodation. In one of them a hardy lad has recently sailed from England to New Zealand. Even though a solo sailor can get by with a smaller boat, I'd say that lad was pushing it.

For crossing a whole ocean, a cat should probably be at least 23 feet on the water, and a tri 27 feet, with two crew. A boat not big enough to carry her required payload must depend on good luck with the weather, which means that she isn't really safe. However, it is a mistake to think that any certain weight or length or beam, or a combination of them, is necessary to encounter a known weather force out there in the ocean. The forces of the ocean are not known and if they were, they couldn't be fitted into such an equation. It is certain that at some times, in some places, there have been hurricanes that no yacht and few commercial ships could have survived.

I cannot emphasize too strongly that the safety of a multihull lies in good design and good construction, not in accessories that are added after the boat is built. Good construction requires good materials, unless the boat is planned for a very short life. Good design requires the closest attention to weight; and even in a multihull, the weight's distance above waterline is of some importance. It requires proper volumes in proper places in the hulls, above and below waterline, and proper spacing of the hulls. It requires the greatest care with the connecting structure, particularly where it attaches to the hulls, for these are the points of maximum stress. I find it bizarre to build multihulls that fold or come apart at just these points, but some designers are doing it and getting away with it. It requires that the rig not overpower the boat, as is often done on racers. My father-in-law, with his good intelligence but complete lack of boating knowledge, would have grasped that readily enough. And of course, safety requires good seamanship. All these points will be covered more fully in later chapters.

Now we must turn, however reluctantly, to the capsize issue. The defenders of monohulls, electrified by the speed, comfort, and economy of multihulls, have skewered this red herring on their forks, and conned the multihull people into swallowing it. The editors of *Multihulls* magazine, who are ordinarily sensible people, swallowed it so hard that they published a whole book, some years ago, called *The Capsize Bugaboo*. The title isn't bad, but *The Capsize Red Herring* would have been better.

All fair people will recognize that a multihull is three or four times harder to capsize than a monohull. What some don't realize is that a multihull is a raft, upside down or right side up. A voyaging monohull carries a raft, because it offers the best chance of safety after a collision or holing or capsize. Often, such rafts inflate with tricky triggers and CO_2 cylinders that, even if serviced regularly, do not always work. But a multihull is a raft, and it doesn't require inflation, either.

It is true that when modern monohulls capsize, as they very often do, they sometimes come upright again. The ballast does it. But there are a good many examples among the wide monohulls that the IOR rule did favor, where they have not come up at all quickly. Overturned, they have become almost as stable as upright. Even a narrow, older-style monohull with fixed outside ballast does not necessarily right herself quickly. In *The Saga of Cimba*, my candidate for the best nautical yarn ever written, Richard Maury describes the 180-degree capsize of his Tancook whaler on the way to Bermuda in December. "Why didn't she right herself? Not sure but that she had not foundered, we knew intuitively that the ton of iron on the keel, now up and down above us, was being offset by the weight of the masts, the bulk of her cabin carlings, by the water that was filling her; and underneath, the foresail was acting as a canvas fin, itself a keel of sorts." They had time to put most of the fire out—the stove had spewed its coals onto the cabin ceiling—before another wave finally did right them. Maury had a very sturdy vessel—one of the last small sailboats built in Nova Scotia for the commercial fishery—and he did not lose his rig in his 360-degree entertainment.

An English friend of ours was not so lucky. He was an Interpol agent, singlehanding home from a summer of fraternizing with a crew of hippies in the Azores, to see whether they had drugs aboard their boat. He was a serious man (though you wouldn't have thought so, to see him dancing down the streets of Horta with his friends, playing finger cymbals), and a good sailor. Under him was the epitome of a good modern monohull: a 35-foot Alan Buchanan sloop, with wineglass sections and lots of ballast. She was in tip-top condition, and he had been sailing her on his missions for many years.

He hit a gale that developed into a storm, though it never became a hurricane. He reduced sail prudently, and by the time he was first knocked flat, he had only storm canvas up. Two or three times it happened, and the boat came up again, just like they're supposed to, so he did what he could to pump her out and clean up the mess. The small, sturdy cabin and its portlights did not break, nor did the mast. Finally, he was knocked down hard enough to do a three-sixty. He was below at the time, and he went "right the way round the cabin, leading with my head." This opened up a very wide, deep cut across his whole skull, and when he recovered enough to stagger on deck, he found that his rig was gone.

Now drifting broadside to the sea, he lost interest in housekeeping. He took innumerable other knockdowns, and was rolled once more, I think. Finally he was pitchpoled, as the boat became too laden with water to move away from the seas at all. In the end, he was staggering around the cabin in water up to his crotch, without any hopes or plans whatsoever. It is scarcely credible, but a commercial ship spotted his mastless sloop in the still-raging storm, and managed to come alongside. He was helped aboard by the crew and delivered to the hospital in their next port of call, which was Horta again. João Fraga, who hasn't much patience with Interpol, did relent and visit him there once. He said our friend wasn't too talkative. When I corresponded with him later, he was still defending ballast for safe voyaging.

Whether or not he had a liferaft, I don't know. When he should have deployed it—supposing that it survived the knockdowns, remained aboard, and all the gadgets worked so that it did inflate—I can't guess. But for sure, if he had been on a multihull, even a bad one, he would have *had* a raft. If he had capsized—and that is less likely—it would only have happened once. I've never heard of a capsized multihull that recapsized and righted herself again. The damage would have been done, and it would have been less damage. He would have been floating, and would have continued to float until the storm abated, whether the ship spotted him or not.

I was told of another capsize tale by motorboat designer Dan McCarthy of Stuart, Florida. Friends of his ordered a 48-foot Rudy Choy catamaran, and it was "the most exciting boat to sail that I've ever experienced." However, one day when Dan was not aboard, "just off the inlet in a puffy westerly," the skipper was surfing her, but with his "attention down." A stronger puff caught her, the skipper put the helm the wrong way, and she went over quick. There were three women in the galley making lunch, and two of them had some trouble getting out. As McCarthy later married one of the women, the incident naturally impressed him. Everyone was picked up within minutes by fishing boats, and the catamaran was picked up a week later off Jacksonville, "pretty much undamaged."

Was this worse than being knocked down flat in a monohull? I wasn't there, and couldn't say. Dan, a sensible person, only concluded that if I insisted on sailing a multihull offshore, I shouldn't let my attention down. Thank you, Dan, I don't plan to. It appears that this Choy cat was being used as a big daysailer, which is fine, as long as you know what that involves. For daysailing, Carol and I prefer 8-foot El Toro monohull prams. We race them often, and take every chance we can. We capsize them regularly. But on our voyaging multihulls, we sail more cautiously, as our Interpol friend did on his Buchanan. We do pay attention. We reef when others might surf. We've seen worse weather than he did, and we haven't capsized.

2

Multihull Evolution

ULTIHULL VOYAGING HAS become so elaborate lately that it's good to be reminded how simply it can be done. Pierre LaPlante and his partner Marie departed Québec in May, 1990, on a 17-foot plywood daysailing catamaran he had built the previous winter. Pierre had designed and built the cat's junk-sloop rig. "The St. Lawrence River is still a very wild place to cruise," he says. They were often among whales, and sometimes the white belugas would make a detour to "gam" with them.

They slept in a small tent, either on shore or on the trampoline of the anchored cat. In two months, the 750-mile voyage took them around the Gaspé, down Northumberland Strait, and into the Bras d'Or Lakes of Nova Scotia. The lakes, says Pierre, are protected, but "breathe with the ocean, like an immense mollusk whose insides you are welcome to visit." In Bras d'Or, they disassembled the cat and brought her home on a pick-up truck. After some thought, Pierre began building a main hull to make the cat into a tri. The main hull will have a small cabin.

Carol and I met Pierre and Marie earlier, in 1987 in Horta, when they—like us—were in the middle of their second Atlantic circuit, from North America to Europe, Antilles, and home. They had a 23-foot mono-hull then, and we had our biggest and most elaborate multihull—our 28-foot 6-inch trimaran. We sold the tri on another visit to the Azores, in 1991, and have since gone back to a smaller boat. A bigger boat inevitably is more work to sail, and a more elaborate boat costs more in upkeep, as well as to purchase.

Nevertheless, the modern tendency in voyaging multihulls (as in most other things in our lives) is to greater complexity as well as greater size. This is a result of the great and increasing wealth of yachtsmen, compared to the world's other people, and to the relentless pressure of advertising. It is useful to compare, with drawings and statistics, two catamarans of about the same length, designed 22 years apart:

	Iroquois Mk II	Shuttle Cat 31
YEAR DESIGNED	1969	1991
L.O.A.	30′ 6″	31′ 0″
L.W.L.	26′ 9″	29′ 1″
Beam	13′ 6″	22′ 4″
Spacing of hull centers	9′ 6″	15′ 9″
Sail area	362 sq. ft.	604 sq. ft.
Masthead above water	36′ 3″	50′ 0″
Weight	5600 lbs.	4900 lbs.

Designer John Shuttleworth gives the very important statistic of payload as 2800 pounds. But like too many production boats, the Iroquois nowhere admits her payload. The two boats do have about the same interior volume.

The Iroquois Mk II was a very successful molded-fiberglass production boat, and a version is still being made, though it has been lengthened 18 inches to accommodate 180 horsepower of outboard engines, and they say it doesn't tack. The original version tacked well and sailed well, compared to other production cats of her length and era. She could touch 20 knots in the right conditions, and even today she will run away from a good monohull her length, upwind and down. Her cabin is low enough to give the helmsman a good view forward, and if you sit relaxedly in the bridgedeck saloon, your head does clear the overhead. To achieve all this, the wing deck is only 16 inches above the water, and in some conditions it can pound unmercifully.

The Shuttle Cat is a new design, and at this writing, the first is only just launched. In my building business I have had more than one inquiry about her; it seems likely that a good many will be built, and she may even become a production boat. Her bridgedeck is 27 inches above water, and she should pound less. The big changes—and this typifies the latest voyaging catamarans—are the longer waterline, the much wider hull spacing, and the immense rig.

The long bow overhangs of the Iroquois were designed to give reserve buoyancy. On the Shuttle Cat, a bigger knuckle and a different hull shape make up for some of what is lost in overhangs, but with such a big rig, an alert skipper also is required. The greater hull spacing may make the Shuttle Cat as stable in a beam wind as the Iroquois. Driven hard downwind, at least one Shuttleworth-designed cat has pitchpoled. Perhaps some badly sailed Iroquois have pitchpoled, too. The Shuttleworth was making 20-some knots in a wind of 40-some knots, so the apparent wind wasn't monstrous. But the waves grew bigger, until she was partly blanketed and lost speed in a trough. On the next crest, the wind was more than she could handle.

Like a modern monohull, the Iroquois is driven by the jib, and the main is almost a trailing flap for it. The Shuttle Cat is driven by the main, and the jib is relatively small. The Iroquois, being narrow and heavily built of molded fiberglass, with wingdeck practically out to the bows, has the rigidity to carry a taut luff on a big jib. Despite having a proportionately smaller jib, the Shuttle Cat's jib luff is 9 feet longer, and the sail actually has as many square feet as a 120-percent genoa on an Iroquois. Most of the extra sail area of the Shuttle Cat simply has to go into the main, whose luff will not sag in strong winds. To get the rigidity to carry such jib as she has, she must go to higher-tech materials and more careful engineering.

Molded fiberglass is a wonderful invention. It allows complex parts to be made quickly and repeatedly by ill-paid labor. It is strong, and relatively weather resistant. Improved resins and fabrics have made it even better since the day when the first Iroquois came off the line. Unfortunately it is heavy, and not stiff, which means that flat panels of it tend to flex, unless they are very thick and heavy indeed. This, as well as spray deflection and extra buoyancy, are the reasons for the knuckle in the Iroquois bow. Still, large areas of the Iroquois are heavier than they would need to be if made of another material.

The Shuttle Cat builder can choose to build with Duracore strips, or with PVC foam. In either case, the core is skinned with fiberglass, outside and in, and the resulting structure is lighter. Looking at the two boats, it seems that the Shuttle Cat should be heavier, with the extra beam and big rig. However, her lightness and stiffness cost more; some builders of production multihulls are still turning out their molded boats for $12 a pound. The Shuttle Cat will cost at least twice that. The core materials themselves are expensive, and usually the skins must be hand-finished on both sides. The two hulls and bridgedeck of the Iroquois were popped out of a mold in one piece, with their outside surfaces glistening and perfect, and another mold took care of the decks, cabintop, and cockpit. Perhaps a couple of other moldings were used for the furniture belowdecks, and they hid most of the inner surfaces of the primary moldings. There wasn't much to building the boats, once the tooling was carefully made.

Other features besides construction materials make the Shuttle Cat more expensive. The rig is vastly more expensive, even without the optional rotating wingmast. So is the hardware to handle it. So are the under-hull rudders, compared to the transom-hung rudders of the Iroquois. The

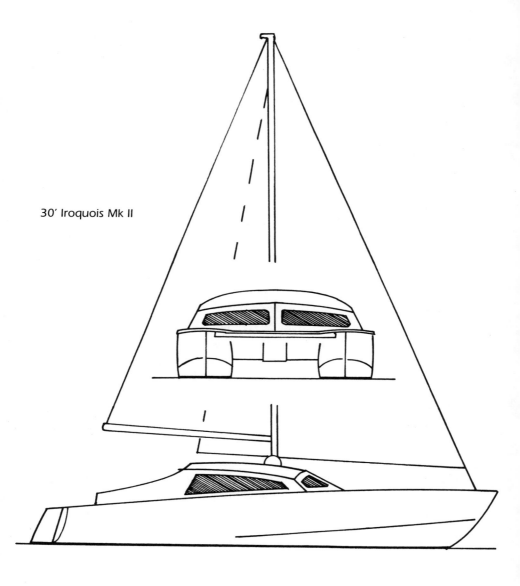

30′ Iroquois Mk II

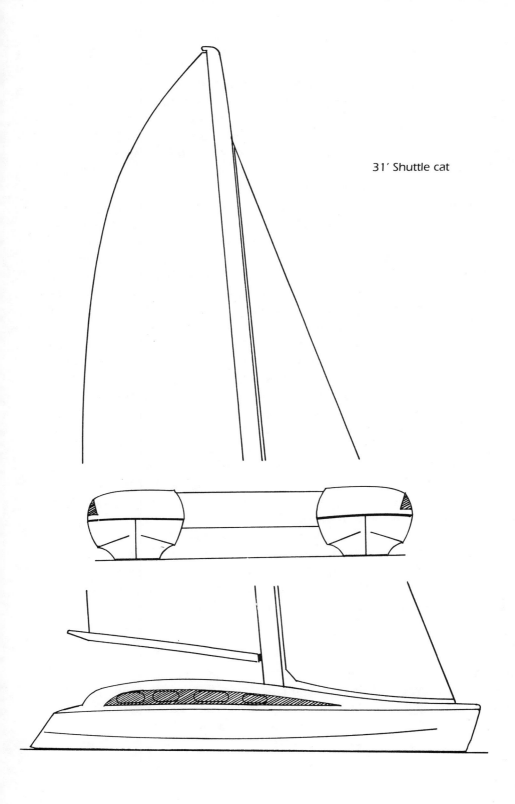

31′ Shuttle cat

Shuttle Cat does have one daggerboard, instead of two pivoting center-boards; this is both cheaper and more efficient. Otherwise she is much more complex and high-tech, and that doesn't come for free.

On a voyage when someone else has paid for the boat, I'd prefer to sail on the Shuttle Cat. The extra speed is not so alluring, because the Iroquois goes fast enough to scare me. Rather, I'd prefer the motion and the arrangement. All cats heel so little that the difference in these two boats is not worth discussing; but in actual movement, in how the boat goes up and down to a beam sea, a catamaran with a wider stance is very much more comfortable to be aboard. Two of our catamarans, *Vireo* and *Dandy*, have waterlines around 23 feet. *Vireo*'s hull spacing is 9 feet, and *Dandy*'s is 11 feet. *Dandy* is incredibly more pleasant in a seaway. Modern cats tend to space their hulls about 50 percent of waterline length apart (Shuttle Cat is somewhat wider, in deference to her huge rig), and this adds as much to comfort as it does to stability.

Arrangement is a more personal matter. Both boats have their bunks in the ends, which is not the most comfortable place for motion. The Shuttle Cat is somewhat worse in this respect. The saloon of the Iroquois would be a nice spot at anchor on a rainy day in harbor, with 360-degree visibility and a chance to mind everyone else's business. The wide knuckle of the Shuttle Cat allows a saloon at least as roomy, aft in the port hull. Windows are smaller, and the starboard hull blocks some of the view. To me, the wonderful open space on the bridgedeck more than makes up. In good weather, both in harbor and at sea, there is no place on any boat as nice as the center deck of a catamaran. The Shuttle Cat has built-in seating. On our boats, we always carry folding aluminum chairs. Take your pick. In harbor, an awning is easily rigged, and at sea my happiest hours always have been spent there, reading or studying the horizon or strolling around to check on the gear and the sail adjustments. I can't think of any structure that could be put on a bridgedeck that would contribute to my pleasure as much as the open deck itself.

*   *   *

Voyaging trimarans have changed less than catamarans, since Arthur Piver designed the first successful one for Jim Brown in 1959. Rigs have become bigger, because Piver had economy on his mind as only the very rich can. That first time, he came near perfection with the proportions. The main changes have been in the placement of the floats, and the shapes of both floats and main hulls.

Throughout the yachting world, Piver catapulted the trimaran into the yachtsmen's consciousness. He was brash and abrasive, and he owned his own publishing company. In America, yachtsmen come from a more conservative element of society than in other countries, and they hated his style as much as his boats. Piver responded with more and more outrageous claims, but most people who bought his plans were not traditional yachtsmen. They were looking for a new challenge after the goat farm had run dry. No building inspector on land would have tolerated the ramshackle structures that they cobbled together for the water, and the hoots of the yachtsmen redoubled. In the midst of it all, in 1968 Piver was lost on a singlehanded voyage down the California coast, on a boat of his own design. That, and the fact that some of the earlier amateur-built boats were already falling apart, seemed to put paid to it.

In England and Australia, Piver's admirers tended to be more knowledgeable and his critics less rabid. Both allowed that improvements could be made, and some of them set about doing it. My profile drawings of a Piver Nimble and a Crowther Buccaneer 28, designed not long after, show what needed to be done. The floats were brought forward, and their centers of buoyancy were brought forward even more. On *Nimble 1*, the 30-footer on which Piver made the first successful trimaran crossing of the Atlantic, the float centers at waterline are 15 feet 4 inches apart, or nearly as far apart as the hull centers of the Shuttle Cat. But they don't have much volume forward, and multihulls do not usually capsize like a monohull, to the side or to the bow. Rather, when driven too hard, they usually capsize in a kind of cartwheel, on an angle more or less 45 degrees to their own axis. The bow of the lee float or hull digs in, and the stern of the windward one goes up. Some trimarans have been designed with floats extending several feet forward of the main hull bow to get more buoyancy out to the leeward forward corner. This isn't necessary.

Another problem with Piver's floats was that, at rest, too much of them was immersed. Skin friction or wetted surface is always a source of resistance, and in light air it is the main source. The reason most tris are faster than most cats is that they have less skin friction. Piver's didn't. Some tris have been built which, at rest and perfectly balanced, have floats many inches out of the water. The consensus now is to have floats that are immersed only a couple of inches when the boat is at rest. Once

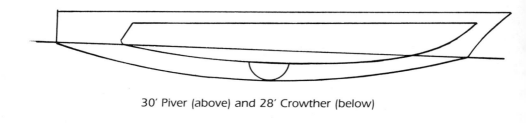

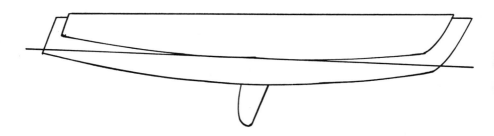

30' Piver (above) and 28' Crowther (below)

moving, and heeled to even a light wind, the windward float comes out, and causes no resistance at all.

A catamaran is easier understood than a trimaran, because it is just two boats tied together and going along together, for lack of other possibilities. But a float is a different thing, a kind of trainer wheel on a single-hulled boat, and there have been numerous ideas about what its shape and function should be. For a while, some designers thought that a low-buoyancy float (a float that would submerge before it had taken the weight of the whole boat) would weigh less, offer less resistance and windage, and give a clearer warning when sails needed reefing. Today such floats aren't seen, except when their low volume is needed for folding and trailering. Most trimaran floats have a different shape, but about the same total volume as Piver's boats—about 150 percent of what is needed to float the whole boat. Experiments have also been made with floats that are flat on the bottom, or hollow on the outer side, in attempts to generate "dynamic lift" or to prevent leeway. To some extent, both ideas do work, but not well enough to compensate for the jarring that they impart to the connecting structure, and to the occupants of the main hull.

The sectional drawing shows the Piver Nimble and a generic modern trimaran of the same 30 feet by 18 feet. Notice that, in addition to creating less drag through the water, the modern float shapes give the boat a 1-foot wider stance for the same overall beam. Very nearly the same shapes can be had with chines and plywood construction.

Piver's main hull shape was a 90-degree V—easier to build than to push through the water. The wetted surface was 10 percent greater than the rounded bottom, and the hull was 4 feet wide on waterline, giving a length-to-beam ratio of only 6.75. The rule of thumb is that multihull hulls should be at least 8-to-1, but some of us think that 9-to-1 is better still. Clearly Piver's hull has more interior volume, and would be a nicer habitation in port. By the time the goatherds filled this space with their refrigerators, dalmatians, and chain saws, and built a pilot house on top of Piver's cabin to hold even more stuff, many a Nimble sat six inches below her marks.

In the early 1960s, these boats were a-building near every waterfront in America, but especially in Florida and in California, where Trimaran City invited amateurs to hack them out. No doubt some well-built boats came from there, and from other yards, too. Good or bad, they fared forth

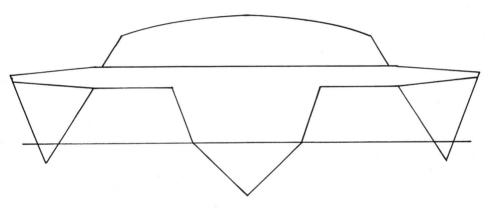

Piver Nimble (above) and generic modern trimaran (below)

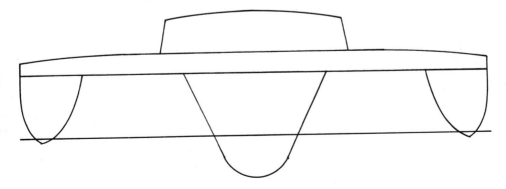

to the Med, the Caribbean, the South Seas. American boating never had an exodus to equal it, and never will again. Most of the tris that got finished (and a good many did not) got their owners where they wanted to go, and their safety record was excellent, despite bad shapes, pinch-penny building, and overloading. It was the money saved in the materials list, and their builders' confident disregard of standard boatbuilding procedures (*not* any bad thing about the designs) that made so many of these Piver tris hulks within 10 years. In 1982, Carol and I visited a trimaran graveyard, disguised as a boatyard, in a northern corner of San Francisco Bay. It was spooky, but some of those boats had voyaged far.

3

Speed, Comfort, and Economy:

A Compromise

THOUGH MULTIHULLS are faster, cheaper, and more comfortable than monohulls, they aren't perfected yet. It is still necessary to compromise these three supremely desirable qualities. Dick Newick used to say that you could have any two, but not all three. I'd say that if you want to go to the limit with any one of them, you must inevitably give up the other two. A really fast boat will be neither comfortable nor cheap, and so on. Most of us prefer a compromise, however, to suit the kind of sailing we like to do. The best way to understand the dilemma is to look at three successful boats which offer, in fairly extreme form, one of these three qualities.

The Gemini 32 is a production boat built in Mayo, Maryland, by everyone's favorite salesman, Tony Smith. Gemini is a very old design, but Tony is a good builder, as well as a good talker, and over the years he has improved the boat's structure and performance. However, he has concentrated hardest on improving her comfort, and today the Gemini is almost like an apartment. She has three private double staterooms, and can sleep more on the rearranged dinette. She has a complete bathroom and kitchen, and closets and cabinets everywhere. She has a light, pleasant feeling below, and you move easily from one space to the next. It's hard to think how more comfort could be packed into a 32-foot sailboat. What is more, the Gemini is not a bad sailer, and her price is reasonable for what you get. The problem is, how to make her faster or cheaper, without sacrificing some of the comfort.

Believe me, Tony has thought about it. Every time I've talked with him, he's been full of ideas on this very subject, and that's the reason he has been the largest builder of cruising multihulls in America for many years. Even appearance, on which many builders and designers waste a lot

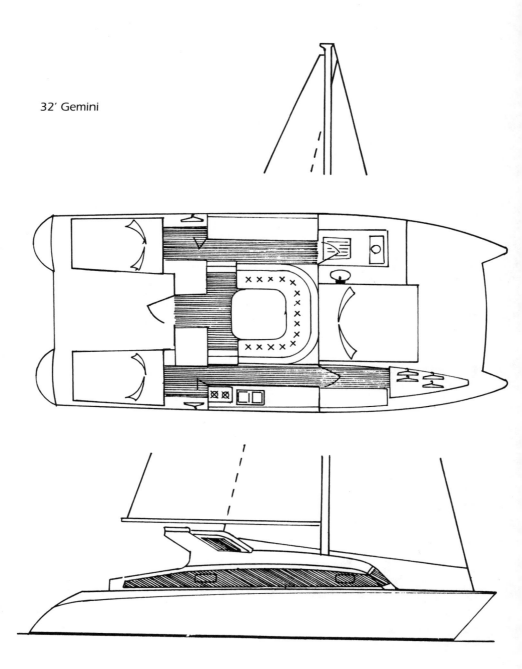

32′ Gemini

of money, has not led him far astray. How much could you save, really, by taking off that wraparound piece of tinted Plexiglas that makes the boat look up to date? And what after that?

Geminis have safely crossed oceans. Of the 300 Tony has built, only two have capsized, and he credits both to skipper incompetence. In one case, three boats left a Texas port together, but two skippers soon turned back, realizing that the weather was bad and getting worse. The third continued, motoring into the rising gale with full main up and most of the genoa still unrolled. No boat is foolproof.

The 31-foot Val trimaran was designed by Dick Newick for the 1976 OSTAR. Several were entered and *The Third Turtle*, skippered by Mike Birch, finished second overall, for the best small-boat performance ever achieved in a long-distance race. A number of Vals were built, and some are still being raced. It takes a tough crew. Access to the aft cabin is through a rat hole, and to the forward one through a manhole. In the forward bunk, you would need to sleep with your legs crossed. The furniture consists of floorboards, a portable toilet, and in the aft cabin a berth bottom of stretched fabric. There's a portlight only in the aft cabin, and no ventilation in either one. Outboard of the cockpit, the helmsman sits in a wet, hammock-like fabric seat, and steers the boat with a Toonerville trolley-style wheel, whose vertical shaft neatly bisects the rat hole. To reach the wheel from the seat, he needs arms four feet long. Oh well, she wasn't built for comfort.

What Newick had in mind was speed at a reasonable price. The speed he did get, and the price wasn't too bad. It could have been more reasonable, if Dick hadn't been so preoccupied with looks. He has a very advanced case of aesthete's eye. Once, when we were sitting on a terrace overlooking Vineyard Haven, our venerable host said to Dick, "You're a trimaran designer. What do you think of that one out there?" He pointed to our *Hummingbird*.

"Oh, that's just a Crowther," said Dick scathingly.

"Thank you very much," said Carol.

The Vals have crossed many oceans, but their safety record is bad. Many have capsized, some more than once, but "the price of speed is accidents," according to Dick. He is absolutely right. All boats designed exclusively for speed have bad safety records, especially if they are small. Voyaging, a small boat can reduce sail earlier, and be as safe as any. A small boat that is trying to keep up with a big boat carries sail far too long. Two attractive young Australians built a Crowther tri about the size of a Val, and campaigned her in a number of major races. They capsized three times; the last time they had to abandon her. Although speed will get you

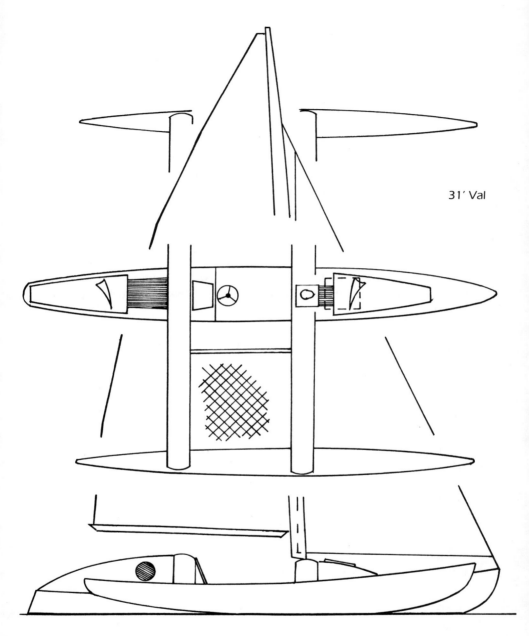

31′ Val

there faster, giving you fewer weather fronts to handle, each front will pose a greater risk than if you had been proceeding more sedately.

How could the comfort of a Val be increased, or how could the price be lowered, without compromising speed? Clearly looks, and especially those beams, is some of what you're paying for. But after that? Would you take the battens out of the main, and make the leech straight? Would you add wings to the main hull, and put bunks in there? That's what finally happened, and the price rose dramatically.

Part of what Dick Newick knows about multihulls he learned from James Wharram. In 1959, Jim and Ruth arrived in St. Thomas, on the homeward leg of the first Atlantic circuit by catamaran. It took Wharram two boats and four years, but his running account of the voyage in *The Rudder* made him a famous sailor, and Newick came up from St. Croix to learn all he could. The Wharrams fed him, took him sailing, and Jim did his best to answer Dick's questions.

James Wharram's book, *Two Girls*, *Two Catamarans*, was put together from those *Rudder* articles. *Rongo*, the boat he built in Trinidad, was the prototype of all his later designs. Wharram has always emphasized safety, followed by simplicity and economy of building, and his Tane is a fairly extreme example.

Tane is a bit shorter than Gemini or Val, and shorter is usually better when economy is the aim. A boat's volume, and therefore its cost, tend to increase with the cube of length. She is built of plywood, which is the cheapest boatbuilding material. I believe it is also the best. Her beams are nothing more than 4x4s. Her mast is also solid wood. She could hardly be simpler, except that Wharram, too, is very concerned with appearance. (Newick may have picked this up from him.)

Tane has a bulwark whose purpose is to conceal the ends of the beams when the boat is seen from the side. *Two Rabbits*, the first voyaging multihull that Carol and I built, was a later Wharram design, a shortened version of Tane with about the same accommodation. By dispensing with the bulwarks and raising the freeboard to bulwark height, we may not have improved the looks, but we vastly increased the interior volume, at no cost in weight, time, or materials. To celebrate our liberation from aesthetics, we let the beam ends stick out a couple of inches past the sheer. They served us well when jousting with quarrelsome docks.

Tane's comforts will hardly compare with Gemini's, but they are better than Val's. The two bunks are amidships, where there is less motion, and they are wide enough to sleep in. Meals can be cooked. The side-opening hatches do have washboards, so going below is not a gymnastic stunt. They will let in some spray, though not as much as forward-opening hatches. The aft side of a cabin is the *only* sensible place for a main hatch on any yacht. The best reason for not having an aft cabin is the water the hatch will take in.

Hundreds of Tanes have been built. For a few years, Arthur Piver sold plans hand over fist, but sales fizzled with his death. Over the decades, James Wharram has been the most successful salesman of multihull plans. Mass-produced boats have yet to equal the mass appeal of home-built multihulls, except of course in daysailers like Hobie Cats. In the next few years, that is likely to change. Slowly but steadily, Tony Smith is increasing his share of the American cruising-boat market. The Farrier-designed trailerable trimarans, discussed in the next chapter, are the biggest marine-marketing success of the last five years. And one by one, the monohull builders are adding catamarans to their lines. The monohull market is saturated, and used ones are so cheap that new ones are almost impossible to sell. To stay in business, these builders must switch to multihulls.

The Tane is not a slow boat, despite her low rig. Notice that the Val rig is also lower than Gemini's. But Tane and Val weigh less than 2000 pounds, while Gemini weighs 7000. A Gemini has been clocked at 17 knots (with all sheets hand-held), and a Tane could certainly equal that, though a Val might do 30. Tane has no leeway prevention beyond the V-shape hulls, but she has very little windage. Upwind against a Gemini, I'd bet on her. Val would get to weather twice as fast as either of them.

Like all Wharram designs, Tane has a wonderful safety record. Peter Sheard, the first person to sail one transatlantic, had both hulls stove in when a curious (or perhaps amorous) whale swam between them, not many days out from the Canaries. However, the boat had watertight bulkheads under the first and fourth beams, so she floated low, but she still floated. Sheard was able to sail back to the Canaries, repair the boat, and complete the crossing. Many other Tanes have made long voyages. The only one I know of that ever capsized did so when the crew left the hatches of the leeward hull open, until it was full and sailed right under. Rumor is that the boat, returning from France to England, was heavy with hooch, and the crew had been sampling the cargo.

A table may help sum up the qualities of these three boats. Where possible, the numbers are those given by the designer or builder. The others are my own best estimates, but they are not far wrong.

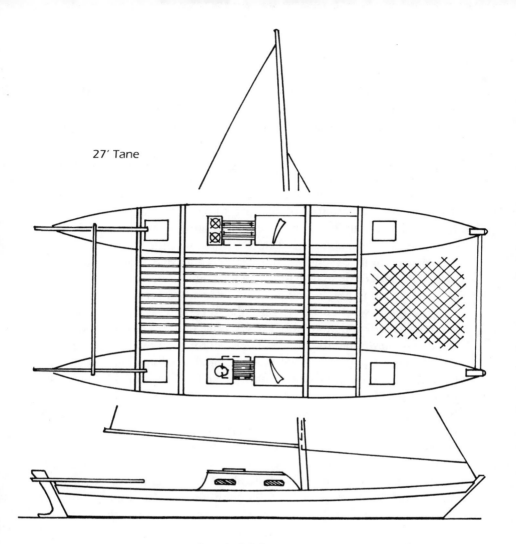

27' Tane

	Gemini 32	**Val**	**Tane**
L.O.A.	32'	31'	27'6"
Beam	14'	25'	12'6"
Sail area	460 sq. ft.	452 sq. ft.	225 sq. ft.
Weight	7000 lbs.	1900 lbs.	1600 lbs.
Payload	3000 lbs.	900 lbs.	1500 lbs.
Likely 24-Hour average	110 mi.	150 mi.	110 mi.
Interior volume	1200 cu. ft.	170 cu. ft.	130 cu. ft.
Professionally built sailaway cost (1993)	$83,000	$70,000	$20,000

Newick was building his Vals in Martha's Vineyard, and Wharram was selling his Tane plans in England. Eventually, their customers revolted, and demanded more comfort at whatever cost. Newick's solution was a "wing-aka Val," which translates to a more conventional-looking trimaran, with cockpit aft and bunks on the wingdeck. He figured this raised the weight by 300 pounds, or 16 percent (and reduced payload to 600 pounds). However, it increased the skin area of the boat by more than 16 percent, so each square foot of skin had to be lighter than before, requiring a higher tech laminate, and more than doubling the price of the boat. From being a reasonably priced racing trimaran with a real shot at winning, she became expensive and less competitive. Dick could have widened the hulls a bit to take the extra load, but he already had the molds. The cost of tooling has an immense effect on fiberglass boat design.

Wharram's solution was to raise the freeboard of Tane 8 inches, and spread the accommodation farther out into the ends. I know this boat pretty well, having drafted the plywood version for the Wharrams. *Vireo*, our own second voyaging multihull, is a modification. The hulls were widened slightly, but the extra weight pushed the Tane shape farther down into the water. For reasons that are not clear even to Jim, his boats have always tolerated overloading better than most multihulls. Weight increased almost 50 percent, and building cost went up in proportion. To drive her, Wharram gave Tanenui a 310-square-foot cutter rig.

Although each of these three boats show either the comfort, speed, or economy that a voyaging multihull about this length can have, other designs have attempted a more even compromise of the three qualities. The Tanenui, for example, may cost more than a Tane, but she is still not an expensive boat. Interior volume has more than doubled, and two people can sit comfortably facing each other with a table between. With her higher freeboard, she is drier, and the Wharrams think she is faster, too.

Two of my own solutions to the compromise are shown in the appendix. On *Vireo* we widened the Wharram V-hull to give two double bunks closer to amidships, instead of four singles nearer the ends. Four people could just about fit into the dinette, so we could invite other couples that we met aboard for dinner. With her simpler rig, she probably cost less than a Tanenui, and Ruth Wharram, who sailed her transatlantic with us, thought she moved as well. Our fatter hulls were still 12-to-1 on waterline, and our wetted surface was less.

Hummingbird, the first voyaging multihull that I designed, was launched 10 years ago. She has about 400 cubic feet of accommodation,

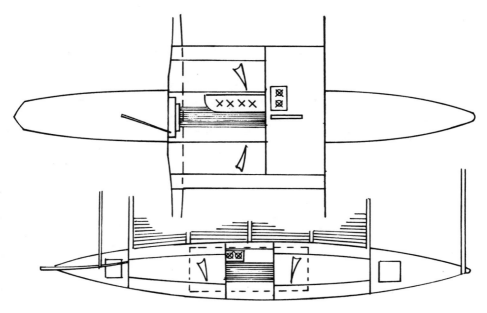

Wing-aka Val (above) and Tanenui (below)

and a comfortable arrangement for four diners or two sleepers, though the bunk for a third crew is a nasty space, with only 2 feet of headroom. With only 1200 pounds payload, she can't take three people on a long voyage, anyway. She cost perhaps 20 percent more than a Tanenui, because her rig is bigger, and like all trimarans, she has more skin than a cat. We never thought that her top speed was higher than *Vireo*'s, but perhaps we pushed her less hard because we were older and smarter. Her present Azorean owner, João Fraga's brother José, is young and very interested in speed, and he has just bought an electronic knotmeter, so we may have numbers soon. She averaged 125 miles a day on ocean passages, and she was especially good in light air and to windward.

These three boats—Tanenui, *Vireo*, and *Hummingbird*—are all built of plywood, which has a bad reputation these days, because too many thrifty builders use bad plywood, and that includes mass-production professionals at least as much as amateurs. I've never seen any but the cheapest plywood go into the transom of a fiberglass outboard runabout. Skin area varies with the design, but *Hummingbird* has about a thousand square feet. The square foot cost for materials in 1993 is about 80 cents for exterior-grade plywood, $3 for the finest African marine mahogany plywood, $8 for foam sandwich, and $12 for Duracore. Labor time is nearly the same for all of them. Other methods, such as cold-molding, are much more time consuming.

Labor on a mass-produced fiberglass multihull, built in a mold, is a good deal less, and materials are not too expensive, either. However, in most cases these savings are eaten up by the cost of shipping, promotion, and salesmen's commissions. In addition, the skipper who buys a mass-produced boat can only choose among the models on the market the one that comes closest to his own desired compromise of speed, comfort, and economy. Shopping must be his substitute for thinking. As multihull popularity grows, more models become available; but as they follow fashions, they are not as different from each other as one might hope.

4

Trailerability:

An Added Complication

TWENTY-FIVE YEARS ago, the fashion in multihulls was for space, as in the many home-built trimarans (most of them designed by Piver), and in the mass-produced catamarans, of which Iroquois and Gemini are good examples. Today, the fashion grows for trailerability, and many reasons are given. A customer once told Derek Kelsall he wanted trailerability because, if a nuclear holocaust closed the Panama Canal, he'd like to be able to trailer across the isthmus.

How to arrange it? "Well," said Kelsall, "you could cut the boat in half with a chain saw and glass it back together on the other side." More commonly, people want to trailer their multihulls because they want to save money on yard and slip fees, or because they do not have the patience (always referred to as "time") to sail the boat where they want to go. They don't see why trailerability should cost them anything in speed, comfort, or economy.

On a very small boat, it need not. The drawing shows the 16-foot Duet, designed by Bernard Rhodes. She has a beam of less than 8 feet, so nothing except the mast needs to fold to get her on a trailer. However, the trailer would have to be very narrow—or the load very high—with the deepest part of the hulls over the fenders. Naturally, her accommodation is limited—a bunk in each hull, and a stove under an open-backed cuddy on the bridgedeck. A 16-foot trailerable monohull wouldn't have much more.

I'm not sure that a cruising multihull this small is faster or drier or has a better motion than a monohull the same size. When Rhodes designed Duet 10 years ago, he wrote an article about her for *Multihulls* magazine. Much of it was devoted to righting her after a capsize. With the help of a masthead float, he was able to manage it himself, at least in flat water. However, the rule of thumb that the centerlines of a cat's hulls should be at least half the waterline length apart best applies to medium-sized cats, about 30 feet long. Bigger voyaging cats can get away with less, and smaller ones probably need more.

16′ Duet

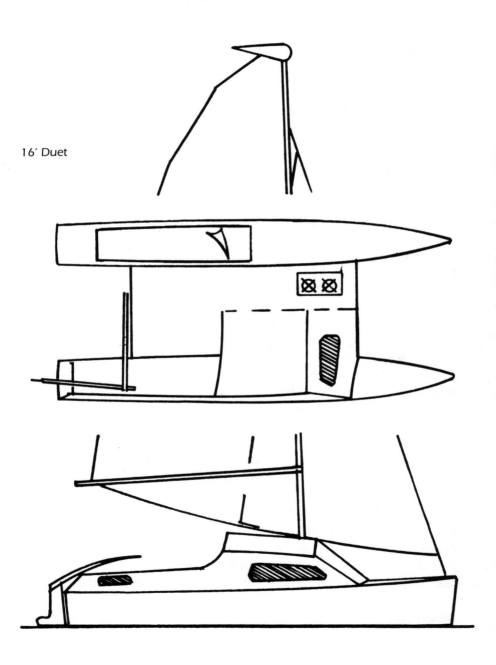

Weekender, my own effort in this direction, takes advantage of the new laws that allow 8-foot 6-inch trailering width, to gain a precious 6 inches more beam. Hulls are 18 feet long, and the skimpy accommodation is entirely within them, with an open wing deck made from a single 4x8 sheet of plywood. Though she has a somewhat wider stance than Duet, and somewhat less sail, lower down, the math suggests that Weekender could still capsize with the sails sheeted flat and 22 knots of wind on the beam. Duet could manage it in 18-1/2 knots. Most designers agree that a voyaging multihull should withstand 30 knots, or about twice the wind pressure of 22 knots, before losing stability in these conditions.

The latest and certainly the bravest effort to make a trailerable multihull that does not have to fold or come apart is a 32-footer designed and built by the Gougeon Brothers. Narrow hull spacing and a high aspect-ratio rig make her an improbable-looking package, but in addition to her 1100-pound weight, she can take on 1200 pounds of water ballast. In that condition, with 500 pounds of people and stores aboard, she would be stable to 21-knot wind. With crew to windward, that number rises slightly, as it does with all these narrow cats.

The Gougeon 32 can also be righted with the help of a masthead float, but whereas Rhodes righted Duet by getting out on the bottom and yanking on a line, in Hobie Cat style, the Gougeon is righted by adjusting the shrouds with special tackles. This should bring the upper hull down more gently than on the Hobies or Duet, which are always in danger of continuing over and capsizing on the other side, as we have all enjoyed doing with Sunfish. The Gougeons even claim that you can stay dry while capsizing and re-righting your 32, but they are an optimistic pair.

With the same tackles, the 32 mast is cranked up to the vertical again, after the hull is righted. The boat costs no more than a Tanenui, and in many conditions she may be as fast as a Val. Her accommodation is tiny, "like a kayak you can sleep in," says her designer, Jan Gougeon. At this writing, 10 boats have been built, and more are planned. I wish the Gougeons luck with this interesting project, and certainly they are to be admired for trying to build and sell a boat that follows no fashion. But I think that, like Wharram and Newick, they may face a customer revolt, with a demand for more comfort at whatever cost.

The majority of multihull trailer sailors want more accommodation than the Gougeon 32 has, and to get it their boats must somehow fold or come apart. This is not a new idea. Piver's earliest trimarans were daysailers, and they folded readily for trailering. The 24-foot Nugget, his first voyaging tri, also folded, as shown in the left drawing (p. 35), with the floats flipping up to narrow the boat to 8 feet. Compared to modern trimarans, strains on Nugget were low, because the rig was small. The 4x4 beams were hinged with ordinary barn-door hinges, though even the economy-minded Piver did recommend springing for the galvanized ones. Obviously the boat could not be folded until it was on the trailer, but not much was sacrificed in speed, comfort, or economy to gain trailerability.

Jim Brown and Norman Cross, two early Piver disciples who later developed their own lines of trimarans, decided that the floats had better fold down, rather than up. This allowed their cabins to be wider than

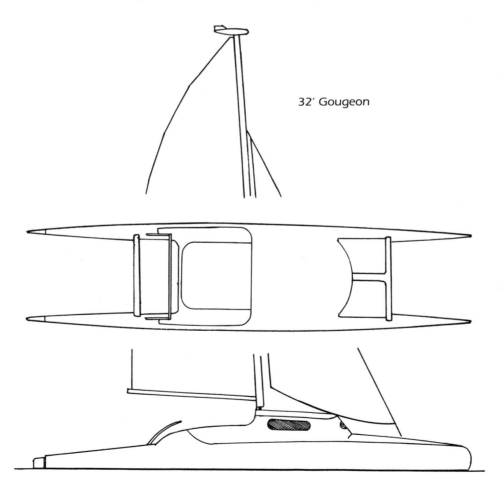

32′ Gougeon

Nugget's, but the boats still had to be taken out of the water on the trailer before they could be folded. These boats were higher stressed, with bigger rigs, and they didn't use barn-door hinges for hardware, so trailerability did increase their cost significantly, and the Brown (I haven't examined a folding Cross) was certainly heavier than it need have been, if built monocoque. When Brown came to designing a 31-footer for trailering, he couldn't figure out how to get all the parts on one trailer. It could be built inland and assembled at the coast, but he said flatly, "A 30-footer is just too big to pack around the highway." Like the rest of us, he had a surprise coming.

Modern trimarans fold in more complex ways. At present, the Farrier system is attracting the most attention. Ian Farrier, a New Zealand designer now living in America, thought it out and patented it many years ago, then applied it to a range of plywood trimarans, for which he sold plans. They were complex and crowded little boats. The 18-foot Trailertri could sleep five, and had a galley with stove and sink. She weighed 1700 pounds with a payload of 1000 pounds, so a fat main hull was needed to take the weight, and a big rig was needed to drive her.

The beams were not hinged. Each one had two triangular aluminum struts, the beam rising up as the float came inward. The float was always touching the water, so the boat could be folded or unfolded while afloat. When sailing, the struts took the strain, though Farrier claims that the beams themselves were strong enough for the load, if the struts ever failed. In fact, I have never heard of a hull-connection failure in a Farrier tri.

Well, it sounds wonderful, doesn't it? If trailerability comes so easily, why not have it? It might be handy sometime. The answer is that the folding mechanism, with its aluminum A-frames, nylon bushings, and stainless-steel pins, is extremely high-tech and expensive, and must be installed much more precisely than the rest of the boat is built. A photo of a Trailertri shows the boat looking like a neat piece of backyard carpentry, and the beam connections looking like parts of a jet fighter. In his literature, Farrier likens these parts of his boats to aircraft parts.

Though Farrier continues to sell his Trailertri plans, he has recently introduced a new series of larger, more complex, and more expensive trimarans, the F-25A and F-9A. For these boats, the folding mechanisms are bought along with the plans, because Farrier has recognized that they are too complex and precise for even the best amateur craftsman to make. The best quote I've heard is $10,000; it doesn't seem to vary with boat size.

Two other Farrier folding trimarans are currently mass-produced in America—the F-24 and F-27. Certainly, it makes more sense to buy one of these boats than to build one yourself, because every surface of these new Farriers, above water as well as below, is a compound curve, that can be popped out of a mold cheaply enough, but that takes a great deal of labor and expensive materials to build by hand. Recently I was asked to quote on building an F-25A, and had to tell the customer that it would cost more than the larger, mass-produced F-27. Whichever manufactured Farrier you buy, the $10,000 beams are included in the price, and if you don't trailer the boat, you have wasted your money.

Another thought haunts me about these folding trimarans, and not just the Farriers: If the float is to fold up beside the hull, then the float size and shape are no longer controlled by what is best or safest in the water, but rather by what will fit onto a trailer. The larger the boat, the more acute the problem becomes. The right-hand drawing shows the F-9A, a gigantic 31-footer that folds to trailerable width. Drawing this design must have been much like solving a three-dimensional jigsaw puzzle, and Farrier's skill is to be admired. We know that it makes the boat expensive, but we don't know what else has been sacrificed, in speed or comfort or safety, to make the boat roadworthy as well as seaworthy. My own opinion, from watching many F-27s under sail, is that the floats are too small.

There's no doubt it's a good boat. In Horta in 1991, we met two young Germans who had bought one in America and were sailing her home. In New England races, the F-27 is rated about a minute a mile faster than an Iroquois, and they often do better than that. But they sail at a very great angle of heel for a trimaran, and in strong winds they can easily put a whole float right under. The crew must brace themselves against sliding down to leeward, as if on a monohull. The boats are wet, and I fear they are capsizable, though I don't know a single instance of it.

A more usual way to fold up a trimaran that is still in the water is to arrange the beams so that the floats swing aft, again winding up under the cabin overhang. Each of the four beams must have a pivot connection at the main hull, and another at the float. Usually, a cable goes from the float to the main hull bow. When it is released, the float swings aft and inboard. The system was first put into production by 505-designer John Westall on the Ocean Bird tri that came out in England when Pivermania was at its height. Today these beams with horizontal pivots are used by Dragonfly and several other production builders. The problem is the same as with the Farrier system: The need to make a package less than 8-1/2 feet wide

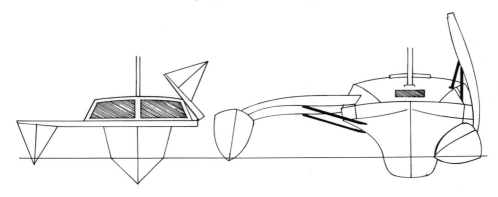

determines the shape of the hulls, and especially the floats. Again, the problem becomes worse as the size of the boat increases. And the folding mechanism inevitably increases the cost of the boat, though it's hard to say by how much.

Voyaging catamarans seem to adapt less well to trailers than do tris. The simplest way is to take the boat apart and put the pieces on the trailer. James Wharram's new Coastal Trek line trailers that way, and for the Tiki 21, it may not work too badly. Wharram has sold over 1000 sets of plans for this design, and each hull is supposed to weigh only 200 pounds, if all gear and personal possessions are removed. With a dolly and a couple of friends, one can imagine doing it. But Tiki 21 has no more interior volume than Duet, Weekender, or the Gougeon 32.

I doubt that Wharram would have designed the boat any differently, if it hadn't been meant to trailer; and so no speed, comfort, economy, or safety have been sacrificed to trailering. All his designs—even the new 63-footer—are demountable, which means that the hulls and beams are connected with bolts or lashings, not glue or fiberglass or welds. Many of them have been built far inland, taken to the shore, and assembled. Few are ever taken apart again, though they certainly could be.

The next size up, the Tiki 26, has a great deal more interior volume than the 21. One 26 was the smallest boat entered in the 1992 OSTAR, and with a very tough skipper, she got to Newport ahead of a dozen other finishers. I'm afraid that trailering her would be almost as big a project as crossing an ocean in her. A sketch in the Wharram catalog shows two nice youngsters who, with the help of a dolly, have hoisted the two 430-pound hulls onto a trailer—and from a sandy beach, some distance from the water! For some reason, they are still smiling. The sketch does not show where the connecting beams, spars, trampolines, and nets will go, nor what has become of the stove, mattresses, anchors, and other gear. If you're a real masochist, Wharram also sells plans for a trailerable 31-footer.

In America, three serious efforts have been made to produce a trailerable voyaging catamaran—the Stiletto, the Sea Wind, and the MacGregor. Several hundred of each were produced, but for reasons that may have nothing to do with the quality of the designs, none is now in production. Tom LaMers, a designer especially interested in folding catamarans, currently owns a Sea Wind 24, and has clarified my understanding of all of them.

The Stiletto was a very sophisticated boat. The hulls were built of Nomex core, a kind of high-class corrugated cardboard, with thin fiberglass skin outside and in, pre-impregnated with resin, which catalyzed when the whole thing was put into an oven. Skin weight was far less than the one pound per square foot that is usually considered minimal for voyaging boats. In fact, the 27, the most popular of several sizes that they built, weighed only 800 pounds, rigged and ready to go. It had a good deal of interior volume too, though the arrangement was trench-like, and you entered through a canopy that looked space-age, but was really a glorified manhole cover.

On land, the boat sat on a trailer that telescoped sideways, with the hulls cheek by jowl. On the launching ramp, the connecting beams were meant to telescope along with the trailer, one aluminum tube inside another, so that in theory, launching was quick. However, Tom says that friction in the various sliding connections often created problems, calling for a good deal of jiggling and starting over. In the water, most Stilettos had a leeboard in the middle of the deck, and like all leeboards, it didn't work very well. A few of the GT models had daggerboards in the hulls, and they sailed very well, thanks to their efficient rigs and very light weight. They have been out of production long enough that inflation must be figured in assessing their cost; but compared to today's folding trimarans, they were not expensive.

The Sea Wind 24 was in production in Florida until quite recently. The factory may still be making a few boats, but without cabins and intended for the rental business. The cabins were entered, more comfortably, from the rear, and the accommodation was as much as should be expected from a 24-footer. With a 35-foot mast, the boat moved well, and the nice people who built her worked hard to improve each example, with better features and better lay-ups of molded glass. The advertised 1991 price was $18,900, and although I have heard that a good many extra dollars had to be spent before the boat could be sailed away, it is less than half the price of an F-24.

The Sea Wind trailered like a Stiletto, though the boat's own beams did not telescope, but were installed after the hulls had been telescoped apart. LaMers says that two people have gotten his boat into the water in less than an hour. He usually figures on two people—taking their time and doing everything carefully and neatly—needing two hours. That's not bad, though you still wouldn't want to do it every weekend. The truth is, there are few voyaging boats, monohull, or multihull, that people want to trailer and launch, retrieve and trailer home again every weekend. When they buy the boat, they think they'll do it. But they get bored with it, and in the end use the boat less than they would if it were kept in the water.

Stiletto and Sea Wind were intended for coastal voyaging, not offshore passages. Not so the MacGregor 36, the largest production catamaran ever designed for trailering. Roger MacGregor, long-time builder of the Venture trailerable monohulls, built nearly 300 of these cats. Sailed well and kept light, they are very fast boats, and have often been first overall in long ocean races. They cost $16,000 in 1981, or about $30,000 in 1993 money.

John Marshall, who races with the NEMA (New England Multihull Association) fleet, currently owns a MacGregor. The literature says it takes two men three hours to launch and assemble the boat, but John says it takes four men eight hours. Another day, he says, must be spent tuning her up, tightening the tramp lashings and the like. On the trailer, the boat is held together by stub beams; she is launched that way, and can be motored away. Afterward, perhaps at a beach far from the launching-ramp crowd, comes the job of substituting the 18-foot sailing beams for the 8-foot stub beams, spreading the hulls apart, attaching the trampolines and nets, stepping the 44-foot mast, and other chores. John doesn't do it every weekend. He says the bolts of his beam connections don't leak much, but I've heard other reports from other owners.

Accommodation on the MacGregor is entered through an aft-facing companionway. Nevertheless, the space itself is an almost comical exaggeration of the trench that must result from a long hull that can only be half of 8 feet 6 inches wide (or, in the days when MacGregors were built,

8 feet). For lack of other use for the space, the forward bunk is 10 feet long. Last summer John kindly invited us aboard to see the layout. We made some excuse. I get claustrophobic easy, and we didn't want to insult him.

Last fall Tom LaMers stopped by to gam about boats in general, and trailerable catamarans in particular. He showed me a very interesting model of an idea he's been working on for some time, and we talked about the trench problem. Even folding trimarans, he thinks, suffer from it to some degree, and don't offer the kind of accommodation people want, and would be willing to pay for, in a trailerable multihull. Half jokingly, I told him the only idea I've ever had on the subject: that a trailering catamaran could be more spacious than a tri if it went on the trailer sideways, and the bows and sterns were detachable sections, to bring her down to 8-foot 6-inch highway width.

These sections would be lighter to lug around than whole hulls. The main connecting structure would be an integral part of the cabins, and would not be disturbed each time the boat was launched or retrieved. The problem, I said, was that the strain on the forestay—most of the strain of the rig, going upwind—would be on the keel connection between the bows and the main sections. The geometry would at least double that strain. Designing a strong-enough piece of hardware required engineering knowledge that I don't have; and anyway, what sensible person was interested in trailering a multihull?

Tom, who lives in Ohio, is very much interested. Last time we talked, he had developed the idea much farther than I ever did. The sketch shows it as far as I had thought it through. You may be able to take it farther, but by the time this book is in print, Tom will have a good head start on you, and he ain't stupid.

I still don't think much of trailering multihulls, and in all but the smallest sizes, the feature costs more than I want to pay in speed, comfort, economy, and perhaps even safety. "What can fold, will fold," says Carol. We now live on a small but navigable river, and haul our own multihull on our own muddy shore. When we didn't have waterfront, we kept her in a marina in winter and on a mooring in summer, and didn't begrudge the cost. It seemed good value, compared to many of the things our money was spent on.

We had no urge to launch our multihull from different sites, and still don't. For us, the pleasure has always been the sailing, and the destination has been little more than an excuse. We find, when we first set sail, that the pace seems slow, because we come to it from our speedy lives ashore. After a day or two aboard, the pace of sailing seems natural and desirable, and the pace of highway life highly unnatural, dangerous, and foolish. The pace of the sailing, it turns out, is part of what we came for.

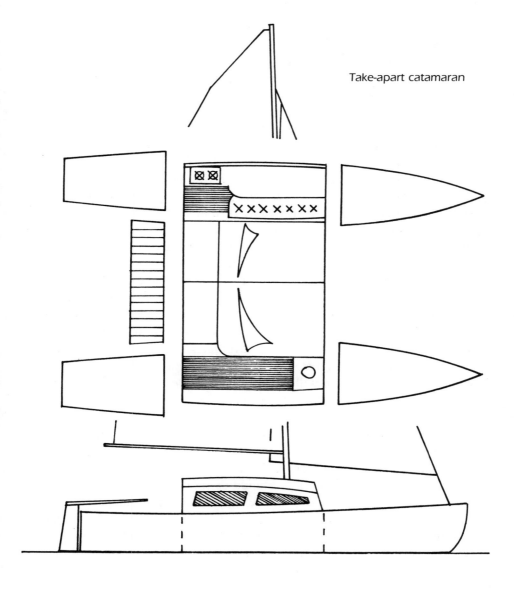

Take-apart catamaran

5

Payload and Size

S EVERAL YEARS AGO, I persuaded the Diamonds, a middle-aged couple who live on the beach of Delaware Bay, to buy an Aquacat rather than a Hobie Cat as their first sailboat. They wanted to keep it in the dunes, dragging it down to the water for launching, and an Aquacat is half the weight of a Hobie. They were new to sailing, and the boomless Aquacat rig with only one sheet to tend is more forgiving.

We assembled the boat on the beach. The tide was high and Bob and I went out to give her a trial. The wind was a perfect 18 knots as we skimmed along on a beam reach, making 7 or 8 knots at times. Bob sat forward on the windward side of the tramp with his feet on the foredeck, looking down at the water. The hull was just touching it, and the bow was spitting out an arc of iridescent water. "Hey, that's pretty good!" he said.

He never saw this sight again. The Aquacat is a small boat, and with two adults aboard, she had her maximum payload. Every time she's been sailed since, it's been with four adults, while other friends and relatives on the beach waited their turns. She does trundle along gamely at 3 or 4 knots with her hulls barely awash. They sail close to the beach, so if anything happened they could certainly swim to shore. They're perfectly safe, but they aren't having much fun. The Diamonds have used their Aquacat less and less, and last year I believe they never launched her at all.

Payload is a subject that some people in the multihull business don't want to talk about. Some will talk around it. "I don't give a payload for my boats," says Tony Smith. "It depends too much on how they're used. You could put two or three tons on a Gemini 32 and go to the Caribbean, and it would be okay. For crossing an ocean, one ton aboard and the bridgedeck wouldn't slam." I wonder how often Tony has sailed in the Caribbean. Our own experience is that on long ocean voyages the wind is usually aft, although the voyager should of course be prepared for headwinds, as well as hurricanes and whatever else may come along. But in the Caribbean in winter, the islands seem to create venturis for the trade winds and their waves. Coming north up the chain from Trinidad, it's always a scramble to get across the passage and into the lee of the next island.

Force 6 is usual, and waves are steep. It seems that you can just lay the course, but the current is pushing you steadily to leeward, and even with a reef in both main and jib, water is coming over the boat in sheets. I wouldn't want to try it in a Gemini with three tons aboard.

Jim Brown, originally a Piver disciple, later designed his own range of trimarans. Piver wasn't gracious about it. Brown published a couple of books about his boats, written in a breezy style and with many very funny cartoons by Jo Hudson. His garrulous irreverence made Brown a cult idol. Aging hippies are still building these old designs of his, though the designer now calls them "dinosaurs." Despite his sociability and flippancy, Brown has always been a cautious man, and his Searunners are careful, complex, and conservative.

In his *Searunner Catalog*, published in 1971, Brown is evasive about boat weight and payload, but he does give a displacement for each of the four boats. On the 31-footer it is 5600 pounds, which is certainly more weight than he would pile onto a 27-foot waterline trimaran today. He also allowed an extra 15 percent of "general plunder," as he said (that is 840 pounds on the 31), if the boat is going to stay close to shore and duck in when the weather turns bad.

Brown, along with most other multihull sailors, has long since discarded the idea that it is desirable to carry "general plunder" on a boat. Last summer, the skipper of one F-27 went aboard another in Cuttyhunk the evening before a race. He looked over the 10 or 20 pounds of new electronic gear and said, "Tony, it's good to see you loading this boat up. Probably you'll be needing a bigger battery soon." These racers do understand the importance of light weight.

It is refreshing to turn to the literature of the late Norman Cross, who began as an aircraft designer, but who, like Brown, began drawing trimarans after owning a Piver. Cross was the deadliest writer that ever wrote, but his meaning was usually clear, and his numbers were impeccable. His boats could be built in sheet plywood, cold-molding, or foam sandwich. The drawing shows the Cross 31. She is a conventional but sound design, with a keel for leeway prevention, moderate performance, and a great deal of interior volume. Her payload is 1550 pounds.

As a catalog, Cross used to send out (and his widow still does) a packet of loose pages, each one a study plan for one of the designs. Naturally, a few other pages were devoted to explaining why Crosses were better than other trimarans. Another sheet, titled "Selecting the Right Size Trimaran," gives us the nub of his thinking, and an example of his prose style: "The *two* greatest mistakes to be made is first: building a boat that is *too large for your budget*, and second: building one that is *too small to carry the load you require*."

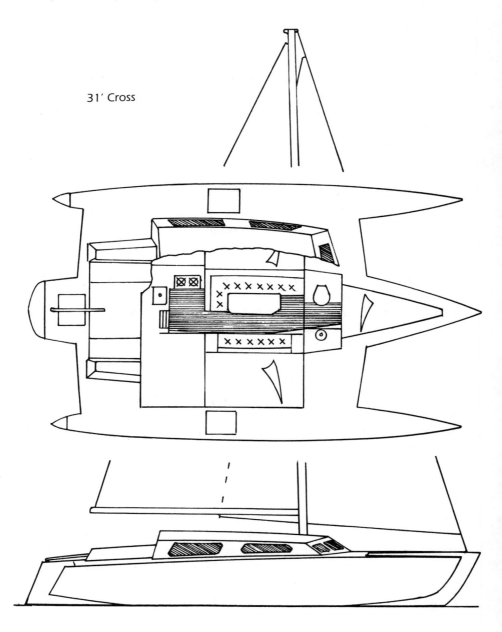

31′ Cross

For most people looking at a boat, payload is a synonym for the number of bunks. For example, the Cross 31 has bunks for five, and an aft-cabin model is available that might sleep two more. It does not take a long study of the plans to see that the dinette could easily be broken down to sleep an eighth person, for a total of at least 1200 pounds of human flesh alone. Whoopee! Let's go 'round the world! But Cross sternly tells us that she will accommodate only "four or five persons for weekend or vacation sailing; two or three persons for extended cruising.'"

As a guide to calculating required payload, Cross provides a sheet to be filled out. He starts with the number of crew and the number of weeks at sea, and by using a chart he calculates the weight that each crew will need for subsistence. This is based on the supposition that you will take more personal belongings if you are going to be gone a longer time. In practice, Carol and I have not found that true. We take nearly as much personal gear for a one-week cruise in Delaware Bay as for a 10-month Atlantic circuit. We figure fifty pounds of clothes and personal gear for each crew. Once this turned out to be badly wrong, when Ruth Wharram joined us in Philadelphia for a passage to the Azores, and brought with her a huge metal trunk (I could hardly lift it) full of plans that she had been selling in this country. Fortunately we had a catamaran, which isn't as easily overloaded as a tri. Meanly, I made her sleep with the trunk at the foot of her bunk (there was no place else in the boat that would hold it), and all went well. It would take more than a trunk as bedmate to make Ruth uncomfortable at sea.

As to stores, racers are extremely weight conscious, and will often cross a starting line with only enough stores for a fast passage. If the passage is slow, they expect to diet. Tom Follet, sailing the Newick proa *Cheers* in the 1968 OSTAR, threw away cans of food every time he made a fast day's run. Most of us are too thrifty for that, and I suggest carrying enough stores for a slower passage than you anticipate. Each of the four times we've sailed to the Azores, it has taken about three weeks; but if we were to start on a fifth passage, we would take four weeks of stores, as we have in the past. This ratio, allowing about a third more time than you think the passage will take, applies only to longer voyages, when the weather is almost certain to average itself out. For shorter passages, stores should be at least twice what you think you'll need. For example, we often sail from the Jersey Coast to New England, and if we leave in the morning, we're pretty sure to be anchoring in Block Island the following evening—36 hours later. We wouldn't think of departing without four days of stores aboard.

It is often said that each crew drinks half a gallon of liquid a day. We have found it less; even in the tropics, with three aboard, we only go through a gallon a day. This does not include any water for washing. At the start of a long passage, we even brush our teeth in salt water. If we make reasonable progress, after a week we may relax and start bathing occasionally in fresh water. Unlike the racers, we find our voyaging lives spartan enough, without the added austerity of short rations. Once, coming across from the Cape Verde Islands to Cayenne, we almost reached the bottom of our stores, because we hadn't been able to replenish them in the island, nor in the last port in Senegal. It was harrowing.

It's best to figure that each crew will eat four pounds (packaged weight) of food as well as drink three pounds of liquid on each voyaging day. A calculation sheet can then be made up that will give the required payload.

Though we once made do with less, Carol and I have now become so addicted to the few voyaging luxuries that we do have (such as an auxiliary engine and a dinghy), that we now feel we need 900 pounds payload for coastal voyages, and 1300 pounds for long ones. How about you?

Start by estimating total crew weight. To that add the number of crew times 50 pounds for personal gear, and for sustenance the number of crew times 7 pounds times days at sea times safety factor. Extra sails, such as spinnakers and storm canvas, are payload, not boat weight. Engine weight times 1.5 will about allow for controls, and for exhaust and propeller systems, or else for outboard bracket. Figure fuel weight at 9 pounds per gallon, to allow for the tank.

Other items that need to be on a payload sheet include mattresses and bedding, head, galley gear, batteries and cables, radios and other electricals, anchors and rodes, safety gear, dinghy and its propulsion, tools and spares, and of course the ubiquitous "other."

"Other" is the easiest number to fudge. "Well, I just won't *take* any other!" But you are a reader, or else you wouldn't be reading this book. How many books will you take? Hardbacks average a pound apiece, and paperbacks half that. Some sailors play musical instruments, and a larger number listen to music that other people have played. How heavy is the equipment? We like to take a pet or two with us—mice or hamster—and more recently a tiny but argumentative parrotlet. She weighs nothing, but her cage and food do. Cats quickly adapt to boat life, and some people claim they are enjoyable. Kitty litter is heavy. Dogs are terrible sailors, and should be left home. They are heavy, eat heavily, and never settle down to a boat. When I think of the worst crew we ever have had, I'd rather take him aboard again than the best dog.

Not until your required payload is added up are you ready to think seriously about a voyaging multihull. Then, if you are thinking about a Cross, it will be easy enough to pick out the minimum boat that will accommodate you. However, if you are buying a built one, you need to be sure that the builder didn't overbuild it. Any overbuilding weight must be subtracted from payload.

If you are looking at boats by other designers, you may find the payload stated, or you may have to ask. Do not be distracted or intimidated. This is information that you are entitled to know, and if the designer was any good, it is information that he used in designing the boat. The most usual reason for failing to state the payload of a multihull is that it is too low. If it were known, the boat could not be sold.

*   *   *

A designer arrives at payload by making a rough calculation of what it will be, what boat weight will be, and drawing the lines of the hulls. He then calculates from the underwater volumes what displacement will be. If he thinks it adequate, he makes a more careful calculation of boat weight, with a list that may be a number of pages long, setting down item by item the square feet of skin and weight of each, the weight of structural members, furniture, spars, hardware, and so on. If boat weight leaves inadequate payload, he may enlarge the underwater volumes by widening or deepening them (frequently a computer does that for him, these days), or he may try to reduce boat weight with a lighter skin, or other methods. However he arrives at it, he wants complete control of the boat's underwater shapes, because he knows that it is crucial to performance and safety.

If you are forced to guess at payload, voyaging trimarans of the following waterline lengths may have the following payloads:

WATERLINE	PAYLOAD
22'	700 lbs.
25'	1100 lbs.
29'	1700 lbs.
34'	2700 lbs.
40'	4500 lbs.

Catamarans the same waterline length often have twice the payload of tri-marans. Some years ago the Simpson-Wild design team was struggling to stay alive in Texas. They hit upon building and selling 26-foot hulls, letting the buyers make cats or tris of them as they chose. Let's suppose that each hull had a 25-foot waterline, and a displacement on its marks of 3000 pounds. Suppose that the tri weighed 2000 pounds. It's unlikely that the cat would weigh more than 2200 pounds. The tri payload would be 3000 − 2000 = 1000 pounds. The cat payload would be 6000 − 2200 = 3800 pounds! When not designed and built in this desperate way, a cat's hulls are usually finer than a tri's. Otherwise, it would take twice the sailing rig to push the cat through the water.

Catamarans and trimarans about the same length generally cost about the same amount. If you cannot afford a trimaran long enough for your required payload, consider a catamaran. The tri will usually be faster, if sailing on her marks, but not necessarily faster and certainly not as safe if you've dumped too much gear into her.

People new to boats often figure that vessels vary in size with their length, not with the cube of length. A 60-footer, they imagine, is twice as big as a 30-footer. In truth, it is eight times bigger. Soon after I began working at Yank Boats, in 1978, a young Frenchman on my crew came to work very excited one morning. He showed me the plans he had just bought for a 42-foot Bruce Roberts monohull ketch. "That's very nice, Pat," I said. "Now, do yourself a favor. Throw it away and send to Roberts for plans for a 30-footer."

He didn't. The extra 12 feet "*çà ne vaut rien*," he said, and he set to work on her. The details of his progress and setbacks are too many and too heartrending to relate. However, after he had put most of his money and energy into her for twelve years, he had her outer shell complete, but no furniture, rig, or engine. The yard where she was then took her over for the unpaid storage bill.

Jim Brown's *Searunner Catalog* spends some time belaboring the point that since boats are three-dimensional objects, their size varies with the *cube* of their length. Apparently he, too, had encountered unbelievers. Some other things that vary with the cube of length are cost (whether "bought" or home-built), building time, weight, payload, interior volume, and maintenance. A 33-footer is *twice* the size of a 26-footer. You *must* believe it.

Most of the boats shown in this book are between 26 and 33 feet, because I believe that boats within those limits will suit most multihull voyagers; and boats outside those limits will offer, with rare exceptions, too little comfort or too much maintenance or something that will make the owner dissatisfied after a time, making him wish he'd never acquired the boat. A liveaboard, unless of minimalist mentality, should have as large a multihull as possible. But people who have a land life, as well as a sailing life, are already stretching their time and budget more than most of their neighbors, and they need to practice restraint.

Very large multihulls are available. Few are more than 50 feet, because the interior volume grows so monstrous that there's no possibility of using it, except commercially. At 46 feet, Cross trimarans bring the cabin all the way out to the sides of the boat, and have standing headroom in the floats, as well as in the main hull. Ed Horstman does this in a 41-footer. Getting back and forth between the various apartments requires lots of stairways. The French are now making a number of huge, luxury catamarans, and would love to sell a few in America. However, the primary purpose of these cats is chartering with paid skipper and crew from Martinique and Guadeloupe. The French government subsidizes the owners with a tax write-off to bring work and money to their islands. No doubt they're pleasant boats, but France won't give *you* a tax write-off for buying one, and they cost millions—not thousands—of dollars.

"I love them," says Tony Smith. "They're wonderful for my business. People see them in big color photographs on the back of all the magazines, and the boats sell the multihull concept. When people find out what they cost, it brings them down to earth a bit, and they come to see me."

6

Arrangement

MONOHULL DESIGNER Tom Colvin is fond of saying that in thinking about a boat: "The primary use is primary. All other uses are secondary." This may sound simplistic, but it doesn't register with many people. In my business, I have too many conversations like this:

CUSTOMER: I want a boat that has two private double bunks, because my brother and I will be cruising with our girlfriends. But I'd like to be able to sleep my parents, too, once in a while.

BUILDER: How often do you think your parents will be spending the night aboard?

CUSTOMER: That's not the point. It's important they feel welcome.

BUILDER: Maybe when they're sleeping aboard, you could sleep on the cabin sole.

CUSTOMER: I don't want to sleep on the sole. It isn't private.

BUILDER: But the primary use is primary.

CUSTOMER: I know, but we're talking about *my mother!*

BUILDER: Let's talk about the boat. To accommodate six people, it will have to be 50 percent larger than if it accommodated four.

CUSTOMER: Couldn't we just have an aft cabin?

Whatever you have, don't have an aft cabin. It is impossible to keep the water out of a forward-facing companionway. As a result, aft cabins are not habitable. Most of the ones I've seen have become storage sheds for junk that should have been taken ashore years ago. Sometimes this junk is stored in the floats of trimarans. Most multihulls have a lot of space, but you'd better not fill it. Even if the aft cabin could be kept dry, perhaps by keeping the boat at the dock and never sailing it, aft cabins that start behind the aft crossbeam of a multihull are never large enough for decent accommodation in boats under 40 feet. You step down onto your pillow, and your oilskin drips into your shoes.

Although Jim Brown's newer designs do not have aft cabins, he put big ones in the *Searunners*, as the drawing shows. They contained the social centers of the boats, as well as bunks. They were as large as the forward cabins, guaranteeing that the galley and chart table, as well as the bedding, got their doses of saltwater. We have sat in "sterncastle lounges" in harbor, and found them pleasant. Owners have assured us that they are not pleasant at sea. Very large multihulls, like very large monohulls, sometimes have a passage like a hamster trail that allows you to go from aft cabin to forward without going on deck. Just the same, I doubt that the aft companionway, even if never opened, remains perfectly tight.

These days it is likely to cost $60 a square foot to have a house built. In the Gemini 32, which gives more space per dollar than any other boat, the accommodation is still costing $300 a square foot; on most other multihulls it is at least twice that, or 10 times the cost of living space on land. This dictates some miniaturization and overlapping of functions, but it shouldn't be taken too far. In the old days, when the structure of a boat took up much of the interior volume, designers resorted to bunks in tiers, folding sinks, and the like. Most people won't put up with that today; but for some reason, they will put up with slithering under a cockpit into a double bunk, poor ventilation, and portlights arranged to look good from the outside rather than to give light to the inside. The best way to deal with accommodation is to think hard about real needs, and to be reconciled to doing without some of the niceties that we are used to on land.

First among the niceties to go is standing headroom. I've never owned a boat with standing headroom, and the only time I miss it is when, pulling up my pants on a rainy day in port, I can't stand up in the hatch. Other annoyances of rainy days in port, such as figuring out how to get ashore, make lack of standing headroom seem minor indeed. Once you stand up in a boat and pull up your pants, there's nothing else to do but sit down again. You can't go for a walk. Everything you need is within reach, sitting down. There really is little point in standing up in a boat except to say that you've done it, or can do it. Yet people will pay a fearful price for it. A 6-1/2-foot-tall customer of Vance Buhler's insisted on standing headroom on the bridgedeck of his 38-foot catamaran. Vance gave it to him, his usual skill keeping it from looking too awful, but the wingdeck does pound of course, and the windage of the boat is pretty high. What's that guy doing in there?

A deep monohull can often have standing headroom on a waterline of 22 feet, as in Carl Alberg's designs. A trimaran has much less depth

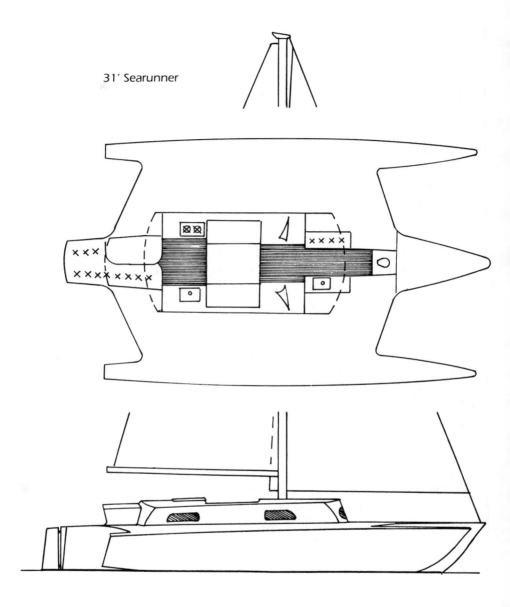

31′ Searunner

below the water, needing perhaps 28 feet of waterline before having 6-foot headroom. A catamaran is shallower yet, and, in my opinion, should not have headroom in hulls less than 30 feet on the water. I know this opinion is not shared by all designers, but the cost in windage, and the extra sail that is needed to overcome it, are more than I'd want to pay for or handle.

A shower is another feature many people unthinkingly insist on, because they have one at home. A shower on a boat is a miserable thing, dribbling where it should spray. We do like one when we reach port, but there we can rent a much better one than any boat has aboard. During a voyage there are other ways to get clean, and it seems less important anyway. In addition to the $600 a square foot that a boat shower takes up, even its dribble uses far more water than a bucket bath, so the water tanks must be bigger, the boat slows down, and so on. Besides, how many showers are actually taken during a voyage? If it's many, then the pump that removes the waste water from the shower sump will periodically clog with hair, scabs, sloughed-off skin, both yours and other people's. It will have to be cleaned out. Have fun!

Another feature often thought desirable is a toilet room with a door. This wastes enormous space, because if a toilet is made private with a curtain, then it can be a seat when it isn't a toilet, and its floor space is also part of the general accommodation. When a potential customer comes to me for a boat with a toilet room and a door, I know that the customer wants the boat, but his wife or girlfriend doesn't, and the boat won't get built.

At the heart of any accommodation plan is the need for a haven. A house on land is a haven, too, but the shelter is less needed, because land is our natural element, and water is not. However majestic the ocean is, however exciting it may be to sail on, all but the toughest of us need a place where we can get away from it, at certain points in a voyage. James Wharram feels so strongly about it that he wants his portlights small, so that he can't see out unless he makes a deliberate effort. I don't go that far, but I do agree with him that the surfaces I see around me in the cabin should remind me of my natural element—land. They should be cloth or varnished wood, not metal, painted wood, or plastic. Despite that, it is true that if the overhead is white, any cabin will be lighter, and will seem bigger.

I want my cabin perfectly dry. I want to sit comfortably, to cook, read, eat, or play cards. I want to lie down very comfortably on 4 inches of foam—more is too hot—in a bunk with at least 3-foot headroom at the head, and not too much less at the foot. I will give up many spurious comforts for these simple and real ones. The motion of a multihull is so much more comfortable than a monohull that it seems sinful to ask for still more comfort; but it is easily available.

Shelves, not cabinets, are the best places to store things on a multihull. Monohulls need cabinets with doors that close firmly to keep the crockery from tumbling out when the boat rolls to 30 or 40 degrees. On a multihull, a one-inch fiddle rail suffices for all but the fiercest weather. With shelves, it is easy to see at a glance what is where, and unneeded junk is more likely to be seen and taken off the boat, not left to molder in a cabinet. Cabinet doors also weigh something, and when opened, they take up space in the narrow hull of a multihull. We like quite a bit of shelving, so that things aren't piled on top of each other.

On all but the shortest voyages, clothing is better kept in hammocks, not under bunks. The circulation of air keeps them sweet. After the trouble of getting yourself clean, it is disconcerting to put on a shirt that smells of mildew. Hammocks can usually be hung above and outboard of the bunks. Chandlers sell them, or, if you are handy, you can make your own that will exactly fit the space available.

At this point, it becomes impossible to talk about catamarans and trimarans in the same paragraph. They are just too different. Let's talk about trimarans first. The first arrangement question is, will the accommodation extend out over the wingdeck, and if so, how far? On the Cross 31, shown in the last chapter, the cabin extends all the way to the inboard edge of the floats. This is not generally done any more, especially in boats this size, and even Cross' last designs showed more restraint about interior volume. He found that everyone filled that big space up with stuff that weighed the boat down, so he shrank the cabins.

A solid wingdeck will also pound, like a low bridgedeck on a catamaran. Even a moderate breeze depresses the leeward float of a trimaran substantially, bringing the wingdeck close to the water. Driven hard, more than one trimaran with solid wingdeck has stove in the underside, and only found salvation in tacking and reefing down. Even if the wingdeck isn't stove, the pounding may make it impossible to sleep in the lee bunk. But it's a lovely arrangement, isn't it? A 40-footer can have it and still have some open wing between where the house ends and the float begins.

Cross put single bunks on the wing of his smallest voyager, a 24-footer. Headroom above them was about 20 inches. On the wingdeck bunks of a trimaran, sitting headroom probably isn't necessary, because a broad view out into the main hull forestalls claustrophobia. Nevertheless, 20-inch headroom is meager. Better not sneeze in the night. On our own *Hummingbird*, I extended the cabin a foot over the main hull, but the extra interior volume was for stowage and visual space, not for bunks. We slept in a double bunk, low down in the hull and not far forward of the center of gyration.

Every boat has a center of gyration, and ideally everything in the boat should be exactly on that center—helmsman, bunk, galley, head. Some designers, in a fit of forgetfulness, put the engine in the center of gyration, spreading the people and their functions out into the corners of the boat. A multihull doesn't waggle around like a monohull, but if you sit on the bow, you'll notice that you're moving up and down more than if you were sitting amidships. The center is usually just aft of amidships, not far above the waterline. That is the choicest spot in the boat.

What to put in this choice spot, and near it? To me, it seems that my bunk and the place where I sit when not on watch are the most important. Steering, I can take some motion, because I'm awake and absorbed in the rhythm of the ocean anyway. You may not feel the same way about it; if you don't, you may justifiably want a different arrangement.

For sure, neither of us wants to be stuffed into the ends of the boat, let alone the corners. This goes for the nasty aft bunk in *Hummingbird*, and the nastier forward bunk in the Cross 31. The motion is just too great for comfortable sleeping. Though a multihull is more comfortable, it's usually going faster than a monohull, and the waves are coming along more often. In addition, both of these bunks are accessed by crawling under beams and over or through heads, so the sleeper, having arrived at his cocoon, must sometimes feign sleep while wishing he could accomplish it. The ends of the boat are there to help get her through the water. They may hold stores, but they should not hold accommodation. This is especially true of the Cross forward bunk. Under the forward beam, or not far forward of that, should be a watertight collision bulkhead.

The saloon of the Cross offers a good example of the arrangement problem in the main hull of a moderate-size trimaran. There are settees on both sides. A tiny off-center table with a leaf allows the crew on the starboard settee to eat from the table, not their laps, but it blocks the alleyway and immobilizes traffic. A monohull much smaller than this would have a wider hull allowing the diners to sit facing forward or aft, and beyond the table and the settees would be a passageway for the cook or the gastronomically unsound. Cross' main hulls are wider than most trimarans', but he doesn't find room for such an arrangement until he draws a 35-footer. Get much beyond 35 feet, and most designers will have you stepping up into the dinette, sacrificing headroom for width. The technique of entering such a dinette is learned after a few head bashings: Step up, and at the same time, stoop down. It's like the samurais in those great Kurosawa movies of yesteryear: They enter a room with a high sill and a low lintel, and their swords never even jangle.

But what a lot of attractive space there can be in a trimaran! Aft in the Cross, notice the wonderful surfaces for food preparation and chart work. As long as they're used for that, not for storing lead ingots, voyaging life will be comfortable indeed. For mental health, long sight lines belowdeck are often as important as actual space; in a well-laid-out tri, you're likely to get longer sight lines than in a cat.

$$* \quad * \quad *$$

Catamarans present a whole different set of arrangement problems. The first question to be settled, as with trimarans, is whether to put accommodation on the bridgedeck. If you do, the space can be palatial, even on a relatively short boat. The usual way to do it is to put bunks up forward, and a saloon aft of them, as in the Gemini. The galley can be aft in one hull, the chartroom in the other. Sometimes, unlike the Gemini, the cabintop has a step in it, so that people in the saloon can see out forward. In the early days, this arrangement was sometimes used in cats as short as 24 feet, but performance suffered badly. Once, we chartered a 26-foot O'Brien Channel Rover for a week in the English Channel. It was a dog under sail, and the motor was broken. Nowadays, this arrangement is only thought suitable for boats over 30 feet, and I'd prefer 35 feet.

Boats with this "classic" catamaran arrangement tend to be very high, and to have very low bridgedecks. The Solaris cats, sold as motorsailers, are intended to immerse the bridgedeck coming down waves, and they're built strong enough to take it. Many other production cats don't intend to immerse, but they all do it. No bridgedeck can be high enough to miss every shape of wave that the boat sails over, so the question is not whether it will hit, but how often, and will it stand it? We met a Prout cat whose bulkheads were coming loose from slamming. It was a new boat, so it probably wasn't overloaded.

For many years the Prouts have built their catamarans with a nacelle down the middle, a kind of third hull which is smaller than the other two. Forward, it is some distance above the water, but aft it comes down to touch. It breaks up the waves that are hitting the bridge, gives more headroom in the saloon, and near the stern it houses the motor, which has a retractable outdrive. I don't know whether the nacelle causes more drag than a prop would. The Prouts are not quick by modern standards, but they do have lovely interiors.

From the cockpit, high houses are hard to see over. The Channel Rover had a "sit bin"—a trash can with a seat on top. You put it behind the wheel and sat on it, until the next wave came. Carol, whose feet didn't touch the deck when she was up on it, found it even worse than I did. Better cats have permanent helm seats, but you're up pretty high on most of them, far from the center of gyration. The publicity shots of one big French cat show the skipper standing up at the helm, and as he's getting paid for it, that may be acceptable.

Sitting headroom in a saloon is 4 feet 6 inches, but in a bunk it's only 3 feet, so a sleeker cat can be built only if the bunks are on the bridgedeck. Then the saloon is forced into a hull, and as a cat hull is likely to be slimmer than the main hull of a tri, placing the table and seats is even more of a problem. On all our boats, we have settled for seats facing forward and aft, with a drop-leaf table between them. It does make traffic problems at times. In addition, when a multihull is under way, it is more comfortable to sit facing athwartships, because the motion is easier to brace against. On *Hummingbird* we had a seatback on each counter, and if you were alone in the seat, you could swing your feet up and turn to face athwartships for reading or wool gathering.

In any catamaran but the smallest, there is some undesirable duplication of spaces, and some problem of what to do with them. On the Gemini, for example, the galley can use its 7-1/2-foot length. The chart room could easily be half that long, but it, too, is 7-1/2 feet, because the space is there. Many catamarans wind up with bigger chart rooms than they need. Over a certain size, many cats have four double bunks, because the space is there.

I prefer an open bridgedeck. As mentioned in describing the Shuttle Cat, I find that space is more pleasant when open rather than enclosed, and even a little slamming under the bunk is too much for me. Most of us do our sailing in nice weather, and both in port and at sea, I like to be on deck as often as possible, enjoying the weather. A catamaran center deck is a very much more desirable place to set up chairs than a trimaran side deck. Even if a side deck is designed to be level at rest, it will slope considerably when two people sit on and depress the float. Also, it lacks that wonderful feeling of protection that the two cabins of a catamaran give. You are in nature, and yet safe from it. What could be more delightful? On *Vireo*, whose beams were flush with the decking, we had a lifeline across the aft beam, 30 inches high, as any useful lifeline should be. On *Dandy*, whose beams are above the decking, we haven't felt the need for a life-line, though we might install one if we planned a long voyage.

Fabric trampolines are the lightest wingdeck material, but I don't like to walk on them, and I mistrust their durability. We have always paid the price in weight to have duckboard decks, an idea that we carried over from the Wharram cats to our newer boats. These decks must be lashed down, because sooner or later a wave will burst under them. I spent one very bad night retrieving an inadequately lashed-down duckboard on *Hummingbird*, in a force 7 on the way to Bermuda. When a wave hits the underside of a well-secured duckboard, the force is far less than it would be if the same wave hit a solid wing, because the gaps between boards relieve the pressure, even if they are narrow gaps.

Nets are sometimes used for side decks on trimarans, and forward and aft of the decks of catamarans. We only ever had one, on *Two Rabbits*, and we enjoyed lolling in it when the weather was fine. In its third season, Carol happened to fall into it one day, while working on the boat at anchor. It didn't even slow her down, and as she spluttered to the surface, she saw a perfect silhouette of her body in the hole in the net. Since then I have seen other multihullers fall through nets, but I won't repeat what they said. Nets and tramps are expensive, and fill me with foreboding. On *Vireo*, we wove half a dozen strands of 1/4-inch Dacron line back and forth between the bows. I once fell into it, and it did stop me. It also kept sails out of the water during jib changes. Rope is more reliable than webbing.

The worst problem with open-bridgedeck catamarans is getting from one hull to the other in bad weather. There's no question that it can be annoying, especially at sea. In port on a rainy day, it is usually possible to wait for a lull and then go across, and it's a diversion to think about visiting a new space, and playing with the new toys that are in it. We don't mind, except when we forget to bring the cigarettes across with us.

Belowdecks, an open-wing cat tends to be plain. Clearly, the galley and saloon must be in the same hull. Often the bigger cats have those four double bunks, and the big chart room in one hull. I prefer to see only one bunk there, and perhaps two bunks with shorter chartroom in the other hull. That brings the accommodation closer to amidships, and surely three doubles are enough on all but charter boats. When a cat hull has bunks forward and aft, companionways must face athwartships, or the aft bunk must be reached by crawling under the aft-facing companionway.

Lately, James Wharram has taken to putting little cabins on his bridgedecks—sometimes just a bunk, sometimes a crawl-in saloon. Among production catamarans, Edel Cat and Louisiane have saloons on the bridgedeck that can only be reached by going outdoors and in again. This seems to me the worst of both worlds, though these deck cabins are narrow, so they offer less windage, and the helmsman can see around them, if not over them. The Edel Cat is offered with or without this extra cabin; I'd certainly take it without.

We have become fairly grandiose, considering that we started by discussing accommodation as a haven. Later, when we discuss the plumbing and electrical systems that many people want in their accommodation, we'll become more grandiose still. To repeat, dryness belowdecks seems to me the first essential of comfort at sea, and only with an aft-facing companionway is there a reasonable chance of it. A hinged hatch can be perfectly dry, if it comes down over the coamings and washboards. However, Carol still bears the mark of where she pinched a finger in one, years ago. A sliding hatch will not be perfectly dry, no matter what baffles are put into it, unless it slides forward into a box. The box, like the hatch, must be stiff enough to stand on, so the whole arrangement becomes complex and heavy. An aft-facing doorway can be dry, if properly made, but aft-facing washboards without a hatch above them will usually leak, especially if the bulkhead that they're mounted on slopes aft. We once visited a Newick tri after she'd won the Multihull Bermuda Race. The crew was bitter about the wetness below, and I think races can be won without that.

Size helps keep a boat dry, as do certain hull shapes, especially knuckles in the topsides. Slowing down also helps, though monohulls are usually slower as well as wetter than multihulls. Overloaded boats are wetter than light ones, of course. But any boat takes some spray, and nasty weather can bring solid water over the cabintops. When sea water dries, it leaves a residue of salt crystals, which are dry in the daytime, but absorb moisture after sundown. Boats are almost always wet on deck at night, except for brief intervals after rain showers. Salt crystals stick to clothing, and then in the night the clothing becomes clammy.

On an overnight passage, wetness can be laughed off, as can many other discomforts. On a longer voyage, perpetual wetness causes saltwater sores. In the tropics, nearly half of all people will develop an allergic reaction to coral spores, ubiquitous in all the warm oceans. The spores keep any wounds or bug bites from healing, so that over a few months, the sufferer becomes a mass of sores. The only cure I know is to wash often in fresh water, and to stay away from salt.

Sailing to the Azores on *Vireo* in 1983, we discovered that the boat had opened up in the two years since we'd last sailed her, because we'd built her with Aerolite, a glue that was supposed to be waterproof, but turned out not to be. She was still held together by screws and nails, but her seams wept saltwater until everything below was wet—clothes, food, bedding. The boat remained spacious, for a 23-foot waterline cat, and the layout comfortable. When we reached Horta, we could hardly wait to sell her.

After dryness comes ventilation, and there can hardly be too much of it. At sea or in port, one washboard can usually be left out of an aft-facing companionway. In our last three voyaging multihulls, and in a number of other boats as well, I've used the baffled cabinfront vent shown in the drawing. For really bad weather, it has a deck plate that screws in from the inside, but we've never had to use it, even in a hurricane. Dorade vents are very dry, but it takes a gale to move any air through them. All vents in cabintops are often in the way, and likely to be tripped over or broken. If I had to have one, I'd paint it day-glo orange. Every inhabited place on a boat should have at least two hatches for cross ventilation. For a fore hatch, we find the lift-off kind with T-bar closer the easiest to make watertight. If you're as claustrophobic as I am, you want this hatch big enough to crawl out. A Windscoop on the fore hatch is a wonderful luxury in port, but not always easy to rig on the hull of a cat with no forestay to hang it from.

When the boat is in port or on land, every enclosed space should have at least some circulation of air, except perhaps the floats of a fiberglass trimaran. Any enclosed space without ventilation will sooner or later become too "icky" to use, even for stowage. The air always contains organic matter, and some of it will find its way in there and putrify. Molds and other fungus can survive on very little, but you can't survive with them.

We like big, fixed portlights. Opening ones almost always leak. I don't mind looking out, and in a gale spend much of my time doing so, searching for signs that the weather's going down. I want to see out of the bunk cabin as well as the saloon, and don't mind using curtains when they're needed. Tacked up with four bits of Velcro, they don't give the trouble that sliding curtains always seem to. The placement of portlights should be determined by structure, utility, and appearance—in that order of importance. Quarter-inch Plexiglas is not strong enough for monohull

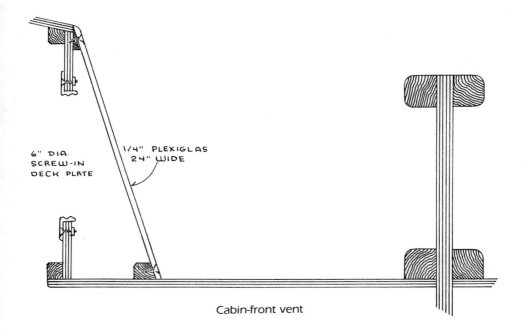

6" DIA.
SCREW-IN
DECK PLATE

1/4" PLEXIGLAS
24" WIDE

Cabin-front vent

portlights, because when the boat is hit by a wave, it stands there and takes it. A multihull moves with the wave, and we've had no trouble with quarter-inch in portlights as big as two square feet.

Most people want cockpits in their voyaging multihulls, but Carol and I prefer to steer from the companionway, sitting on the deck with our feet inside. When we are off watch, we want to be below in strong weather or at night, and in a chair on deck in nice weather in the daytime. Steering from the companionway, we are halfway between the exciting outdoors and the reassuring cabin, and can see both. We can reach down to a shelf for the binoculars, or lean down and glance at the chart lying on the table. On catamarans we usually steer from the windward hull, which takes less spray. The compass is mounted in a box, or on a square piece of wood, so that it can be set down on the hatch or on deck beside the helmsman, and squared up with the boat. In rain showers, I sometimes steer from below, with one arm reaching out to the tiller and the compass on a shelf near me.

Almost all monohull yachts have cockpits, though Tom Colvin has no time for them. He says, "This supreme robber baron, vandal, thief, pirate, is found aboard too often, threatening the safety of a proper seagoing vessel: the cockpit." Well, Tom, we agree, if not quite so strongly. A cockpit often takes up a good deal of the interior volume of a hull; or, if built entirely above deck line, it puts the helmsman up as high as he would be on a sit bin. On a monohull, the cockpit is usually the only comfortable place to be outdoors. But if a multihull is not entirely covered with cabin, outdoor space is plentiful.

Cockpits are confining, and not pleasant places to relax. The space that is left below them is usually pretty nasty. You will often notice that the companionway is the most desired space on a sailboat, where people like to stand or sit, to watch what's going on. Why isn't the helmsman entitled to that most-desired space? He's doing the work, and its comfort will help him do it better. If the bottom of the companionway is 2 feet wide, and the top a few inches wider, crew can get past the helmsman without much trouble. They can make do with some less desirable spot, until it's their turn to take the helm.

7
Sailing Rigs

THERE IS NO question that the most brilliant multihull designer yet to come along is Australian Lock Crowther. He is no barrel of laughs, and I'd rather get drunk with Wharram or Brown. What's more, Crowther hasn't bothered too much with yacht design in recent years, because he's been determined to make a living at his business. Monohulls still account for most of the pleasure-boat market, and even *their* designers have a hard time scraping by. With multihulls, it's that much harder. Every other designer that I know much about supplements his design earnings with another source of income—perhaps boatbuilding (which is not a very profitable enterprise, either), or a daytime job with the government or some other institution, a pension, or inherited money.

When I visited Crowther's design office in 1982, it seemed modest enough. Many a small-time house architect has premises at least as imposing. Three or four men worked at drafting boards, and the drawings on them were commercial multihulls—ferries, excursion boats, fishing boats—a hundred and more feet long, some with sailing rigs, but many without. That, Crowther has found, is where the multihull money is. At the 1988 Multihull Symposium, he was asked whether, if the money was the same, he wouldn't rather be designing yachts. Briefly he looked wistful and said that, yes, he would. Then the business-as-usual look came back to his face.

Crowther began designing multihull sailing yachts in the heady, Piver days. His boats were so much better that only the geographic isolation of Australia kept them from dominating early racing. They won many of the local races, often with the designer aboard, but news of these victories didn't make headlines abroad. Soon he had developed a whole line of excellent cats and tris, and he did sell some plans, but not enough to make a living. He turned to commercial boats, and although his yacht designs have been upgraded over the years, they haven't received as much of his energy as some of us would have liked.

There is very little about multihull sailing rigs that Crowther did not know many years ago. When I visited him, I was having a problem with

Vireo. Her helm seemed balanced in moderate going, but as the wind picked up, she developed strong weather helm, like a monohull. However, the monohull solution of reefing the main and continuing with the jib only changed the helm balance insofar as it slowed the boat down. What to do?

Multihulls aren't like monohulls, he explained. In the one, heeling makes the underwater shape asymmetrical, and carries the center of effort far out to the side. In the other, strong wind across the sails pushes the fine bows down, and moves the center of resistance too far forward. To solve my weather helm problem, I needed to do the exact opposite of what a monohull did, and move my whole rig aft.

I did, and it worked. Long before then, Crowther had realized that a multihull's center of effort had to be kept well aft. The Shockwave 29, designed for mass production in 1977, illustrates how far he often goes with it. *Twiggy*, his 31-foot trimaran that came so close to eating up the bigger boats in a number of ocean races, was designed at about the same time. She had a fractional rig with the mast stepped 56 percent aft on the waterline, and a forestay chainplate more than 4 feet inboard of the bow. The reason he couldn't move the whole thing even farther aft, he explained, was that for helm balance, the daggerboard had to move aft with the rig, and if it were any closer to the rudder, it would interfere with steering.

Crowther does sometimes use a masthead rig, but the mast can be alarmingly far aft. On *Shotover*, a 60-foot catamaran, it is stepped 64 percent aft on the waterline. Some of his other designs are visually less extreme, especially after he developed the bulbous bow, to be discussed in the next chapter. For decades, Prout has stepped the masts of its production cats 60 percent aft, with a foretriangle more than twice the size of the mainsail. Robert B. Harris once advocated stepping the mast nearly 75 percent aft, and driving the boat entirely with headsails, using no main at all. The problem with these schemes is that the whole structure of the boat must be very rigid, or the headsails will lose their drive to windward. A Prout is so heavily built, with the bridgedeck coming nearly out to the bows, that the jib luff does remain relatively taut. In a modern, lighter boat with wider hull spacing, it's less likely to work.

Among multihull designers, a consensus has developed favoring a fractional sloop rig, with the main providing most of the power. Masts bend less than wires, and often a little bend can be used to change the shape of the main for different strengths of wind. For all-out racers, the jib is sometimes dispensed with entirely; but a voyaging boat needs a mini-

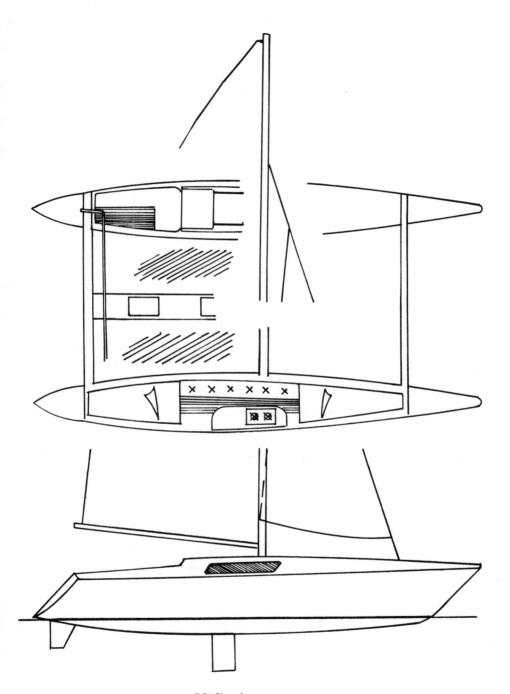

29' Shockwave

mum of two sails, so that one can control her while the other is being changed or reefed. Increasingly often, the main is fully battened, and this can yield 50 percent more area than a conventional 12-inch roach. The extra area can be applied to having a faster boat, or a shorter rig. Sailmakers have worked hard to make full battens more reliable than they used to be. There is less chafe now, and less batten breakage. But chafe and breakage still do happen, and a fully battened main is almost impossible to store, except on the boom.

Sometimes a fractional sloop will have a rotating mast that smoothes air flow. Commander G. C. Chapman, a member of the Amateur Yacht Research Society (AYRS), decided to go the whole hog with it, and in AYRS #76 he describes putting a jibless rotating wingsail onto a 14-foot clinker monohull, which formerly had a conventional sloop rig. He found that the wingsail, with 12-1/4-percent less sail area than the sloop was only 4 percent slower, averaging all points of sailing. However, putting a rotating mast—even a rotating wingmast—on a rig that continues to have a jib will not yield as great an improvement.

Naturally, rotating masts are more flimsily connected to the boat than fixed masts, and failures are more frequent. Approaching Gomera in the Canaries, Carol and I lost the fixed mast of *Hummingbird* when we couldn't reef fast enough for a 35-knot squall. Jury-rigged, we crept back to Tenerife, and built a new mast on the marina's floating dock, out of the inferior wood we found on the island. We made it shorter than the old mast, and cut the mainsail down to the first row of reefing points; it did get us home.

Jan Gougeon, on the other hand, lost the rotating mast of his Gougeon 32 in 15 to 20 knots of steady wind. Rigging stretch was all it took. Unfortunately, he had a man from *Sail* magazine aboard at the time, testing the boat. The man was nice enough to come back another day, when a redesigned rig with more wires and struts did last out the test. There is no possibility of getting as much extra drive out of a rotating mast as out of full battens and a bigger roach. On a voyaging boat, I'd say full battens make a radical enough rig, and rotating masts are best left to the racers. A wingmast certainly is the most dangerous single feature that a voyaging boat can have. It is too high to be used as a stormsail, and can overpower the boat.

Some experimenting has been done with unstayed rigs on trimarans, but no voyaging catamaran has yet succeeded with them. Catamarans are just too stiff, and would put too much strain on the mast base. Even with trimarans, the floats must be small or the mast won't take the strain. Dick Newick's proa *Cheers*, which finished an excellent third in the 1968 OSTAR, had an unstayed schooner rig. Ten years later, Phil Weld, looking for some humanitarian use for his money, put Jim Brown and Newick to work building a prototype "water-borne pickup truck" for the Third World. Astonishingly, *SIB* turned out to be a trimaran, the worst possible load-carrier. To save "yachty hardware," she had an unstayed schooner rig.

For some time, Brown traveled to third-world countries on foundation grants, teaching the natives how to build their own pickup trucks. Vance Buhler, whose shop employs twenty people in St. Vincent, a very third-world country, is skeptical. "Sure, if Brown comes in with the epoxy and veneers and Dacron, the people pitch in and get themselves a couple of boats," he says. "But once Brown is gone, the people go back to hacking down the few remaining trees in the place, and banging them into boats with ungalvanized nails. They wouldn't waste a piece of plywood on a boat; that makes a dining table at home."

At any rate, the unstayed masts of the pickup truck did not fail. Chris White, at first a disciple of Brown just as Brown was a disciple of Piver, was keen on the building method of *SIB*, and on unstayed masts. (Brown and White have remained friends since White started designing his own, because Brown is a nice man, and Piver really wasn't.) White built an unstayed 53-foot ketch for himself, and sailed her for six years that way, before converting her to a stayed rig. In his book, *The Cruising Multihull*, he gives an interesting analysis of the problems he had. Essentially, he was only able to control sail shape in some conditions, not in others. From the pictures I've seen of *SIB* sailing, she, too, had problems with sail shape.

Few ideas work perfectly the first few times they're tried. Chris White has hold of an interesting idea here, and, by his own admission, part of the sail-shape problem was caused by the masts he built the first time. He implies that he'll try again, and I hope he will, and will keep us informed.

Aspect ratio (the ratio of height to length) is important to the performance of any sailing rig. Until recently, multihulls had lower aspect ratio rigs than monohulls, as well as less sail for their length. Safety and economy were concerns. However, it was a revelation to us when we put the new rig on *Hummingbird*. The first mast was 30 feet, and the boom 15 feet. The mast clobbered up in the Canaries was only 27 feet. When we got home, needing new sails anyway, I drew a new rig with a 33-foot mast and 13-foot boom. The jib also became taller in proportion, and to maintain balance, the new mast was raked farther aft. Sail area was little changed.

We expected a faster boat, and we got it. The surprise was how much easier she was to handle. The main was easier to vang and reef as well as to sheet. We had more control, with less effort. Aspect ratio was still only 2.3-to-1, and I would not suggest going to the 4-to-1 common among monohulls. Michael Ellison, long-time editor of AYRS publications, once told me he thought 1.7-to-1 was the ideal aspect ratio for the whole rig, not just for individual sails. Of the boats shown in this book so far, only the Shockwave 29 and the Shuttle Cat have it. They look frighteningly high to me.

A very old idea is the four-sided sail. There are many varieties of it—square, gaff, sprit, and the various lugs. Almost all sails were four-sided until the invention of wire rope in the nineteenth century made it possible to carry a tall-enough mast to drive the boat with a three-sided sail. We hear a good deal about "lofty clipper ships," but on the fleetest of them, the distance from the tallest masthead to waterline was only three-fourths of waterline length. In proportion to length, the Optimist pram has a loftier rig than any clipper.

I have cherished a preliminary drawing from James Wharram Associates, showing their 63-footer with two masts, no jibs, and two square sails. The naked crew are steering her with an oar, pulling on ropes, or relaxing in the shade of a grass hut on the bridgedeck. I can't think of a multihull that would be more fun to see, or less fun to sail.

When Wharram built one for himself, he went to rudders, a schooner rig with gaffs on both masts, and double headsails. This still sounds lunatic enough to most modern sailors, but Wharram has been working with four-sided sails all his designing life, and he has made them work astonishingly well. His most recent gaff rigs are tall, and the sails are sleeved over the gaffs as well as the masts. Comparing them to airplane wings (which is what all sails would look like, if keeping them up and allowing them to rotate were no problem), it is hard to find a three-sided sail that so nearly approaches the wing shape. And then there is Bob Beggs who finished the OSTAR so well with his 26-foot gaff-rigged Wharram. How to account for it?

As said before, Bob is tough. But the sails, though they aren't as good as Bermudan, are nothing like as bad, upwind as well as down, as everyone usually says. Our first Wharram cat, *Two Rabbits*, had a boomless sprit mainsail, and in the last year we owned her we replaced it with a Bermudan sail. That raised our daily average 8 percent, but we thought we could have made as big an improvement by putting a boom on the spritsail. I still choose sprit rig over Bermudan when designing a sailing dinghy. However, there is a limit to the size of sprit that anyone can handle, and the 16-1/2-footer on *Rabbits* came very near my limit.

Unlike a spritsail, a gaff sail can be any size, and the gear will still be manageable. On a monohull, its sheet can't be eased very much before the gaff jaws touch the shrouds, because the sail tends to twist more than a spritsail. But on a cat the gaff can be vanged to the windward stern with a light line, and with a boom vang as well, twist can be largely eliminated. If I had a good reason to have a gaff sail on my multihull, such as a fixed bridge between my anchorage and open water, I wouldn't be unhappy. You may be scoffing still, but watch out for Bob Beggs!

Wharram's schooner and White's ketch both have two masts. The designers put up practical defenses for their rigs, but I suspect that the romantic appearance of two sticks attracted both of them. No racing multihulls have two masts, and neither do the big French luxury cats. In 1961, Piver put two masts on all his trimarans over 30 feet, but since then the size at which two masts become desirable has been steadily edging upward. It is demonstrable that one 400-square-foot sail does more work than two 200-square-footers. Crowther put a ketch rig on a 59-foot charter boat in 1981, but I doubt that he would today. Wharram's schooner and White's ketch would probably sail better with sloop rigs, but might be less pleasing to their owners' eyes.

At least Wharram and White put some sail area onto their aft masts. They are clearly meant to help drive the boats, and I'm sure they do. The more usual ketch rig uses the mizzen mostly for "balance," as is politely said. When a friend of ours bought a Piver AA36 with such a rig, he immediately chopped it down. He said it didn't change the balance that he could see, and it saved considerable weight.

Biplane rig—a mast on each hull of a catamaran—seems so logical that when you see one you have to look twice to realize it's unusual. Like a trimaran or monohull, it puts the rig loads on the hulls, not the connecting structure; and "you can get more sail force for the same capsizing moment, therefore you should be faster," said Lock Crowther when I consulted him about it. "The drag of the rig is not as important as the actual force produced. Water drag and aerodynamic drag of the vessel itself are of a high order, and the parasitic drag of rigging wire, etc., is relatively small." Lock, I wish you'd been right.

Crowther sent me a drawing of a 28-foot x23-foot daysailing biplane cat that he designed ten years ago. It was like an iceboat in that, whatever the course or wind strength, it had the speed to bring the apparent wind forward of the beam. When we put a smaller version of his rig on *Dandy*, with her 23-foot waterline and 1000-pound payload, she couldn't do that. On a reach the leeward sail flopped idly about, and we were driving the boat with only half her sail area.

Dandy's biplane rig had two mains and no jibs, though we could set a small drifter off the wind. We were hoping that two 26-foot masts would do the work of one 30-foot mast. The clutter of the masts, two booms, and twelve rigging wires oppressed us increasingly, during the two seasons and 2000 miles that we sailed her. But it was the poor performance on most points of sail that finally made us abandon the rig.

It did have several virtues. It tacked faster than any other catamaran I've sailed, and of course it tacked without any sheet handling. It pointed phenomenally high: the sails filled and the boat made some progress to windward tacking in 60 degrees. Downwind the sails didn't blanket each other at all, and it was certainly faster than a sloop under working sails. We raced four times with NEMA, and our handicap meant that the F-27s had to give us a minute a mile. Downwind we didn't need that much, but on other courses we needed embarrassingly much more. Because the effort was low, we very seldom needed to reef, and in our first race we may have been the only unreefed boat in the fleet.

By the second season, we realized that although our biplane rig was close winded, it wasn't fast upwind, even when we eased the sheets and tacked in 90 degrees. It just didn't go. We could move away from most of the bigger monohulls that we met while voyaging, on the rare occasions when they weren't motoring with their sails up. Most such boats are sailed incredibly sloppily; but when we found ourselves in a racing fleet, in the Buzzards Bay Regatta, we couldn't stay with anyone upwind, not even monohulls our own length. Perhaps the drag of the rig was important after all, or perhaps its proportions were wrong, and the aerodynamic interaction was harmful. A jibless rig usually is faster upwind than a sloop rig the same size, but our two jibless rigs sure weren't.

In addition, there were so few courses that we could sail. From the 360 degrees circle, most boats can't sail in the windward 90 degrees, and most fast boats should tack downwind, avoiding the leeward 60 degrees. That leaves them 210 degrees to sail in. But our windward sail blanketed the leeward one through 50 degrees of wind on each side, leaving us only

110 degrees to sail in. And most boats, especially multihulls, are most fun to sail when they're reaching.

The first season, we tried a squaresail between the two masts. With the mains wung out and the beam of the whole craft nearly 35-foot, it made grand theater, and we once put the fear of God into a sports fisherman, who was approaching a narrow bridge. However, the boat covered more ground jibing downwind, with the two mains on the same jibe, though care had to be taken to jibe the windward sail first, or the booms could tangle. Jibing downwind, the squaresail wouldn't fill, no matter what the wind strength, and in the second season we didn't bother with it.

Close-hauled and with only the windward sail sheeted in, a biplane rig gives a boat terrific lee helm; with only the leeward one sheeted in it has equally great weather helm. It's like a monohull heeling. Phil Bolger recently told me that he was thinking of a catamaran with the rig on one hull, to free up the other for accommodation. At the very least, he will need a different daggerboard for each tack.

The rig of *Planesail*, the larger of the two Walker Wingsails, is a biplane rig that seems to work, but the whole rig is mounted on a base that rotates. The driving sails are rigid wings, and their angle of attack is controlled by a smaller wing behind them. For 25 years Englishman John Walker has been saying, "A boat should be as easy to sail as a motor car is to drive." On the big luxurious trimarans that he is now marketing, the skipper can sit outdoors, but is more likely to be indoors, in a cockpit full of computers, gauges, and levers. "No shouting, no ropes, no winches, no nasty surprises," says Walker.

The Wingsails use electricity to run the computer and control the rig, but that is supplied by solar panels and windmills on the wing base. The wings are much more efficient than soft sails, but also much smaller. Walker is not looking for a record-breaker, but a boat with the same performance as a good soft-sail trimaran, only easier on the crew. The wings cannot be reefed, and instead are feathered in strong winds: a hard-sail equivalent to luffing. A prototype was sailed to America for the boatshow season, and weathered a hurricane 60 miles from the eye.

Though I'd certainly like to try a wingsail, I doubt I'd want to own one. My fascination with sailing has always been arranging and adjusting the sails, and I don't think I'd like a computer doing it for me, even if the computer did it better. Nevertheless it was a wonderful treat to see the prototype at a show two years ago. Walker has spent half a lifetime developing this idea, and he has brought it very far along.

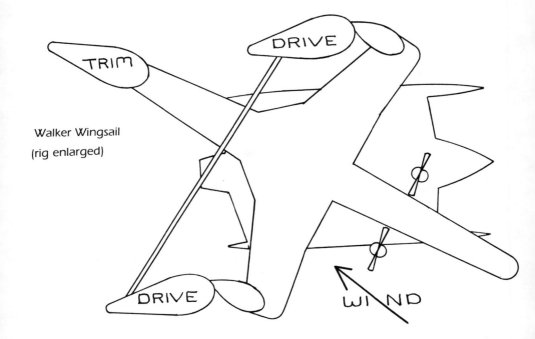

Walker Wingsail
(rig enlarged)

8

Hulls and Appendages

T ODAY, WHEN MOST multihull owners are buying factory-made boats, it is easy to say too much about hull shapes; but even those who choose not to build may want to understand what they are buying. It used to be commonplace to say that hull sections were evolving from V-shaped to round, and that round was better because it had less wetted surface. However, the Farrier shape shown in the folding section in the second chapter is a rounded rectangle; both because Farrier's boats are heavy for their length, needing a large underwater section to support the weight, and because, at high speed, Farrier boats plane like powerboats, requiring a lifting surface. Orthodox multihull thinking is that the hulls should be fine enough to slice through their own wakes, not ride up over them. All I can say in refutation is that Farrier's hulls do work. They make a big wake, but they go right along.

Section A in the drawing shows a hull with a single chine, such as Norman Cross used on his plywood designs and I used on *Hummingbird*. It has only 3 percent more wetted surface than a semicircular hull, section B. Round the chines ever so slightly, as must be done anyway, if the bottom is to be fiberglassed, and the difference is even less. I do not think that chines make as much turbulence in a narrow multihull as they do in a fat monohull. Even Piver's 90-degree V-hull (section C) has less than 13 percent more wetted surface than the semicircular section. That wasn't the biggest problem with his shapes. Rather, the 90-degree V made the hull too fat, and his fore-and-aft shape was worse than his section. He also didn't put enough sail on his boats.

To have a perfectly semicircular section, a hull must have a knuckle like the Shuttle Cat (section D), or it will contain too little interior volume for voyaging (section B). Flare it out for accommodation (section E, which is *Dandy*) and some of the wetted-surface advantage is lost. Anyway, underwater shapes look better on the drawing board than they do in the water. The next drawing shows a cat and a tri, heeled to normal windward-going shapes. There isn't much left of semicircularity.

A modern hull shape not too different from Piver's is the constant camber (section F). This building method was developed by Jim Brown, and is often used by him, Chris White, John Marples, and others. The idea is to make plywood sheets with compound curves on forms by a kind of cold-molding. This takes less time than usual, because all the veneer strips have the same shape, and don't have to be fitted to each other. It works, but the disadvantage is that the camber is constant, and usually a designer wants the camber to be greater below the waterline and less above it (section E), both for good performance and for habitability. Constant camber hulls have about 8 percent more wetted surface than semicircular bottoms. Nevertheless they do work satisfactorily, partly because the designers do pay attention to longitudinal shape, and because they put adequate rigs on the boats.

Most designers have discarded round bottoms for the floats of trimarans. Derek Kelsall tried them first, and defended them for quite a while, again because they have the least wetted surface. However, his latest designs are again showing some V-shape, because the round bottoms slam too much. It seems that 100 degrees may not be far wrong for the bottom of a trimaran float. James Wharram, the eternal iconoclast among multihull designers, continues with deep V-hulls on his catamarans, some as narrow as 45 degrees (section G). He claims many advantages for these shapes—leeway prevention, safety, ease of construction—and there is some truth to all of it. The wetted surface penalty is greater than what Piver paid, and as until recently Wharram canvassed his boats conservatively, all the ones I've sailed have been logy in light air.

Wetted surface—the frictional resistance of the water that the hulls are passing through—is the main source of resistance in light air. Wave-making is the main source at speeds higher than 1.2 times the square root of waterline, though both forms of resistance are present at all speeds. Wave-making resistance is more complex to analyze than wetted surface, but it is caused principally by weight, and secondarily by shape. Weight is so critical that Edmund Bruce devised a simple formula that predicts very accurately what high-speed performance will be, and allows boats of different sizes to be compared. The Bruce number is the square root of sail area in feet divided by the cube root of displacement in pounds. One, Bruce said, was about the dividing line between slow and fast boats, and many monohull cruisers come in near that number. A Tahiti ketch has a Bruce number of .65. Many modern voyaging multihulls are about 1.2, but all-out racers without accommodation can have a Bruce number near

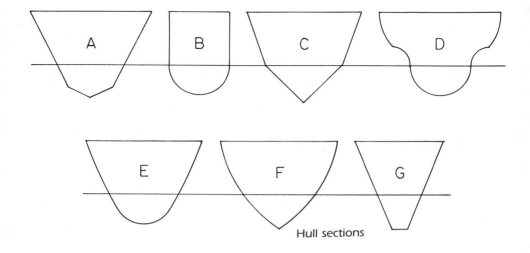

Hull sections

2.0. To judge light-air performance from statistics, the best formula is sail area divided by wetted surface. It should be at least 2.0 on a multihull, and 10 percent more on a monohull.

Piver's longitudinal shapes were bad because, for apparent simplicity of construction, the chine was at waterline the whole length of the boat, and because there was too much volume in the middle of his hulls, and not enough in the ends. Comparing the Piver Nimble underwater profile with the Crowther 28 in Chapter 2, the keel line of the Nimble looks like the arc of a circle, while the Crowther is flatter amidships, and deeper almost out to the ends. Monohull designers squeeze their ends in fine, trying to get a sharp entry and exit for a fat boat; but multihulls will inevitably have fine ends. As well as increasing speed, these relatively greater volumes in the ends are the reason that multihulls pitch less than monohulls.

A further reduction of pitching, Crowther thought, could be achieved by using the kind of bulbous bow seen on tankers. They had been tried on yachts before: Twenty years ago, an Australian challenger for the Six-meter cup (a kind of half-pint America's Cup) had a bulb, and she won at least one heat race, but not the cup. A number of Crowther's cats, such as the 42-foot *Bagatelle*, were built with bulbs. They worked fine, but unfortunately Crowther was not interested in pitch reduction for greater comfort, but rather for greater speed. The bulbous bows were faster in some speed ranges, but not in others. Crowther is less interested in them these days.

Waterline length-to-beam ratio is very important to the performance of any boat. Who would bet on a coracle against a kayak? Even the fattest multihulls are relatively slim on the waterline, but from the drawing of the six sections, it is obvious that although their areas are about the same, their beams are very different. If B and D are 10-to-1 hulls, then C is 8, F is 8.5, A and E are 9, and G is 14. Actually, Piver's main hulls were not much better than 6-to-1, and constant camber boats usually manage to be 10-to-1. When hulls become too long and slim, wetted surface can become a problem; so for many years, most designers thought that 8-to-1 was the best compromise. Today, 10-to-1 is thought more desirable for a voyaging boat.

It is difficult to draw a trimaran with 10-to-1 main hull that has any payload at all, unless she is a 50-footer. We settled for 8-to-1 on *Hummingbird*, and she is a fast boat. For years our Azorean friend Dino Silva has been buying and building boats, trying to beat her in the local races, which are handicapped on a simple square-root-of-waterline formula. He's had the old *Olympus Photo*, and Olivier Moussy's last tri, and

Heeled trimaran and catamaran

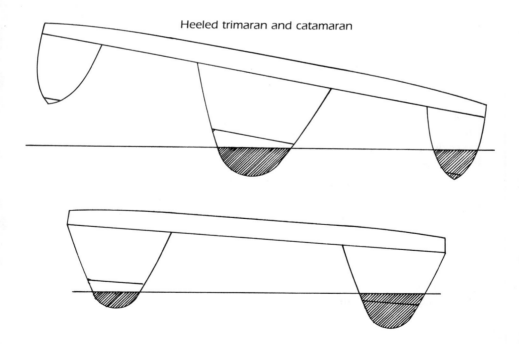

a very stripped-down cat of *Hummingbird*'s length and racy French design. He hasn't succeeded yet.

Hummingbird's hull speed is 6.9 knots. She exceeds it regularly. Once she averaged 8.4 knots for 11 hours, coming up Chesapeake Bay. However, when she goes through this barrier (it is a brick-wall barrier for most monohull sailboats) she sticks her nose up a couple of degrees, and begins to throw out a big wake. An F-27 with a wider main hull does this even more noticeably. I don't enjoy the wake's noise, though many people seem to. A worse problem is that she becomes harder to steer. She's not out of control, and maybe with a deeper or better-shaped rudder it would be less noticeable. After all, most things that you drive become harder to steer as speed increases.

Two Rabbits and *Vireo* have 12-to-1 hulls, and *Dandy* has 10-to-1. All three of these boats pass through the hull speed barrier without the slightest notice. They don't squat, and they don't make more wake. What's more, as 10 knots is approached, steering becomes lighter and more positive. At the highest speeds we've driven these boats—perhaps 15 knots—the steering is feather-light and thread-needle perfect. I don't think it's because they are catamarans, not tris, but rather because they have narrower hulls.

*　　　*　　　*

Piver's first Nimble, on which he crossed the Atlantic, had a daggerboard in the main hull, but when he came to draw plans for amateur builders, he used the dinky float fins shown in the drawing in Chapter 2. Perhaps these fins aren't worthless for leeway prevention, but they certainly are inadequate. To sail well to windward, a multihull needs a daggerboard of at least 2-to-1 aspect ratio, with one square foot of surface for every 50 square feet of sail area. If the leeway preventer is a less-than-perfect shape—a low-aspect-ratio keel, for example, or an arc-shaped centerboard—the area must be increased to compensate, because boards or keels are foils, like sails, and their leading edges do much of the work, while their power loss occurs at the top where they meet the hull, and especially at the bottom.

Nearly all multihulls will go to windward to some degree without any leeway preventer at all. *Hummingbird* does it quite well, and as our river has many shallow spots, we often tacked her down to the bay without a board. In deep water she also trucked along merrily that way, pointing high and making a good wake. When we put in the board, the wake almost disappeared. It was caused by pushing the hull sideways through the water.

For years, both Rudy Choy and James Wharram tried valiantly to design catamarans that would go to windward without daggerboards. Many of Wharram's designs still don't have them. Some of his builders put them in anyway, and others put in "vortex generators." People who are attracted to Wharram cats tend to originality. Vortex generators are long shallow fins that stick out perpendicular to the sides of the hulls, and allegedly trap water and keep the boat from slipping sideways without deepening draft. People who have installed them like them, and claim that they improve light-air performance as well. When this technology reaches the aircraft industry, it certainly will make airport runways less congested.

The Hobie 16 goes to windward pretty well without a board, but the windage of her hulls is low, and her rig is large and efficient. If you scaled a Hobie up to 42 feet—three times her present length—the hulls still wouldn't have any interior volume, and the rig would then be 2000 square feet, on a mast 78 feet off the water. Instead of her crew as live ballast, she would need at least four tons of sandbags. I don't believe that the asymmetry of the Hobie hulls helps much in getting her to weather, though the V-bottoms certainly do. Little about the attractive Hobie can be profitably applied to voyaging boats.

Nearing the Azores in 1983, *Vireo* had two days of steady headwinds. Sometimes she managed with plain sail, and sometimes she needed a single reef. She made a good 60 miles each of those days, which isn't terrible, but it was weary work, and with a daggerboard she certainly could have made 80. All boats make leeway upwind, since it is the different pressure on the two sides of the board that make it work and resist further leeway. Only with toed-in boards is there any hope of eliminating leeway altogether. Leeway costs a boat direction, but it also costs speed, because a hull doesn't move as fast diagonally as it does straight.

Because daggerboard trunks take up interior volume, boards are sometimes mounted on the bridgedeck of a cat, as on the standard Stiletto 27. Her board is really a leeboard, and it doesn't work very well. Power loss at the top, where air and water meet with no hull to end-stop the board, is greater than at the bottom. When *Hummingbird*'s board was to windward, just after tacking, it was much like the leeboard of a Stiletto, and you could see a big bubble of air going halfway down its immersed length. That top half of it was providing no leeway prevention at all.

On *Dandy*, to avoid hacking up both hulls with board trunks, I put a larger board in one hull only. The earliest MacGregor cats had the same single board, and so does the Shuttle Cat. Eventually MacGregor's customers objected to it loudly enough, perhaps for aesthetic reasons, and a second board was put into the later models. "Symmetry is always in fashion," as Carol says. I wonder how many Shuttle Cats will be built with two boards.

In both *Dandy* and Shuttle Cat, the trunk does not bisect the accommodation, but goes down one side of it, so the board is about 12 degrees from plumb. This is still much nearer to plumb than the daggerboard of a monohull going to windward. All it costs is the lost depth—in *Dandy*'s case, one inch.

The single daggerboard of *Hummingbird*, shifted from float to float, was just fine in a seaway, where we were often on one tack for days at a time. When racing, we always carried enough crew to have one person on each float, and they got the board across and reset almost as quickly as the boat tacked. Once we sailed up the Hudson, almost to Albany, and naturally we had a north wind going up, and a south wind coming back. Shifting the board then was a great nuisance, and in the narrower stretches we didn't bother. I have seen a Simpson-Wild trimaran with a daggerboard in each float, and above them a kind of pulpit, with multi-part tackles for raising and lowering the boards from the cockpit. This hardware may have cost as much as the entire materials list for *Two Rabbits*, and it had considerable windage.

Centerboards are another possibility. "Daggerboards work fine, but they're not a cruising option," says Tony Smith. I disagree with him, but he knows the market better than I do. One problem with centerboards is the turbulence of the large trunk opening. Another is that unless they are heavy—and multihull boards certainly shouldn't be—they need gear to hold them down, as well as up. If they are under a bunk, where some designers like to put them, the routing of the lines to control them can be tortuous. And of course the hold-down line must have some release mechanism, or the kick-up advantage will be lost.

The big objection people have to daggerboards, apart from having to handle them, is that they don't kick up. Because of that, we broke two boards in the 20,000 miles we sailed *Hummingbird*. We hit the board on the bottom and on floating objects far oftener than that; but boards are strong, and will often survive such encounters. The time ours didn't, we hit a packing skid, barely awash, when we were just beyond sight of the

Jersey Coast, bound for Bermuda. We continued, mostly with the wind forward of the beam. We passed through some of the atrocious fronts that always mark that Gulf Stream crossing, and the passage time was 4 days 18 hours. No doubt a board would have shortened the time, but the point is that a board may be desirable for windward sailing, but it isn't essential. Compared to breaking a mast, breaking a board is a trifle.

We made a new board in Bermuda, which gave us something to do while resting up. In finding the lumber, getting it milled, and transporting it to the boat, we met a number of local people, and that was a pleasure. Often the best things that happen to us in foreign ports happen while we're tending to ship's business. The new board lasted 9 months and 9000 miles, until we stuck it into the mud, beating up Pamlico Sound. We knew we were inside the channel markers, but we were cold and tired, and thought we could skin the point. The board grounded softly, but the wind pressing on the hull and sails snapped it off sideways.

Hummingbird's board was 13 times longer, fore and aft, than it was thick. That's not ideal proportions for a foil, but any foil will be many times stronger fore and aft than it is sideways. A number of schemes have been invented to keep a board from breaking on forward impact; but side force, resisted by something denser than water, seems to me the most likely way to break a board. Nevertheless we continued to sail, sometimes to windward, until we reached Norfolk and found wood for a new board.

Fixed keels are the final possibility for leeway prevention. Norman Cross championed them, and in addition to putting them on all his own designs, he drew them up for other boats, particularly Pivers. In the Bahamas, Carol and I met a young Florida couple and their two kids, who regularly spent six months a year among the islands on their old Kantola tri. The husband explained that she had been a centerboarder, and had suited him fine when he was single, but for the family the trunk took up too much space in the saloon, and the boat was down on her marks. Cross drew him a foil-shaped hollow fin keel that, in addition to freeing up the accommodation, gave the hull considerable extra buoyancy. It seemed a good solution for them.

Ordinarily, Cross put these foil-shaped fins, with an aspect ratio of less than 1-to-2, on his racier models. His cruising models, like the 31, have narrower solid-wood fins. The 31, for example, has a keel almost 12 feet long, protruding 19 inches below the hull, for an aspect ratio of 1-to-7. It has more than 40 square feet of wetted surface, while a daggerboard for this boat would have 16 square feet. And yet Cross was right that if a keel was to be that shallow, it *had* to be that long to do the job. Cross claimed that his keels protected the rudder, and on larger models the propeller as well. However, the longest of them stops far short of either rudder or propeller, so they might protect from groundings, but not from floating objects.

People often say that a keel is fine in the ocean, but a daggerboard or centerboard is better for shallow water, near shore. I feel just the opposite. Weekender, my little trailer design, has fin keels, and so does the Rhodes Duet, because there isn't room in the hull of either of them for a board trunk and a person as well. Drafts are 18 inches and 16 inches, respectively. The Cross 32, one of his racier models, draws 4 feet 2 inches, which doesn't close many anchorages. No matter what the draft of your boat, you can find the bottom if you've a mind to. Probably we grounded *Two Rabbits* more often than any other boat, though she drew 16 inches. The less a boat draws, the more chances we find to take.

I do not trust a boat with a keel in bad weather in the ocean. I've never tried one, but in the accounts of knockdowns—both of multihulls and of monohulls—when the skipper has been prudent and the boat is snugged down for the blow, almost always there is a sideways tripping. A wave hits the boat, and she trips and goes over. What she trips on is the keel. A hundred years ago, sailors of coastal freighting schooners learned to trust the centerboarders in really bad weather, and to mistrust the keelers.

Dozens of times, I've been in the cabin of one of our multihulls, in a gale or storm or hurricane, and a wave 20 or more feet high has hit the boat. The boat skips away from it so fast that I am plastered against the seatback or the planking. What would have happened with a keel down deep in the water? I don't know, and don't want to find out. A fixed keel is a tremendous help to a monohull, because it can carry the ballast, which is more effective when lower. It has no comparable advantage in a multihull, and I do not recommend it.

We were talking about floating objects breaking daggerboards, and how it doesn't happen often, and isn't disastrous anyway. What floating objects do break—and it can be an immense disaster—are rudders. In his three books about his voyages, Arthur Piver never mentions breaking a rudder, though he sailed his boats tens of thousands of miles, and his rudders were completely unprotected. That is the big change in the world's oceans in the last 30 years. They have become the world's trash heap, and the trend is likely to continue. Oceans have always had some debris in them: trees that were hit by lightning and fell into rivers, and 80-foot whales that died, and floated to the surface filled with the gas of decomposition. We once came upon such a whale halfway across the Atlantic, and took care to sail well to windward of him. But this natural debris is often visible from a sailboat, and not too damaging if struck. Man's own debris, a good deal of it deliberately thrown into the ocean, is what gets the rudders.

There is a lot of small stuff, annoying but not threatening to a sailor: light bulbs, styrofoam cups and peanuts, deliberately corked bottles. We once sailed through a sea coated with tiny, plastic-enveloped servings of mustard of the kind you take away from a Chinese restaurant. And in a calm, you will see that every square foot of the ocean's surface has its little black balls of crude oil—some of it spills, but much of it from cleaning tanks. Occasionally you see a whole container from a freighter, 40 feet long and weighing dozens of tons, barely awash in the seas. But it's lumber, packing skids, and oil drums that clip off multihull rudders.

Carol and I made our first three Atlantic crossings on *Vireo*. Like all Wharram designs, she had skegs in front of the rudders, and that is very good protection. As much as one third of the rudder area can be put into a skeg, without having to enlarge the total area and without harming the ability to turn. Rudders and skegs should be higher aspect ratio than Wharram uses. The ones on Searunner trimarans look good to me, and I've never heard a complaint about them.

Naively, we started our fourth crossing on *Hummingbird*, with a fixed rudder and no skeg. Much of the 10-month trip was spent working on the rudder and its hardware, and the rest was spent worrying about them. The second night out from Bermuda, we hit something that holed the bow, rumbled aft, and sheered off the rudder at waterline. It would be tedious to recount all of our other rudder disasters that trip; but it's worth mentioning that the rudder hardware that got us home was mild steel, not stainless, and was welded up by eye by a motel handyman in Dakar. Mild steel does rust predictably, but it takes more of a beating than stainless, and isn't so prone to fatigue and stress cracks.

Of course we should have had a skeg or a kick-up rudder. The one I built when we got home is shown in the drawing. The blade is held down by a rope going around it, and up to a cam cleat. The cleat is mounted on a thin piece of fiberglass that will bend under strain and release the tension. The setup was suggested by a German-Swiss, whom we met in Georgetown, Bahamas, on the way home. It does work, but it's too elaborate. Rudders don't kick up every day in 1993, though they may in a few years when the ocean becomes even junkier.

On *Dandy*, our rudders are held down simply by the friction of the pivot bolts. When one kicks up, we loosen the bolt and push the blade back down with our feet. The bolt of a kick-up rudder needs to be some distance above waterline, if it is to kick up on hitting floating debris. If it is only wanted as protection against grounding, the bolt can be anywhere.

In a kick-up rudder, the blade is subject to chafe by the box. We lost one blade blasting up the West Passage toward Newport, leaving all the monomarans in our wake. We were lucky to get an anchor down in that deep water, and were ignominiously towed to a mooring by the Coast Guard. The blade needs to be protected by a glass band from the chafe of the box bottom, and the band needs to be inspected and renewed periodically.

In his book, Chris White shows us several schemes for having a kick-up rudder underneath the hull, rather than hung from the transom. They are ingenious, and underhull rudders do work somewhat better and cause somewhat less resistance than transom-hung rudders. The difference is nothing like the difference between leeboards and daggerboards, because where a transom-hung rudder pierces the surface, it is in water that is going nearly as fast as the boat, while a leeboard pierces the surface of still water. I would say that these rudders in trunks that slot into the hull (on other types, the whole aft end of the hull hinges up like a parrot's beak) are not to be considered, if cost or building time are even a slight concern.

A skeg on an under-hull rudder will do the job very well, and a kick-up rudder on the transom will do the job pretty well, too. A rudder no deeper than the hull usually will not steer the boat adequately, and at any rate, like Cross' keel-protected rudders, it will only save itself from groundings, not debris. That stuff is floating, which is why you hit it in the first place, and it will certainly float up as it slides along the keel, and hit your rudder a good one.

On older catamarans, you often see transom-hung rudders in boxes, like daggerboards. They don't kick up, but can be pulled up. These boats were built in England, where tides are 20 feet and more, and most moorings are "on the hard" part of each day. On mooring or anchor, the skipper pulls up the rudders to keep them from grinding on the bottom as the tide falls. If you don't berth your boat in a similar place, you won't find rudders like that especially helpful.

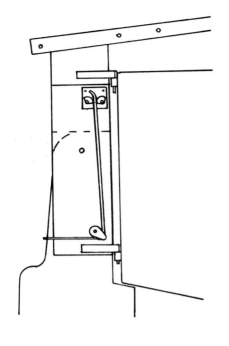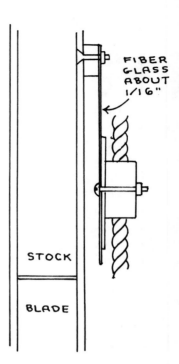

FIBER GLASS ABOUT 1/16"

STOCK

BLADE

Kick-up rudder

9

Tri, Cat, Proa, and Foiler

THE DIFFERENCE BETWEEN trimarans and catamarans may be grasped most easily by comparing *Hummingbird* with a hypothetical cat of the same length and sailplan. The drawings show the arrangements and sections, but not the profiles or sails, as those would be virtually identical. The statistics are:

	TRI	CAT
Displacement	3600 lbs.	4350 lbs.
Weight	2400 lbs.	2550 lbs.
Payload	1200 lbs.	1800 lbs.
Interior volume	357 cu. ft.	551 cu. ft.
Headroom	5' 6"	5' 3"
Hull draft	20"	16"
Waterline length to beam	8:1	10:1
Bruce number	1.20	1.13
Wetted surface	127 sq. ft.	175 sq. ft.
SA/WS	2.67	1.94

The weights can be argued, because it assumes that the cat will be loaded with an additional 600 pounds. Most people who buy all that interior volume have some intention of putting things in it. In addition, though the tri could sleep three in a pinch, the cat could sleep six with little more pinching: two under the aft decks, and two more in a rearranged dinette. All six of them could find seats in the dinette-galley. The daggerboard trunk, piercing the table, will slope inward as it goes down, but won't interfere with foot room too much. The folding chart table in the port hull is, as usual on catamarans, bigger than it needs to be. But what a lot of space there is belowdecks in this cat! On deck, what a luxurious living room there is, between the hulls!

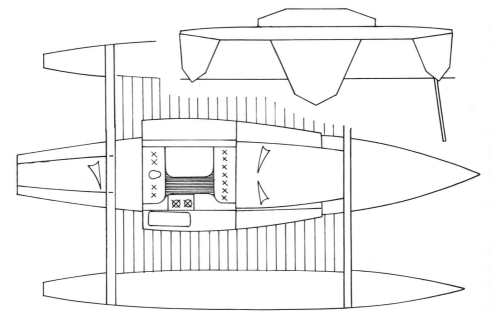

Hummingbird trimaran

When it comes to going somewhere, the trimaran must be the winner. I'm not sure she'd have more top speed, because the narrower hulls of the cat might make up for the greater wetted surface and lower Bruce number. However, top speed is seldom touched on a voyage, and certainly can't be averaged. Multihulls are always wet at their fastest speeds, and the necessary strong wind and flat sea are not found in too many places. The "French trench" is a ditch close to shore and perpendicular to the prevailing wind, dug for the setting of sailboat speed records. Most voyaging itineraries don't include sailing down it.

It is in moderate and light air that the tri will walk away from the cat. In the wind that will allow the cat to do 4 knots, the tri will easily do 5; and the tri will keep moving when, for all practical purposes, the cat has stopped. It may be nice to sit in chairs on that big deck, but it's nice to be moving, too. The cat could of course have enough more sail to overcome this light-air disadvantage, but it would require 10 feet more mast, and she has no more inherent stability than the tri. Even if she didn't capsize, the stresses on her would be very much greater; and the stresses on a cat already are much greater, because the hulls are farther apart.

If the cat really were carrying only 1200 pounds, she'd float an inch higher than shown, and her wetted surface would shrink to 165 square

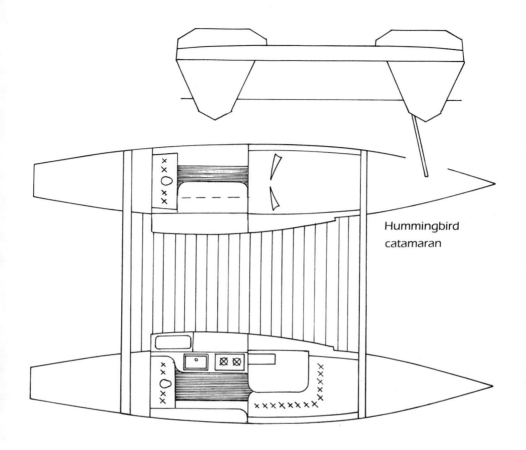

Hummingbird
catamaran

feet. That's an improvement worth making, but it's still 30 percent more
than the tri, and she still wouldn't be competitive in light going. Among
racing boats, cats do as well as tris. In small sizes, they do better, because
a trimaran under 20 feet becomes too complicated for its length, and with
complication comes weight. For the same reason, boats under 12 feet are
better off with one hull. Big ocean-racing cats and tris spend as much time
as possible sailing on one hull. Many of the racing tris now expect to have
the main hull out of the water often. To make that possible the rudders
have been moved out to the floats. It may be fast, but it's sailing too close
to the edge to suit most voyagers.

It is difficult to compare the motion of cats and tris objectively. The
motion of either is incredibly better than a monohull's. Downwind, nearly all monohulls roll rhythmically at certain speeds, and we have never
met a monohull sailor who came across in the trade winds and didn't
complain about it. Even after you get used to it and stop being scared, it's

nauseating. Multihulls don't do it *at all*. They also roll very little and pitch very little, compared to a monohull.

It may seem niggling, then, to say that Carol and I prefer the motion of a cat. It goes to windward at only 3 or 4 degrees of heel, where a tri may heel 10—15 degrees in gusts. That's not much by monohull standards, but we find it excessive. Some sailors complain about a "snap roll" in a catamaran, short but too quick for them. We prefer it to the longer roll of a tri. On *Dandy*, with her modern, wide hull spacing, we find the side-to-side motion even easier to take. And we definitely do not like the way a tri periodically touches her windward float to the water, sending a jet of spray at the main hull, where one of us may be trying to sleep. Tris also walk back and forth from one float to the other on wakes in harbors. It's true that there shouldn't be wakes in harbors, but usually there are. Tris and cats are as different from each other as they are from monohulls, and it's worth trying both out, before settling on one.

                              *   *   *

Two other kinds of multihulls deserve consideration: the proa and the foiler. The traditional proa carried her single float to windward of the main hull, and she "shunted" or changed ends instead of tacking. This required moving the rig and the steering gear, and although the float was a fairly heavy log, more than a little wind required that the crew scamper out on it, as human ballast. Until recently, voyaging multihull sailors were not willing to be ballast. They sat at their steering stations and jeered at the monohull crews, with their goose-pimpled legs hanging out over the windward rail. However, multihull rigs have become so much taller lately that advertising photographs now show the crew of voyaging boats perched out to windward, as if this were a fun way to go places. Perhaps this advertising (it is for trimarans, not for proas) will soften the public up, and make mass-produced proas feasible.

Over the years, Jim Brown's son Russ has worked hard and with commendable modesty to develop traditional proas. A 40-footer of his that we saw on the beach in Vineyard Haven looked like a very attractive and habitable boat, but Brown doesn't recommend his proas to others, because he knows they have less stability than cats or tris, and need careful watching. James Wharram found out about it. He built a 31-footer, also attractive, and touted it as "the top-speed seagoing boat of the future." Then one day he was waiting for the breeze in her and it came from an unexpected direction. Over she went, and Wharram turned his attention back to catamarans.

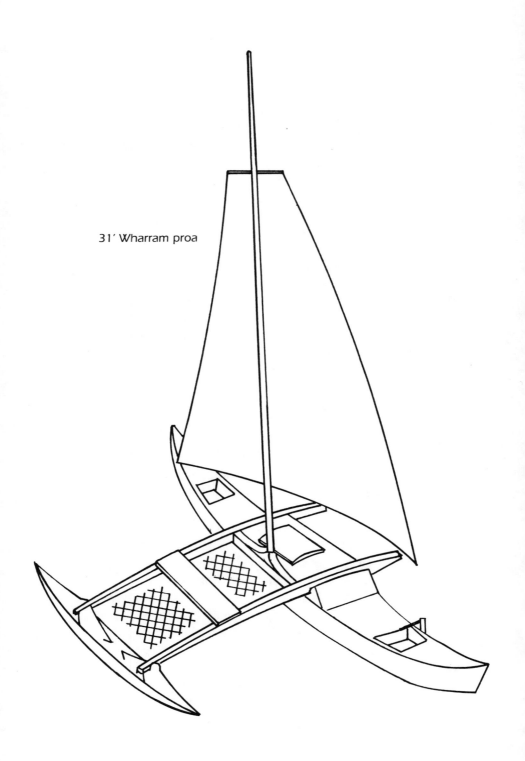

31′ Wharram proa

Long before Brown's or Wharram's proas, Warren Seaman was selling plans for the 19-foot Malibu Outrigger, a tacking proa. The float was
to windward on one tack, and to leeward on the other, and the rig and
steering gear didn't have to be shifted. Later, and for a relatively short
time, Alcort sold a tacking proa, smaller than the Malibu and made of
fiberglass. Malibus were briefly popular on California beaches. A friend
of ours who had seen them there built one and sailed her out of Cape May
for a couple of seasons. He said she went fastest with the float to windward and barely touching the water; but just when she seemed in a nice
groove there, a gust would come and over she would go. A couple of years
later, he was back in California, and saw that all the Malibus had been
replaced by Hobies. If a tacking proa big enough to have accommodation
has ever been built, I haven't heard of it.

Dick Newick has built a number of what he calls "Atlantic proas,"
with the float always to leeward. Like traditional proas, these boats also
must shunt. Most successful of them was the 40-foot *Cheers*. Designer
Newick, Skipper Tom Follett, and banker Jim Morris wrote a very good
book about the project. On a trial run, *Cheers* tacked herself and capsized
one night while Follett slept. A sponson was then grafted to the windward
side of the main hull to keep capsize from going beyond 45 degrees. Once,
in deep twilight in Cape May Harbor, Carol and I spotted a "Pacific proa"
with a similar sponson to leeward. She was about 60 feet, and breathtak-
ing to see, but in the morning she was gone.

Other designers have tried "Atlantic proas", and the French have
built some especially radical racers. The attraction of the type is the potential weight saving over a tri or cat, but the problems have been the risk of
capsize and the complicated gear. Most proas use two centerboards, with
a flap at the back edge to do the steering. This makes the forward rudder,
which is not being used for steering, very subject to damage. Wharram
used a kind of steering oar, as did the Polynesians. Last time I saw
Newick, he was still willing to talk proas. But so many of them have capsized that they are now banned from most races, and they have never
caught on as voyaging boats. They continue to intrigue many of us.

Nearly forty years ago, J.G. Baker was subsidized by the Navy to
build a 25-knot sailboat. Some authorities doubt that he succeeded; at the
least they question the accuracy of his measuring methods. But no one
doubts that under sail power alone Baker's *Monitor* did come a couple of
feet out of the water and scoot along on her foils. She can be seen today

at the Mariners' Museum in Newport News. She is a monohull planing dinghy, but since her time foilers have usually been tris or cats.

From the time when sailboat speed trials were first held in Portsmouth, England, some of the entrants have been foilers, and today nearly all are. However, foilers for voyaging are difficult to design, because they tolerate weight even less well than conventional multihulls, and because, when there isn't enough wind to get them out of the water, the foils must be retracted, or else they create intolerable drag. It would be worse than towing half a dozen unused propellers along under the boat.

David Keiper spent nearly 10 years developing *Williwaw*, a 31-foot trimaran foiler. She had four foils: one on each float, and bow and rudder foils on the main hull. All could be retracted. Though boat weight was only 1600 pounds, the aluminum foils weighed another 400 pounds, and then there was the payload. The foils not only lifted the boat, but steered her and prevented leeway and capsize, so the strain on the hinges must have been considerable. It made designing a folding trimaran look like a piece of cake.

Keiper did his experimenting in San Francisco Bay. By 1976, he reported from New Zealand that he had logged 14,000 voyaging miles on *Williwaw*, once covering 1650 miles in 10 tradewind days, with the foils continuously down. When *The Third Turtle*, a trimaran the same length, finished second in the OSTAR that year, she averaged 5 knots, and Keiper had averaged 6.9. No doubt Keiper had more favorable winds, but his achievement still is impressive.

I don't know Keiper, but despite his occasional weakening and taking "woman crew," as he described her, I suspect he traveled light. *Williwaw* was not his only attempt to make practical sailboats of foilers, but commercial success eluded him. Recently Greg Ketterman has been developing a series of daysailing foilers that he calls Trifoilers. He has broken some records with them, and unlike other record-breakers, the Trifoilers sail well on a variety of headings. He hopes to market a mass-produced model soon. However, it's a long way back from there to where Dave Keiper was twenty years ago.

It must be emphasized that no aspect of yacht design calls for as high engineering skills, or as careful fabrication, as do foils. Dimensions of lifting surfaces are not to be guessed at. Angles of attack must be calculated to fractions of degrees. In most of the marine welding I've seen, heat distortion has not spelled the difference between success and failure. In foil building, it can. There are good books on the subject, such as *Hydrofoil Sailing* by Alexander, Grogono, and Nigg. They need to be memorized. Foilers are the worst possible place for the tyro to begin his experiments in multihull design.

10

Auxiliary Power

ARS AND PADDLES are too often ignored as auxiliary power for
multihulls. If the multihull is small and light enough, an oar can
move it along pretty smartly. It never fails to work, and it needs
no maintenance. In the first 10 years of our voyaging, Carol and I never
had a motor, and when we did put one on *Hummingbird*, the chief reason
was that we had moved upriver of three drawbridges, and a new federal
law required that motors be used under drawbridges.

I rowed *Two Rabbits* facing backward, sitting in the sail locker hatch,
using a 9-foot oar and an oarlock on the inboard gunwale. Rowing is a
very efficient use of the body's energy, and it wasn't much trouble to keep
her moving at 2 knots. However, the loaded boat weighed less than a ton,
and the human body isn't happy generating more than a fifth of a horsepower, except in brief spurts; so power-to-weight ratio was minimal.

Vireo, fully loaded, weighed nearly twice as much as *Rabbits*, and
rowing her was a lot less fun. One evening we were becalmed in the lee
of Bequia, about a mile from the harbor mouth. The lights came on, and
across the water we could hear the steel drums tuning up. In those days
Bequia was not stuffed with cruise ships, and the town looked inviting.
But after a day in the tropical sun, no one on board felt like pulling that
oar for an hour, so we stayed outside until a morning breeze allowed us to
tack in. Later, coming home up the Inland Waterway, I must have rowed
Vireo 25 miles in all. We should have bought a kicker in Miami.

A yuloh is a Chinese sculling oar, rigged with a trip line to make it
easier to feather at the end of each stroke. Some multihull designers have
recommended yuloh propulsion, but I doubt they've tried it. In 1977,
when I raced on *Raka* from England to the Azores, the scrutineers for their
own inscrutable reasons required all boats to have at least three means of
propulsion, and Skipper George Payne built a yuloh for the 40-foot cat.
This did pass scrutiny, but I was glad we never had to use it. Perhaps
yulohs, like sculling oars, are not too cumbersome in boats where the
operator can stand with his feet at waterline level or below it. Standing on
the deck of a multihull means that the yuloh must be monstrously long to

hit the water at an efficient angle. *Raka*'s yuloh was at least 14 feet long when assembled, and, despite having hollow sections, it wasn't light. Besides, in the Western world, sculling has always been for short-distance propulsion, when seeing where you are going is more important than getting there efficiently. If an oar won't move a boat satisfactorily, I doubt that a yuloh will either.

Although very few outboard motors were designed to be auxiliaries, they are still the only choice for multihulls under 30 feet, and usually the best choice for multihulls under 40 feet. Inboards are now common in monohulls of 25 feet or less, but multihulls are less able to carry the weight of an inboard, and better sailing performance is expected of them. Inboards degrade performance with their weight, and with the drag of their shafts and props.

An ideal outboard auxiliary should use a 4-stroke engine,which burns not much more than half the fuel of a 2-stroke, and so saves fuel weight as well as cost. It should have a very long shaft, by which I do not mean the 19 inches that masquerades as a long shaft, because this will simplify installation, as well as keep the powerhead away from the spray. It should have a gear reduction of at least 3-to-1, which will allow it to swing a large prop. The Italians make a couple of small diesel outboards which meet all these requirements, but they are extremely heavy. The 9.9 horsepower Yamaha also comes close to meeting them, and at 100 pounds it is plenty heavy enough. However, I have seen one push a 40-foot cat with luffing sails into a stiff wind and chop at a steady 5 knots, and at a small throttle opening. James Wharram is using two of them to power his 63-foot catamaran.

Other outboards sold as auxiliaries are slight modifications of the 2-stroke motors used to push small powerboats. The shaft is a little longer, but gearing is the same. The prop is little if any bigger, because if it were, a different casting for the motor foot would be needed. Prop pitch is somewhat reduced, and the blades are somewhat widened. The most significant change may well be the decal on the cowling that says "sailboat motor." Yet many of us are stuck with these motors, because a Yamaha 9.9 is far too powerful and heavy for a multihull under 30 feet.

Electric motors are tempting, because they do have very long shafts and big, slow-turning props. We tried a 2-horsepower model on *Hummingbird*, and found that it would just about move the boat at full throttle, but would consume the juice in a good-sized battery in minutes. The next lower throttle setting gave better battery life, but did not move the boat as well as an oar would have. Looking down at the prop flipping lazily around, I wondered whether a wind-up motor wouldn't be better.

Mounting an outboard on a trimaran is difficult. Sometimes it's in a lazarette, so that the prop comes out under the hull in about the same place that an inboard prop would. This gives good performance under power, provided enough air reaches the engine (2-stroke combustion uses a great deal of air). Under sail, the outboard should be drawn up and a plug slipped into the hole that it occupied in the hull, to present a smooth bottom to the water. What will all this gear weigh, and where will it stow? Most often, the main reason for mounting an outboard in a lazarette is to get it out of sight, and pretend the boat has an inboard.

A trimaran outboard can be mounted on the side of the main hull, aft of the aft beam, as Norman Cross recommended. There, it takes a lot of spray from the float. It can be mounted on the transom, "hanging an egg-beater over the stern," as Jim Brown says. In flat water, it will push better than a side-mount. But in waves or wakes it will cavitate at one moment, and plunge toward the depths at the next. After trying both arrangements, we settled on the transom-mount for *Hummingbird*. The conventional spring-loaded, hinged bracket seen on many small monohulls does not work well on the stern of a multihull because, when lowered, the power-head is too far away from the operator. These brackets weigh 12 pounds or more, much of it in a huge hunk of chintzy plywood, which inevitably is varnished.

A sliding bracket, as shown in the drawing, can be lighter and will work better. Though on a catamaran beam these brackets can chatter alarmingly when the prop is disturbed by chop, on trimarans they stay quiet, because they are pressed firmly against the transom, and the prop is protected from chop by the wave train of the hull. We are told *never* to pull on an outboard starter cord at right angles to its spool, and the fastidious may want to avoid doing so by attaching a small snatchblock to the cord. I have had no trouble with lowering outboards off the sterns of multihulls and pulling the starter cord straight up. The cords outlast the motors.

A catamaran takes an outboard auxiliary better than a trimaran. Usually the transoms aren't wide enough to mount both a rudder and a motor. Anyway, the motor is better protected and runs smoother if it is mounted farther forward, between the two hulls. By the time a wave reaches it there, the hulls are already lifting, and a cat's hulls don't throw spray like a tri's floats. Some cats drop the motor straight down through a

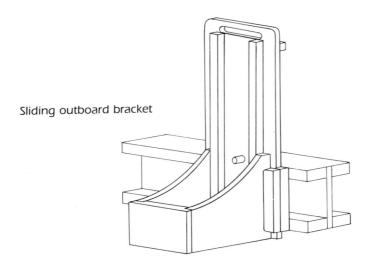

Sliding outboard bracket

hole in the center of the deck, and it works fine, though it can't be turned for close maneuvering. The problem is that an outboard without a hull in front of it to smooth out its water flow will cavitate if run at any speed through the water. It will suck air down from the surface, and the prop will turn more in air than in water.

One solution is to make the front of the bracket a kind of boat shape, and to lower and raise it along with the motor. The thrust on such a bracket is often taken on a hinged A-frame, going out and forward to the insides of the hulls. Such a bracket is often heavy and doesn't allow the motor to be raised as far above the water as does a simpler mounting. The most elaborate solution is to make a real boat of the bracket, a sled buoyant enough to float the motor, that can rise and fall with the waves, independent of what the hulls are doing. This is of course the heaviest solution of all, and the most bulk under the bridgedeck.

On *Dandy*, I have fitted a shaped piece of wood to the front of the outboard shaft, as shown in the drawing. It weighs ounces, and in flat water it eliminates cavitation at any throttle opening. In chop and wakes it works less well, because the waterline is alternately above and below the shaped piece. Slowing down will usually solve the problem. I have been told that a larger cavitation plate, perhaps made out of plywood or aluminum and bolted to the extant plate, will also work. Unlike the oversized plates that are used to lift low-powered motorboats onto a plane, this one should have its extra area forward of the shaft, because that is where the air enters. You can also buy a nozzle to fit around the prop, supposedly curing outboard cavitation, but they're nearly as expensive as a motor.

How much power should an outboard have? A multihull will often exceed hull speed under sail, but to do so with an outboard requires an engine so big that its weight and the weight of the fuel will cripple sailing performance. Better to settle for one that will take you to hull speed. In practice, you'll usually find that the square root of the waterline length—5 knots for a 25-footer, 6 knots for a 36-footer—is as fast as you feel like pushing the boat under power. Commercial ships get this performance from one horsepower per ton of displacement, but their props are better situated and their drivetrains more efficient. Two horsepower per ton is better, and that is exactly what we have on *Dandy*. Her 2-1/2-horsepower engine gives her 5 knots at quarter throttle, and weighs 28 pounds. Who could ask for anything more?

Streamlining for outboard shaft

*   *   *

If a multihull has an inboard engine, sometimes a voyage of several days can be made without even raising the sails. It isn't too unpleasant, and the crew still has the multihull advantages of less pitching and rolling, wider decks to relax on, etc. Nevertheless, I don't see the point of it. My house on land rolls and pitches not at all, and her decks are wider yet. The usual excuse for motoring is that the wind has died, but so far it has always come back again, sooner or later. As for appointments and schedules, they should not have been made. The point of sailing is to sail, not to get somewhere. It is a wonderful sport, but a terrible means of transportation.

Multihull voyaging under outboard power is equally pointless, and very much less pleasant. The thing is noisy, and its fuel needs more looking after, and sooner or later it acts up in a seaway, cavitating or getting itself wet or just quitting, for reasons best known to itself. An outboard is

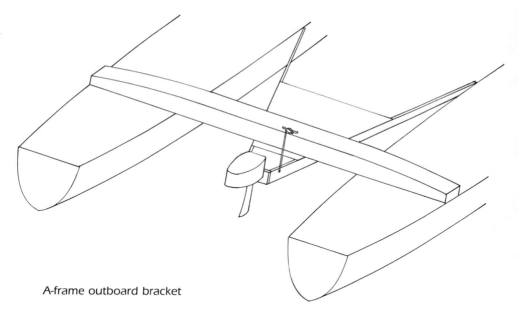

A-frame outboard bracket

more truly an auxiliary, suitable for maneuvering in harbor, threading a narrow river, or getting under a drawbridge. It is less truly an alternate way of driving the boat in open water. The smaller multihulls that typically carry outboards are easier and more fun to sail than the larger ones. So, unless an appointment has been made, the outboard need not be used often.

Though modern outboards still do quit sometimes, they are more reliable than the older ones, thanks in good part to modern ignition systems. In the years that I worked as a motorcycle mechanic, we had a standard routine whenever a bike that didn't run was brought in. We put gas in the tank, whether we could see gas in the tank or not, and we replaced the spark plugs. More than half the time, the bike ran like new, and we charged our customers for the aggravation, as well as the work. A tool kit should always contain extra spark plugs, and a new one is the one to try, not a good used one. And do make sure you have gas.

If the motor still won't start, remove a spark plug, hold its threads against bare metal somewhere on the engine, and pull the starter. If you see no spark, the problem is often wet wiring, and can be cured with paper towels. Deeper analysis of modern ignition systems is seldom possible at sea. If you do see a spark, the problem probably is a clogged fuel line or carburetor. It is possible to take a carburetor apart, clean its parts, and put it back together, even if you don't know what the parts do. Since many of the parts are tiny, this work should not be started until the motor is removed from its bracket and laid down where the parts can't get away from you. Sometimes it's just water that has collected in the float chamber, and draining that will get the motor started again.

Though I did once work as a mechanic, I do take an outboard to a mechanic trained to work on that brand every couple of years. I tell him to do whatever servicing he thinks it needs. It's not expensive, and it's good insurance.

If an outboard is small enough to have an integral tank, like ours, topping it up under way can spill gasoline into the water. An old liquid-detergent bottle, well cleaned out, can be filled with a funnel on deck. Its cap is then inserted in the outboard tank and opened. The bottle is squeezed until the tank is full.

A possible compromise between outboard and inboard is the "longtail" motor used in water taxis all over Southeast Asia. A stationary engine (a lawnmower engine, for example) is mounted on deck, and drives a long, flexible shaft to a prop some distance astern of the boat. The height of the deck of a multihull would require a very long shaft indeed, if its angle weren't to be steep. However, the engine would be relatively safe from spray and waves, and the prop could turn in deep water.

One imaginative owner of a 40-foot Wharram cat installed an automobile engine, complete with transmission, on his bridgedeck. He said that although reverse was a bit low-geared, second was fine for motoring into a wind and sea. He sometimes used third for motorsailing. If the boat could be persuaded to make 6 knots under sail, the prop could be let down and the engine bump-started in fourth. I imagine he gave up much of his bridgedeck to this engine.

Inboard motors are sometimes wanted on multihulls over 30 feet, though a trimaran has a smaller payload than a cat, and should be several feet longer before an inboard is considered. The lightest inboard on the market is the Brown 10-horsepower, air-cooled gasoline engine. It weighs 80 pounds, but with shaft, prop, stuffing box, and bilge blower, it must weigh a good deal more than a Yamaha 9.9, and it is not what most people have in mind when they say *inboard*. What they have in mind is a diesel.

Horsepower for horsepower, diesels weigh more than gas engines, because heavier castings are needed to take the strain of their higher compression. Some of this weight can be recouped in their stingier use of fuel. Diesels vibrate and make more noise than gasoline engines, again because the compression ratio is higher, but people still want them because diesel fumes don't explode. Mandatory bilge blowers now make gasoline explosions less likely, but you still read about it happening several times a year, up and down the coast.

A great problem with inboards in multihulls is the drag of propellers and running gear. This is primarily wave-making resistance, not frictional resistance, so the faster the boat, the greater the problem. Monohullers, who often care less about sailing performance, will sometimes just hang a three-blade prop out there, and let it drag. Multihullers are told to use a two-blade folding prop. However, the best folding propellers have only 20 percent of the efficiency of fixed, three-blade props.

We had a friend who told us he was thinking of repowering his recently acquired Searunner 40. It had only an 18-horsepower diesel, he said, and Jim Brown recommended 40 horsepower. Much of his time underway was motoring up and down the Inland Waterway, and contrary winds nearly stopped him. However, he knew that a 40-horsepower motor might cost him $10,000 installed.

If he had switched to a 3-blade prop, his 18-horsepower would have given him as much power in the water as a 90-horsepower engine with a folding prop. Propellers can be changed on a beach at low tide, or a diver can be hired for very little money, because divers like their work and don't get many chances to do it. But I don't think our friend ever did switch props, because it would have blurred his picture of himself as a sailor. Certainly, if I were going down the Waterway with an inboard auxiliary, I'd do it with an efficient prop, and have a folding prop in the toolbox, ready to install before heading out to the Bahamas. Nevertheless, if an inboard really is to be an auxiliary and not a prime mover, it's worth putting up with a folding prop. Folding props have a great deal less drag than fixed props, but they and their shafts and struts still do have some drag, while a raised outboard has none. Folding props can be troublesome. If at all fouled, they may not close or open completely. At least one brand does open when a multihull's speed under sail exceeds 12 knots. If the engine is in gear, the prop will bump-start it, according to Vance Buhler. His shop in St. Vincent, West Indies, builds catamarans to sail tourists from their hotels out to the reefs for a day of snorkeling. These boats are 50 to 60 feet, but many of them do fine with outboard auxiliaries. "Yes," you may be saying, "but I still want an inboard."

A folding prop under the hull is better located than an outboard prop, which somewhat compensates for its inefficient configuration. Because of that, 4 to 5 horsepower per ton of displacement is enough inboard power. Small diesels weigh 15 to 20 pounds per horsepower, and shafting, exhaust and the like weigh half as much again, so about 5 percent of the weight that an inboard auxiliary is pushing is the weight of the engine itself. That does not include batteries, tanks, or fuel. Typically, outboards weigh 5 to 10 pounds per horsepower.

Unless a catamaran is an outright motorsailer, she doesn't need two inboards. We are again butting up against the old symmetry problem, but please bear with me. The smaller engines are, the more they weigh per horsepower. A 30-horsepower Yanmar diesel, for example, weighs 368 pounds, but two 15-horsepower Yanmars weigh 476 pounds. The multiple shafts, exhausts, batteries, tanks, and controls will make the weight difference even greater. Cost will be roughly comparable to weight. Two engines will make a cat more maneuverable; but for the money and weight saved, it is worth learning how to maneuver with one engine. A cat with a single engine will readily turn in either direction, though it will make a smaller-radius turn in one direction. Even that can be minimized, if prop rotation is taken into account. A prop mounted on the centerline of a tri or a monohull has a tendency to turn the boat anyway, which is why the better twin-screw powerboats have props that turn in opposite directions. An engine with a right-hand prop should be mounted in the port hull of a cat; with a left-hand prop, it should be mounted in the starboard hull.

For a catamaran skipper who *must* have a prop in each hull, it may be better to power them hydraulically from one engine. Hydraulic systems are very efficient, and at least it won't be necessary to have two sets of tanks, batteries, exhausts, etc. However, hydraulic systems are expensive, and when they fail, they can make an extraordinary mess.

Diesel motors are pretty easy to troubleshoot: The problem is almost always the fuel. Regular cleaning of the filter and replacement of its element will be well rewarded. Even if the filter has been serviced recently, it's worth checking it if the engine balks. If the fuel is badly contaminated, it may be necessary to bleed the lines. This is messy but not difficult work.

Motors do have a place in multihull voyaging. I'd hate to spend another night drifting off Bequia, far from the rum punch and the steel drums. But an auxiliary engine that is used too much takes the fun and the sense of accomplishment out of the voyage. Even in a multihull, sailing is a slow way of getting places. If you don't make a conscious effort to change the pace of your thinking when you step aboard your boat, you find yourself turning on the motor as soon as there's a lull in the wind. You leave it on thereafter, no matter what the wind is doing, because with the motor running, you're not aware of the wind. I've fallen into the trap myself.

37' Russ Brown-designed proa, rafted to a small monohull. David G. Bolduc

HUMMINGBIRD (VERDELHÃO) leaving Cuttyhunk reefed. John Kettlewell

Pierre LaPlante's 17' HITIA in Bras d'Or. LaPlante

HUMMINGBIRD self-steering with sheet and shock cord.

54' Walker Wingsail. John Walker

TWO RABBITS in Bermuda.

32' Comanche. Multihulls magazine

VIREO minutes before she entered the trades.

A big but affordable multihull: 40' Wharram cat. Dolf Kruger

F-31 trimaran folded. Ian Farrier

F-27 sailing. Ian Farrier

An old Piver, perhaps in her final berth.

36' MacGregor on a trailer.

DANDY with biplane rig.

Sea Wind with harbor tent by Tom LaMers.

Iroquois Mk II dropping her jib. Jonathan Eastland

11

Accessory Power

A LL OF US want energy for lighting and cooking, and some of us want it for self-steering, heating and air conditioning, freezers, televisions, etc. At dockside, the ideal source of this energy is 110-volt shore power, because the weight of the generator and its fuel are on land, and because we're often paying for electricity anyway, as part of the slip fee. Naturally, we'd like to take away from the dock as much of this paid-for energy as possible, and use it later at anchor or underway. Unfortunately, that means storing it.

Carol and I once met a thrifty sailor who took away from the dock not just water, but the energy to pressurize it as well. With a series of tricky valves on his water tank, he half filled it with water, but without allowing any air to escape. The compressed air in the top of the tank then gave him a pressurized water system, while it lasted. Most of us just leave with a charged storage battery, but it takes over 50 pounds of wet-cell battery to store one kilowatt-hour of electricity, and dry cells are even worse. By contrast, a kilowatt-hour of energy can be achieved from 7 ounces of diesel fuel. So for our weight-sensitive multihulls, it is better to get our energy from fuel wherever possible, rather than from stored electricity.

In multihulls under 30 feet, a wet-cell battery is a large percentage of the available payload, and should be avoided if possible. Carol and I have never had one on any of our boats, though *Vireo* and *Hummingbird* both had them soon after they were sold in Horta, and *Hummingbird* is still winning races there. However, her present owner does not voyage often, and has little other gear aboard. *Vireo* is just plain heavy, and she no longer wins.

For light, Carol and I use lanterns that we fuel with paint thinner. It is cleaner than kerosene, and cheaper than lamp oil. Lanterns make heat, as well as light, but that only bothered us in the Bahamas one windless July. In the Antilles in winter, the heat of lanterns is adequately drawn off by an open hatch; and on many a summer evening in temperate waters, the heat is welcomed and treasured.

On *Two Rabbits*, we heated food with Sterno, and didn't really cook. This sounds expensive, but in five seasons of voyaging, we spent less on Sterno than a marine stove would have cost. Besides, on a boat so small, it was good to be able to put the stove away after each use. The food wasn't very tasty, but we're always so hungry on a voyage that food quality hardly matters.

On the last three boats, we've cooked with propane. Most marine propane stoves have electric thermocouples that turn off the gas if the flame goes out, removing some of the danger of propane finding its way into the bilge where it can collect and explode. For fear of explosion, some sailors use natural gas instead, which is lighter than air, and won't collect in the bilge but it is harder to find, especially outside the United States. The fear of explosion is not imaginary; a 14-ounce cylinder, often used with a plumber's torch, contains enough propane to blow a 30-foot boat to kingdom-come. Some sailors use these cylinders in portable stoves, and let the spare cylinders roll around in the bilge.

We use flush-mounted camper stoves that are smaller, lighter, and cheaper than marine stoves. They don't have thermocouples, but we mount the stove in a self-draining well, and the propane bottle (aluminum bottles are in every way worth the extra cost) in another self-draining well, with the gas line going out one drain and in the other. The drawing shows the setup on *Hummingbird*. The bottle well also holds gasoline, paint thinner, and everything else that might possibly explode or even burn. This system has been foolproof, even when wind has blown out a burner. On long voyages, 10 pounds of propane lasts us about four months.

Propane can also make light—a great deal of light—with a cheap mantle lantern, but a lot of heat comes with it, as with all pressure lanterns. Propane can refrigerate economically, and as there are no moving parts, there is no noise. However, it is difficult to mount a propane refrigerator high enough to drain gas leakage overboard. Tony Smith does use it successfully on the Geminis.

We light our cabins and cook without electricity, and we light our compass and our running lights with dry cells. We survive without heating or refrigeration. The one accessory we occasionally wish we had is electric self-steering, which is covered in another chapter. So far, we haven't wanted it enough to put aboard a wet-cell battery and its charging apparatus.

Twelve-volt electricity can't be used for cooking; 110-volt can. My cousin Chris Mayer has lived aboard an aluminum houseboat for eight

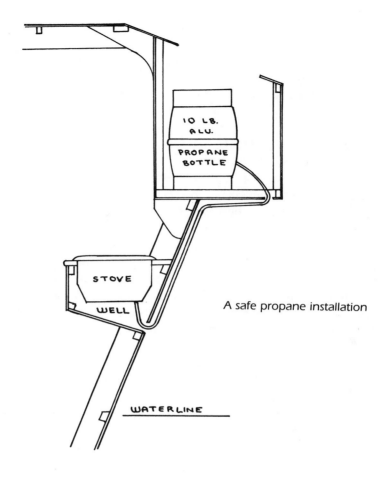

A safe propane installation

years, and although he can run a few lights off 12-volt, everything else aboard is done with 110-volt electricity. This means that he does not need two of every appliance—one for dockside, and the other for the anchorage. He does need to have a 110-volt generator (110-volt doesn't store well), and he does have to start it to make himself a cup of coffee; but for him it's probably the best system. An air-cooled gasoline generator can weigh less than a storage battery, and can generate any amount of 110-volt electricity. Chris has a water-cooled marine generator mounted in the bilge, and it weighs as much as an auxiliary engine.

Besides electricity and propane, a number of fuels can be used for cooking. Briefly, we had a wood stove on *Two Rabbits*, but only a small part of its heat found its way to the burner, and the rest of it stifled us. For the heat it produces, wood weighs six times what diesel oil does.

Relatively inexpensive "absorption-type" alcohol stoves are sold for boats, but they use enormous amounts of fuel, and give very little heat. They work just like a Sterno stove, except that the alcohol is held by a wadding instead of a jelly. The burner seals less effectively than a Sterno can, so more fuel is lost by evaporation. Alcohol delivers about half the heat of other liquid fuels, and costs 5 to 10 times as much.

Liquid fuel burns better when pressurized. Twenty years ago, pressure alcohol was the standard stove on sailboats, but high cost and low heat have put it out of fashion. Pressure gasoline stoves work very well, and are often used by campers; but the fumes-in-the-bilge problem is more severe than with propane, and they are never seen on boats. Pressure kerosene or diesel-oil stoves are the choice of some perpetual voyagers, who claim that you can learn to keep them running. I never did. After pumping up the tank pressure, you preheat the burner with alcohol, before turning on and lighting the kerosene vapor. Any impurity in the fuel—and there seem to be plenty of them—puts the flame out, and the burner must be cleaned or "pricked" before starting the process again. Increasingly, what people use for cooking is propane.

For cabin heat, away from the dock, small wood- or coal-burning stoves work better than they do for cooking, though they are bulkier and dirtier than propane and kerosene heaters. They weigh no more, but their fuel does. All stoves used for heat must have chimneys to guard against carbon monoxide poisoning, which is why cooking stoves should not be used for heat. Eventually, sails backdraft any chimney, causing soot and confusion below. Hot-water heaters are best powered by sunlight.

Dry-cell batteries are another source of accessory power, and although they are expensive for the energy they hold, their light weight makes them attractive for multihulls. On a longer voyage, they can be replaced in new ports, so it isn't necessary to start with a whole carton of them. We run our radio direction finder and our VHF radio on dry cells, but we turn them off when we aren't using them. GPS and Loran can also be run on them. A dry cell gives many more hours of use if it isn't discharging continuously. A one-pound, 6-volt lantern battery, turned on and off as needed, will run the 12-volt bulb of a compass light 40 or 50 nights.

Nevertheless, most voyaging multihulls do have a wet-cell battery. It is the wretchedest of man's inventions. Energy stored as compressed air is given back with negligible loss. From a wet-cell battery you're lucky to get back half the energy you put into it. The older a battery, the less well it will work, deep-cycle or not. In the past 50 years, while most electrical components have improved beyond recognition, batteries have improved hardly at all. Currently, batteries with a jelly electrolyte are touted everywhere to replace batteries with liquid electrolyte. Watt-hour for watt-hour, they weigh 20 percent more, and cost three times as much. They may be a little better at taking or holding a charge. Compared to the improvement that transistors are over tubes, they are a laughable improvement. Whoever invents a battery as efficient as a compressed-air tank will deserve a Nobel Prize.

Most inboard engines—and some outboards—must be started with a battery, though Volvos and Saabs can still be cranked. The thought then occurs that if the battery is there, might as well run a few other things off it. The next thought is that if other things are running off it, it might be too discharged to start the engine, so better have two batteries. Batteries weigh more than half a pound for each watt-hour that they hold when new. Whatever you charge them with weighs something, too.

One horsepower is 746 watts, or 3/4 of a kilowatt, or 62 amps of 12-volt electricity. Therefore, a 62 amp-hour battery (very modest size, though large enough to start most auxiliary diesels) is supposed to produce one horsepower for one hour when new. The most usual way to charge it is with the alternator on the diesel, running at idling speed. Typically, an alternator produces 50 amps, so it should charge the battery in a little over an hour, but in practice, it takes at least two hours, because energy is lost in the battery in various ways, one of them heat. Somehow, the damned battery just dribbles the energy away. Meanwhile, the engine has been producing at least three or four horsepower for two hours, most of it wasted. Alternators on outboards are usually tiny. The Honda 10, for example, has a 5-amp alternator, and would need to run at least 12 hours to charge the same battery.

Under sail, plenty of electricity can be generated by dragging a propeller—either the engine's propeller or a separate one—through the water, but the loss of sailing performance would hardly be acceptable in a multihull. Windmills can also generate electricity. One manufacturer claims that his 36-inch-diameter model will make 2 amps at 9 knots wind, and 6 amps at 19 knots. Windmills make a loud, ominous drone, and one owner told me proudly that his could cut my hand off.

Solar panels don't produce quite as much energy as we'd like, and cost a bit more than we'd like, but they do charge a battery silently, and without taking off anyone's hand. They charge slowly, so less energy dribbles away in heat. Each square foot of panel costs $60 to $100, and weighs

1 to 5 pounds, producing about half an amp of electricity. They are rated at maximum output, and can be expected to produce an average of four and a half times their rating in amp-hours a day. An average panel of 4 square feet might cost $300 and weigh 8 pounds, be rated at 2 amps, and produce 9 amp-hours in an average day. It would then need 7 days to charge the one kilowatt-hour battery. That may sound minimal, but a careful voyager can make do with it. He can run his compass light all night, turn on other lights when he needs to see a chart or let another boat know he's there, take a few fixes with the GPS, talk on the VHF when he has anyone to talk to, and still be sure the engine will start when he reaches port. I find it lots more attractive than running a generator every other day.

Solar power charges batteries slowly, but it heats water quickly. The very cheap and lightweight "solar showers" can sometimes get so hot after an hour in the sun that cold water has to be added before they can be used. Wind cools them, but they can often be sheltered behind a cabin or insulated with a towel. Until you've tried one of these gadgets, you can't believe how very well they work.

12

Accessories

THE MONOHULL OWNER must find a space on his boat for each accessory that he'd like aboard. On a multihull, the space can usually be found, but the wise owner will not fill it unless he is sure his boat can carry the weight.

One of the heavier accessories is a plumbing system, but not because the hardware is so heavy. Piping usually is plastic, and sinks and shower heads don't weigh much. Rather, a plumbing system is heavy because it encourages the heavy use of fresh water. This is especially true if the pump is electric, not manual. One of our friends took his beloved for a one-week cruise to Block Island, and she went through the 80-gallon water tank in four days. At home, most of us probably use more than 80 gallons of water in four days, but the 640-pound weight of it is less important. This nice young woman thought she was being careful, but she was used to showering and washing her hair every day, and to washing dishes under running water. The taps were there, and she turned them on.

Carol and I carry our water in one-gallon plastic jugs. We have one on the shelf in each hull, its handle taped with Velcro to a bulkhead. We never give a thought to how much water we drink. At the beginning of a long voyage, we bathe with wads of paper towels saturated with rubbing alcohol. A quart of alcohol lasts for many baths. On shorter voyages, or when the long voyage is going well, we bathe in a bucket on deck, often in water heated by the solar shower. One gallon of water does for two of us, because we use a washrag, instead of pouring the water over ourselves. We don't bathe in saltwater because we don't find that "saltwater soap" works very well, and we feel less clean than if we'd bathed in alcohol.

Keeping our water in gallon bottles, we always know how much we have left. If one bottle grows algae, it doesn't contaminate the whole water supply. We wash dishes in a dishpan on deck, in saltwater. Joy is the detergent that rinses off best.

A sink in a galley is more useful for storing dirty pots and dishes than for washing them. Some boats have sinks without drains set into the counter; these can be lifted out and taken on deck for the washing up. If you have the counter space to hold one, it may be a good idea. Old-fashioned yachts often have pumps for both fresh and saltwater beside the sink, but the saltwater pump inevitably means an extra through-hull fitting below waterline. A pump operated by the foot leaves both hands free for the washing.

Showers have already been mentioned—the need for a sump pump, and the nastiness of cleaning out its filter. Also, the shower stall (in practice it's often the whole head compartment) becomes funky at sea quicker than it does on land. The organic particles that bounce off your skin and stick to the walls grow mold quicker in a marine environment. It's not my idea of luxury.

Heads are not usually part of the plumbing system, because most of them don't use fresh water. A number of overlapping and conflicting laws govern them. A Canadian law requires holding tanks for heads, and it is vigorously enforced in some parts of the Dominion. American federal law requires a holding tank or macerator-chlorinator, but it is not enforced at present. It's just another of those laws that we have around to teach us contempt for the law. Some states have laws about heads, and attempt to enforce them. Before deciding on a head, local knowledge is needed.

We use a bucket head at sea, with a comfortable seat above it. This is always clean and sweet; apart from wiping it out after use, there is no maintenance. In ports with no tidal current, we use a very simple kind of holding tank that is really just a bucket with a seat on top, and a lid on top of that. We dump it when we're well out of harbor. We use it below, but we stow it on deck when not in use. We find that the chemicals you're supposed to put in a head smell worse than nature. There is small merit in most portable heads, with their separate toilets and holding tanks, and pumps to circulate the contents (more parts, more maintenance, and more weight). Whenever possible we try to use a toilet ashore, because dumping sewage into the ocean is certainly the part of our voyaging that gives us least satisfaction.

It may be true, as one of my friends says, that the present federal law doesn't forbid the dumping of sewage into the ocean, but rather the pumping of it through a hole in the side of the boat. I haven't read the law, but I know that a macerator-chlorinator does comply with it. This silly machine chops the sewage up fine enough so that it's less visible when it exits the boat, and then sterilizes it with chlorine, to retard bacteriological breakdown. The whole setup weighs at least 70 pounds, and uses considerable electricity.

A conventional marine head will only weigh 15 pounds less, but it needn't use electricity, thus saving weight in battery capacity or in fuel to run the generator. It will still need through-hulls, seacocks, hoses, and a vented loop. However, it can be placed anywhere in the boat, and a bucket head needs to be near the companionway. If everyone aboard can be persuaded not to put trash down a marine head (the discharge line is only half the diameter of a toilet discharge at home), it will only need servicing every few years. When that time comes, the work won't be fun.

Most other accessories that people want on multihulls use electricity to a greater or lesser extent. The compressors of refrigerators and freezers can run on propane or can be belted directly off the engine. Usually, they run on 12-volt, and they consume an enormous amount of it. Eric Hiscock, certainly the most experienced and respected voyager of our century, wrote, "At least two hours of battery charging or compressing in the morning and another half hour or so in the evening are needed, and it seems that more delays in port are due to refrigeration problems than any other cause." These problems can be desperate, because if it is assumed that a refrigerator will work, there may be little unrefrigerated food aboard, so the refrigerator has to work. The weight of the fuel to run the generator, the weight of the batteries to store the energy, and the weight of the refrigerator itself (20 or more pounds per cubic foot of capacity) would make refrigeration a questionable proposition on a multihull, even if it was reliable.

Recently, a *Multihulls* reader wrote a letter about a catamaran charter he'd had in the Virgins. The batteries were charged by the 13-amp alternators of two outboard engines. A little math suggests that, even in that climate, it should have been possible to keep the fridge cold and the batteries charged. However, due to the power losses of the system, the writer found that he "never fully charged the batteries, regardless of how long one ran the engine."

Carol and I make some use of a cooler for the first night's provisions and when we're in port. Bought ice cubes may seem expensive, but compared to cubes made with 12-volt electricity, they are very cheap. Sometimes a guest will ask for ice, but if we don't happen to have it, he seldom refuses a drink for the lack of it. In a built-in icebox, food can be kept fresh a week or more, and it will weigh less than a refrigerator, give many less problems, and of course consume no electricity.

Electrical systems are less reliable afloat than ashore because they don't like a salty environment that corrodes terminals before your eyes.

The electrical system that we had on *Hummingbird* was a dry cell running the compass light through a toggle switch, and we were astonished at how much time we spent repairing it. Nevertheless, many multihullers want *some* accessories powered by a wet-cell battery, so it may be worth compiling a wish list. It is emphasized that these accessories are wishes, not needs, and it may be necessary to reduce or eliminate some of them, if one also wishes to get by with solar panels, or run the generator fewer hours a day. Current drain figures taken from manufacturers' specs are minimal, and appliances may use a good deal more.

Even small economies in electricity are worth making. Fluorescent cabin lights are nearly twice as efficient as incandescent. Sailboats under 20 meters can show a bicolor bow light, instead of two side lights, or a tricolor masthead light, though that will require elaborate wiring and a sturdy mount. On that race from Plymouth to Horta, George had plenty to say about the economy and especially the safety of *Raka*'s masthead tricolor. On the third night it fell to the deck and nearly brained him. Thereafter, we heard less about it. Probably Carol and I should be using our dry-cell running lights all the time, but we only turn them on when we see other boats, or in sight of land. Someday we may meet another boat offshore that is using the same system. We do keep a good lookout, and usually find that steamers don't change course for us anyway. Indeed, by the rules of the road, we're obliged to get out of their way. We've tried kerosene running lights, but have found them better for living room decoration. They seldom stay lit in a breeze.

The electrical wish list should be in four columns: the appliance, the amp draw, the hours per day, and the amp hours. Adding the amp hours will give the wished-for battery charge per day. As examples, a compass light draws only 0.1 amp, and a fluorescent cabin light 0.7; but a water pump draws 6.0, a macerator-chlorinator 8.0, and an anchor windlass 40.0 and up. With radios and navigation gear, it is distinctly more blessed to receive than to give. Talk is cheap ashore, but listening is cheap at sea. Radars and depth sounders, which are senders, consume about 5 amps; but GPS and Loran, which are receivers, make do with a tenth of that. It takes five times as much power to broadcast on VHF as to receive on it. Radar detectors, which pick up other boats' radar and sound an alarm, also consume little electricity, but are not much use offshore, because only naval ships use their radars after the first night out. The same is true of radar reflectors.

Salesmen would like you to have aboard many electricity-consuming accessories. It is possible to buy an inverter that converts 12-volt to 110-volt power, and plug in skilsaws, hair dryers, and other nautical necessities. They will run briefly. To drain a battery slower, there are "sailing instruments" such as speedometer, apparent wind speed and angle, etc. These can be integrated with Loran or GPS, and run continuously even with the autopilot. There is a reason for having every one of these accessories, and an even better reason for not having them.

However pleasant, convenient, or entertaining marine electrical accessories may be, none of them should be depended upon. A friend of Vance Buhler was delivering a new cat from France to the Antilles. He had to reprogram the GPS at least 30 times, he said, and the electric autopilot "started spitting out plastic parts three days out from the Canaries." You must work on sailing the boat, or you must work on the systems that sail it for you. I'd rather sail the boat. GPS and Loran give wonderfully accurate fixes. The sets don't weigh much, and if they aren't left on all the time, they don't use much electricity. If you enjoy them and can afford them, there's no harm in having them. But like every other electrical accessory on a boat—like electrical systems, in fact—they are a sometime-thing.

A relatively new accessory that has caught my eye is a manually operated desalinator. Tough Bob Beggs used one in the OSTAR (racing transatlantic didn't keep him busy enough) and never had to break into his emergency supply of water. When you consider that on some ocean passages, each crew may need to take along his own weight in drinking water alone, and that if fresh water could be made on board, some freeze-dried foods could also be carried, it seems that these desalinators offer a bigger chance to save weight than can be found anywhere else on a multihull.

They are not like solar stills that gave Steve Callahan so much trouble on his *Adrift* crossing, but did in the end save his life. They are pumps that squeeze sea water at great pressure through a membrane, just like an electrically-powered desalinator. Unfortunately, they are intended for life raft use, and so are operated by the hand, not the foot. The $500 model produces a quart an hour, and the $1400 model produces 1.4 gallons an hour, with correspondingly more elbow grease. After a few days of a voyage, we are eager for exercise, and these desalinators might be just the thing. Beggs thought they were just great.

13

Dinghies and Liferafts

ON THE TWO 10-month trips Carol and I have taken, in 1979-80 and 1987-88, the two big changes that we noticed among habitual voyagers were that by 1987 most had GPS navigation, and most had motors for their dinghies. Dinghies are undesirable weight and clutter on very small voyaging multihulls—and on very high-speed ones. But for the rest of us, a dinghy is the very first luxury to be put aboard (and aboard it must be put, because good multihulls sail too fast to tow a dinghy). Though the cost of dockage has remained reasonable in some areas, such as the southeastern United States, in many areas it has risen far faster than inflation. In New England it is now 20 times what it was 20 years ago. This is partly the result of the extra amenities that have become standard—floating docks, water and electricity at every slip—and partly the competition for water frontage by non-marine users. Of these, condominiums are surely the worst, because they close the waterfront to the public, as well as to sailors.

In deciding on a dinghy, the first consideration is how it will be propelled—by oars, motor, or sail. The easy answer is, why not all three? But that's not too different from saying that a multihull should be cheap, fast, and comfortable. The different hull lines can scarcely be compromised in a boat less than 15 feet long, and on most multihulls, a 15-footer will take up too much deck space, and be too heavy.

For a motoring dinghy, the ideal shape is not too far from a shoebox. Even a small outboard will drive it at a trifle more than hull speed, bringing the bow up and keeping the passengers dry. The shoebox shape stows in very little deck space, compared to its payload, and is seaworthy enough in harbors, provided the throttle is kept twisted. Motors will punch through wakes better than oars, and they appear to be less work. I'm not sure they are less work. They are some trouble to mount, and they often need refilling with gas-oil. Even the Japanese ones are not entirely reliable. American dinghy motors are substantially less reliable, and as for British Seagulls, another sailor once said to me: "These people must love their Seagulls to spend so much time rowing them around the harbor." Of all the gear on your boat, the dinghy motor is the most likely to be stolen.

Most inflatable dinghies are roughly the shape of a wobbly shoebox, and are well matched to outboards. They sure aren't much fun to row, and they are expensive. Cheap inflatables, the ones sold in camping-goods stores, are even more expensive, for the time they last. A good Hypalon-covered inflatable will stow in a few cubic feet of space, will weigh less than 40 pounds, and will last 10 years or more. But best not to row it.

We always rowed the Repimpa. We bought her at the factory in Lisbon in 1979. She was a Portuguese copy of an 8-foot Avon, and sold at a government-subsidized price in a effort to get industry started. Soon after, the government became harder-nosed, and the Repimpa factory shut its doors. We had some nuisance with the brass valves, and had to put a couple of patches on, mostly from folding her too often in the same places. After a few years, I made a plywood floor for her, so the bottom was at least flat, not concave. She was aboard *Hummingbird* and still giving service when we sold the trimaran to José Fraga in 1991. "*A ultima Repimpa do mundo!* " said João. Hail Repimpa! How I hated rowing you!

Besides compact stowage, inflatables have two other great advantages: They are easy to enter from the water when swimming or snorkeling; and when tied astern and coming up to nuzzle the mother ship (as all dinghies eventually do), they caress where a rigid dinghy smashes. On daysails, we often brought the Repimpa on deck and lashed her down. If we expected to be out overnight, we always deflated her and stowed her below. That seems like work that might be avoided, but a voyage is more pleasant and safer with no dinghy on deck, and if you never deflate an inflatable, you are wasting much of what you paid for.

The terminal use of inflatable dinghies we have seen only in Cayenne. French sailors often go to Brazil, where they hang out in various "savage" backwaters until the cupboard is bare. Then they sail to Cayenne, where they can get the same jobs they had at home for more than home pay. They stay for a year or so, building up a kitty for the Pacific. A fleet of aged inflatables brings them ashore to work each morning, and many are past holding air. One last time, they are patched with whatever is at hand, inflated, and glassed. The pumping continues until the glass goes off.

I never heard of anyone making his own inflatable, but plans can be bought for building folding dinghies. These are composite boats, plywood-and-fabric prams up to about 8 feet long. An 8-foot by 4-foot boat typically will stow in a space 8 feet by 2 feet, and only a few inches high. Pierre LaPlante has built a couple of them, and says the problems are getting good enough fabric, and keeping the joins between plywood and fabric waterproof. His boats have leaked, and they have weighed more than plywood prams the same size.

For a while, similar folding prams were manufactured in England, and they were excellent. Fabric was Hypalon-coated, seams did not leak, and the shape was as good as any plywood pram. They cost half as much as good inflatables, and assembled easier and quicker than inflatables inflate. In Horta, our British Interpol friend let me try his, and it was wonderful to row, after the Repimpa. It went down with his sloop in that storm on the way home.

In Europe, folding dinghies up to 10 feet long are made from a curious plastic. They are four-panel double-enders, and when launched, they look like white bananas floating impudently on the water. The plastic of the panels thins out at the seams, and apparently this makes satisfactory hinges, though I'd want to keep the sun away from them. Underway they flex alarmingly with each oar stroke, but they don't seem to buckle. They stow flatter and weigh less than composite folding dinghies. Length-for-length, they are more expensive than the good inflatables, which hasn't helped their sales.

I prefer rowing a dinghy to motoring it because the gear gives no trouble, it offers exercise that I often welcome on a voyage, and it connects me to a great tradition. So many people made their livings under oars until this century that the shapes of rowboats had reached perfection by 1900. However, these shapes suit only the longest dinghies. A working rowboat was seldom less than 15 feet, and if its lines are shrunk to 8 feet, its ends are too sharp and it digs a big hole in the water, out of which the oarsman is forever trying to pull it. This happens because the working oarsman was content to move his boat at the square root of waterline, or about 4 knots, but the dinghy oarsman hopes to move his boat at the same 4 knots, which is more than hull speed, and creates a whole different wave train calling for a blunter-ended boat.

The flat-bottomed pram, which looks like it wouldn't work and doesn't work at all well in larger sizes, is not a bad 8-foot dinghy. A slight V-shape to the bottom makes the boat quieter through the water, at some cost to stability. A round bottom is no advantage in a dinghy. The stability decreases more rapidly than the wetted surface. Inevitably, round-bottomed dinghies are wider on the waterline than chined ones.

A rigid dinghy should be a pram or square at both ends. It will carry more load and be drier than a sharp-ended dinghy. Bow transom should rake 60 degrees to the water, and its base should be several inches above waterline when the boat is in normal trim. Such a pram, in plywood, is fun to build and not expensive. Eight feet long, it can weigh as little as 50 pounds, compared to 80 pounds for a fiberglass pram the same length. We are always amazed that more people don't have them.

A dinghy, like any boat, should be no bigger than needed for the load usually carried. An 8-footer is adequate for two people, and a 10-footer will do for four. Sometimes, when friends come down from shore for a party, it will be necessary to make several trips to bring them all off; but that is better than lumbering around in a big half-empty dinghy on most days, and the boat is less weight and space when stowed.

Nesting dinghies stow in less space than one-piece dinghies. Inevitably they are slightly heavier, because they need two bulkheads approximately amidships, where the two halves join; and one or both of these bulkheads could be eliminated in a rigid boat. A number of designs are on the market, both as plans and as completed boats. Most ingenious is a "bifurcating dinghy" whose two halves can be launched separately, and connected by one man standing in one half, working a set of tricky hinges. This might be useful on a monohull, with its scanty deck space, but a multihull should have enough room to put a nesting dinghy together on deck.

Most nesting dinghies break amidships, in a double bulkhead under the oarsman's thwart. *Dandy Dinghy* breaks forward of the accommodation, and is a kind of multihull herself, having a float and a main hull. Connection is by two bolts epoxied into the bow float, and two wingnuts in the main hull. The bow is decked, and serves only for flotation and to lengthen the waterline.

The boat weighs 53 pounds, less oars, and is 9 feet by just over 3 feet. The bow stows in the main hull, and when inverted she takes up only 6 feet by 3 feet of the mother ship's deck space. She is not tippy; her bottom is as wide as most 8-foot prams, but her scant flare diminishes her stowed bulk and allows the efficient use of shorter oars. There are two rowing positions to allow for different loadings. In her first season's use, she never took water over the splash guard, and only once or twice onto the decked bow. *Dandy*'s biplane rig allowed us to pull the dinghy aboard over a trailer roller on the center of the forward beam. Carol and I are in love with this little boat.

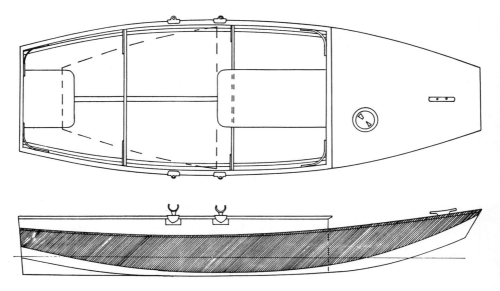

DANDY dinghy

It seems cruel to say, but sailing dinghies have a place on only the largest multihulls, where the weight and bulk of gear are of less concern. Dinghies are wonderfully responsive and fun to sail, which is why so many monohulls carry them. They are the antithesis of the stodgy, lead-ballasted cruiser whose skipper voyages under power more often than not, and sails his dinghy after he arrives. A sailing dinghy is less of a treat aboard a voyaging multihull which, if kept light and uncluttered, can be almost as much fun to sail as a dinghy, and can make its passages under sail. Most multihulls can also sail in water as shallow as a dinghy can, and can be brought within wading distance of the beach, though if the bottom paint is valued, it is better not to touch the sand.

You may have special requirements, such as children to be entertained on lay-over days in port, which will justify the weight and clutter of a dinghy rig, daggerboard, and rudder, and the inevitable compromise of rowing or motoring performance that comes with fitting a dinghy for sailing. If so, it had better be a good-sailing dinghy, because no lug-rigged leeboarder is going to entertain the kids for long, the day after they come in from reaching across the bay at 12 knots and beating the ferry into harbor. Like a lot of other unnecessary gadgets on a cruising multihull, a sailing rig for the dinghy is something you can have if you really want it. The bigger your multihull is, the more of these gadgets you can have. But every one of them will degrade the performance of even the largest multihull, and too many of them will make the boat unsafe as well as unpleasant to sail.

A liferaft is a survival dinghy, meant to keep the crew alive after the mother ship goes glug-glug. But a multihull is a raft itself, whether upright or inverted. In many offshore races, multihulls are required to carry liferafts. But that is a monohull rule, applied to multihulls with no more thought than to say, "Why not? What can it hurt?" It hurts the buoyancy, the crew's ability to get around on deck, and the ability of the multihull to slide sideways when creamed by a wave. The liferaft in a canister with its tripline and CO_2 cylinder weighs a minimum of 75 pounds, costs $3000, and must be serviced annually. Writing about his Dart racing trimarans shortly before his death, Arthur Piver said, "As the rapidly increasing list of safety requirements is making the overall boats heavier than foreseen, these particular ones may be driven through waves with a minimum of frontal interference." Sounds like fun, doesn't it?

More lives have been lost in multihull accidents by the crew abandoning the mother ship than by staying with it. Even in monohulls, the sailing literature is full of tales of boats being found still afloat, while the crew in the liferaft are long gone and never seen again. More than one multihull story relates that after capsizing or holing, all the good stuff on the mother ship was put into the liferaft, after which the painter parted, and the raft with its cache of survival gear went bobbing merrily away.

A multihull, upright or inverted, is easier seen by rescuers than is a liferaft. It has aboard not just survival gear, but everything that was put there at the beginning of the voyage, and if you are trying to survive for long enough, you will find good use for much of it. In a liferaft, capsizing and bailing out after every breaking sea, you'll wish you had the comfort and security of the mother ship.

Some advisors want us to take not only a liferaft but an "abandon-ship bag." This will contain a duplicate of nearly everything on the mother ship—not just food and water, but an extra EPIRB, an extra VHF, fishing gear, medical kit, clothing, binoculars, eye glasses, a harmonica. Dummy, all that stuff was on the mother ship you just left! You loaded your multihull with safety gear until it gave you more cause to need it. People whose minds work that way are better suited to monohulls, and should stick to them. A monohull can carry a back-up coffee maker, and go through the waves instead of over them. The essence of multihull voyaging is to trust your vessel, after making sure that it is a vessel you can trust. The trustworthiness is in the design and the seamanship.

PART

TWO

THE VOYAGING

14

In Port

I F YOUR MULTIHULL does not live on a trailer, you must find a place to keep her when you aren't sailing. Her wide beam can make this difficult. On the East Coast, from New Jersey southward, there is so much more dock space than anyone needs that negotiating a slip for a wide boat usually is not a problem. New England is more crowded, and California is very much more crowded. In Gibraltar, the most crowded yachting port I've seen, the only marina used to charge twice the monohull rate for cats, and triple for tris. I hope you have better luck.

Some marinas will want to put a wide multihull on the end of a finger pier, to avoid taking up two slips. They do that at Horta Marina in the busiest season, and yours is the boat most likely to be crunched by another boat that is not in control. It is difficult to tie a trimaran safely to the end of a pier—or to the side of it, for that matter—because, in the wakes of other boats, she will lift her float enough to kick out the best-secured fenders, and sometimes enough to put her whole float up onto a floating dock, like a drinker putting his foot up on the bar rail. It is desirable to tie any docked boat up from both sides so that she doesn't depend on fenders to keep her away from the dock. With a trimaran, it's ever so much more desirable.

I raced from England to the Azores against *Three Legs of Mann II*, Nick Keig's 53-foot Kelsall tri. With one float in the water, the other was several feet out. She was a very fast and pleasant boat underway, but at dockside few boats ever kicked out fenders as gleefully as she did. In wakes on anchor she could walk back and forth from float to float like a perfect mechanical toy. In port, Nick used to transfer all movable weights, such as anchors and water bottles, to one float; but this was laborious, and in a big enough wake she still did some walking.

Docks are convenient, especially when loading up for a voyage, but not necessarily the best place to keep a multihull all the time. I prefer a mooring or the anchor, if we're going to be in port more than a night or two, because the boat will usually swing to the wind, and it's easier to arrange the ventilation to keep her fresh and sweet-smelling below. Even in a crowded mooring field, such as seen in many New England harbors, the extra beam of a multihull usually is not a problem. If rented, moorings are cheaper than dockage, as well as more private. The other sailors that you want to meet are usually on moorings or anchors, and the sportfishermen are in the slips.

We set our own mooring each spring, and haul it each fall. It is a 50-pound mushroom which has never dragged, even with very short scope and a 28-foot trimaran on it. According to *Chapman*'s, any boat over 25 feet should have at least a 125-pound mushroom. In storm conditions, all boats will edge forward toward their anchors, and then pull back on them. The elasticity of the rode pulls them forward; the force of wind and waves drives them back. The instant they snub off aft is the instant of maximum strain, when they will be most likely to drag anchor. The force applied at that instant is to a small extent windage, but otherwise entirely the weight of the boat.

A mushroom is a better mooring anchor than any other anchor its weight, because it does not have to reset itself with every shift of wind and tide. With each shift it digs itself farther in, unless the bottom is grass or rock, so that at the end of the season, only the tip of its shank is above the mud or sand. In grass or rock, a mooring anchor must hold by weight alone, and there had better be plenty of it. A big hunk of iron—an old engine block, for example—is a much better choice than concrete. In air, concrete weighs 144 pounds per cubic foot, and iron weighs 450 pounds. But saltwater itself weighs 64 pounds per cubic foot, so submerged concrete only weighs 80 pounds, while iron still weighs 386 pounds. This and the shape of the mushroom anchor explain why I almost lost a catboat once, in a moderate summer gale.

I had two of them, sisterships, anchored out in the river, one on the 50-pound mushroom, and the other on a 250-pound block of concrete. We were away sailing on *Vireo* when the gale sprang up, and the boat on the mushroom stayed put, but the other started dragging toward the railroad bridge. Fortunately, we have good neighbors, and they somehow got out to her and towed her away from the bridge. When we came home and heard the story, I bought each of them a bottle of gin, which they received without thanks, one of them saying very simply and appropriately, "That's right."

For a working anchor we prefer a standard Danforth. We have tried ploughs and fishermen, but not every kind of anchor, because there seem to be new kinds every year; no doubt some have merit. We do not like the high-tensile Danforths because, to get the same dimensions and holding power in a lighter weight, the parts are made very fine and sharp, especially the fluke points, and they can do considerable damage to topsides, or to bare feet on deck.

James Wharram says that an anchor for any boat ought to weigh at least 40 pounds, because a lighter one will not dig through certain kinds of grass and bite into the bottom. He's probably right, but I am so unwilling to burden my multihull with such an anchor that I'd rather not stop in anchorages where that grass grows. (It may be more common in England.) Usually a grass bottom is visible from a boat, because grass won't grow in opaque water, and there will be patches of sand or mud to throw the anchor at. In the Caribbean we have found that if we drop a Danforth into a sandy patch and it slides over to a grassy patch before taking hold, it does hold very well.

It may seem wrong to weigh down a multihull with two anchors, but even if the greatest care is taken, an anchor will occasionally be lost, and if there is no spare aboard, the next stop can only be a mooring or a dock. There is no worse feeling of helplessness than being on a boat without an anchor. Books often recommend carrying a "storm anchor," twice the weight of the working anchor, presumably to be plopped overboard when the working anchor starts dragging. We prefer to carry two anchors about the same size, and set them both when the weather looks threatening.

Admittedly, it doesn't always work. One July we entered the Choptank River in midafternoon and soon found a pretty cove, closed to every direction but north. Wind was southerly and light. An hour later, dramatic thunderheads burgeoned on the northern horizon, and we set the second anchor. When the front arrived, with winds of 40 knots and more, both anchors were soon dragging in the mud bottom, which was about the consistency of Cream of Wheat, and they went on dragging until we touched. I don't know whether a storm anchor would have saved us, but probably not.

There wasn't much to be saved from. The bottom was the same consistency where we touched as where we had dragged, and the boat wasn't damaged. The next high tide floated us off. We once found bad holding ground and a potentially lethal shore in a cove on the northeast corner of Madeira. The bottom and the shores were all slick rock. We dragged even though there was hardly any wind, and awoke in the morning to find our transoms almost kissing the rock face. However, we knew that that cove was not recommended for anchoring. Five miles south at Machico was a good anchorage, where we spent many nights and weathered some strong winds without alarm.

We like our two anchors of different pattern, even though we find the standard Danforth the best pattern for most bottoms. For a second anchor we like to carry a plough or fisherman of about the same weight. A Danforth is not the best for rocks, and if it doesn't hold in whatever bottom, we'd like to try something different, not just another of the same. We carry about a fathom of chain on each anchor, 1 or 2/16ths heavier than the catalogs suggest, and the rest of the rode is 3-strand nylon, as light as possible. The lighter the rode, the more it stretches, so it shocks the anchor less when the boat snubs back. On *Two Rabbits* one of the anchors was a 4-pound Danforth with 1/4-inch rode, and it never dragged, though we finally lost it when it became entangled with a wreck, and we replaced it with an 8-pounder.

Quarter-inch nylon has a breaking strain of 1500 pounds, and so it should hold a 22-pound Danforth, which is not rated at any more holding power than that. Quarter-inch line can chafe through pretty quickly, however, and I don't recommend it. Three-eighths-inch line has a breaking strain of 4000 pounds, and will do for any multihull under 40 feet. If the boat is to be anchored for any length of time, the rode should be protected from chafe where it goes through the chock with leather, old inner tubing, or a piece of garden hose slipped on over the end.

One anchor definitely not needed in a multihull is a "lunch hook." For one thing, it's enough fun sailing a multihull so that you won't be stopping for lunch often, and because the platform is stable, there's no problem about preparing or eating lunch under way. The lunch hook is by definition an inadequate anchor, lighter and easier to handle than the working anchor, that can be set for a few hours when you're around to watch it constantly. How lazy can you get? And to pay for it, you have the weight and clutter of this third anchor aboard. In a light multihull, your working anchor will be light enough to be handled easily.

On the East Coast, and even in the steep-to Azores, we have found 75 feet of rode enough to carry. Five-to-one is plenty of scope, and on the rare times when we anchor in more than 12 feet of water (freeboard must be added to depth in figuring scope), we'd rather tie on another line than have a long rode on deck all the time. A carrick bend is the most elegant way of tying two ropes together, but two bowlines work just as well. However much anchor rode you have on deck, it all has to be overhauled every time you raise anchor. It is always wet and therefore surprisingly heavy. Unless you regularly anchor someplace where you know you'll need it, don't be stumbling around in 200 feet of anchor rode on your deck.

I make the following recommendations for multihull anchors. They are based on experience, and have no relation to charts seen in chandlers' catalogs. The key number for determining anchor size is boat displacement, not boat weight, unless you are certain that the boat will be in light condition every time she is at anchor.

Mooring mushrooms: 25 pounds for each ton. Enough chain to reach the surface at high tide, and three times that length of nylon rode plus whatever is needed for cleating off. Chain minimum 5/16-inch, and inspect it annually. For mushrooms above 100 pounds, square root of anchor weight divided by 30 equals chain size. Rode minimum 3/8-inch, and 1/2-inch gives better chafe security, if your anchor cleat can take it. However, inch for inch, nylon rope has about the same breaking strain as does chain.

Standard Danforth working anchor: 9 pounds for each long ton. One fathom of chain; size equals square root of anchor weight divided by 12. Seventy-five feet of nylon rode, minimum 1/16-inch thicker than chain-link diameter.

Second working anchor: preferably a different pattern from a Danforth. About the same weight, unless you trust the manufacturer's claim that you can get by with less. Northills were good, but are no longer made. Bruce anchors have their enthusiasts, but are expensive and hard to stow. Fortress aluminum anchors sound ideal for weight-sensitive multihulls, but somehow seem contrary to the whole idea of an anchor. John Kettlewell reports good results with them. Holding pound for holding pound, they are lighter but larger than standard Danforths. They are the same pattern as Danforths, so if one doesn't hold in a certain bottom, the other probably won't either.

A trimaran usually is anchored just like a monohull, with the rode led to the main hull bow. Some cats with bridgedecks coming far forward are anchored the same way, from the middle of the bridgedeck. Like many other catamaran sailors, we prefer to anchor to a bridle. We put the anchor down from one bow and cleat it off. We tie a docking line around the rode with a bowline, carry it around to the other bow, and pull it in while letting out the rode a bit, until the bowline is about in the middle between the two bows, and the angle formed by the two lines is about 90 degrees. Notice that to make this work, the anchoring chocks should be on the inboard sides of the bows. If a bridle is used, a cat faces the wind like a tri, which decreases windage, gets the ventilators working to maximum advantage, and means that whatever waves are in the anchorage will be taken head on.

However, some cat sailors like to anchor by one hull only, so that the boat lies cattywumpus to the wind. For this, the chocks should be outboard. I've heard skippers claim that they like the motion better, or that it's easier to do, or done from habit. Once in a while you'll see a trimaran anchored by a float, not by the main hull, and the skipper will claim that he, too, prefers it. I guess it's his business.

We haven't had much luck with a Bahamian moor, where two anchors are put out in opposite directions so that the boat will pull first on one and then the other as the tide changes. The theory is good, because the time when an anchor is most likely to foul and drag is when it is pulled out by a reversing tide and must reset itself. Multiple hulls often seem to foul one rode or the other, and often at slack water there comes a time when the wind is pushing the boat perpendicular to the tidal stream. The strain is then taken by both anchors, but with powerful mechanical advantage. Although the anchors don't exactly drag, they usually creep toward each other a bit, so that there is considerable slack when the tide starts running again. If you take up this slack, after several tidal changes you won't have enough scope, and will have to reset one of the anchors. Whatever you do, don't put an anchor out from each of a catamaran's two hulls, because that will make the damnedest cat's cradle you ever saw. For two anchors, use two bridles or cleat off both rodes to the same hull.

Many sententious books will tell you to back down on an anchor under motor. I guess that before the days of motors, anchoring just couldn't be done. The engine manufacturers must have dreamed up this goofy idea that serves no possible purpose. Half the time, you are mistaken about which way the boat will swing, so the first job of the anchor will be to dig itself out of the hole you have made for it, and reset. If you aspire to be a sailor you should be making your anchorages—and your docks and moorings, too—under sail as often as possible. There's no telling when you'll *have* to make it under sail, and you'd better know how. Besides, that's the fun of it.

Once the anchor is down and the right scope paid out, you need to take a compass bearing of land or another boat, or line up two fixed objects that are more or less abeam. Periodically for the next hour, check that bearing again. Keep an eye on the anchor, especially after a wind or tide shift. If the water is clear enough, I like to take a look at the anchor through a snorkeling mask. It's no more trouble than starting the engine, and much more secure.

Multihulls, especially the modern wide ones, are often hard to haul, because travel lifts aren't always wide enough to accommodate them. Before buying or building a boat, it's worth making sure that at least one yard near where you plan to keep her can handle her. Railways are good, but increasingly scarce. Cranes, too, can sometimes handle a multihull, but often just for a bottom job, because the yard may lack the equipment to move the boat around on land.

Any multihull strong enough to stand the seas can stand being hauled by a travel lift without damaging her connecting structure. In Los Christianos, Tenerife, *Hummingbird* was hauled by one-eyed Juan, who had hauled an aged Piver only the day before and folded it into a mono-hull. He was terrified that he'd do the same to us, and had plenty to say about his lack of insurance, but there were no problems.

Advertising photos like to show multihulls beached, and their shallow draft does make it possible, but we avoid the practice. Even the softest sand takes off bottom paint, and can go on to take gelcoat, too, and eventually glass or wood fibers or whatever your bottom is made of. Sand is the preferred universal abrasive, and is only slightly kinder than rocks to your multihull's bottom, especially as the pretty little waves are constantly moving the boat back and forth, back and forth, with a motion very similar to sandpaper held in the hand.

A friend in Massachusetts keeps his fiberglass dinghy on the beach, and drags it up beyond the high tide. He adds glass to the bottom every year, but he can hardly keep up with it. This boat weighs 80 pounds, but it can't take it. Will a two-ton boat take it better? Richard Suriani took the bottoms right out of a Hobie 18, shooting her across a narrow beach in James Bond fashion. In retrospect, he thinks it was worth it, but I've never known a toy wrecker like Richard.

We haul our multihull each winter on our own beach, but it's mud, not sand, and we use rollers. Most successful so far have been the heaviest F-series Polyform fenders, 9 inches by 30 inches. Polyform doesn't guarantee them for this use, especially if rocks are present. But they conform to lumps in the ground better than steel rollers, and they can be used right against the hulls, while steel had to be insulated from the hull with a rolling cradle. Very little jacking is required, because the compressor can be brought down to the shore in a wheelbarrow, the fenders can be deflated and slipped under the hulls, and then blown up. We may put a thousand-pound weight on one of these fenders at times, but I think they'd stand more.

15

Get Ready, Get Set...

SETTING A SCHEDULE is certainly the easiest way to spoil a sailing voyage. On land, we arrange our lives with schedules, and could hardly manage without them. On a sailboat, it is impossible to predict when the weather will allow prudent departure, let alone how long the passage will take. Setting a schedule and insisting on following it is sure to lead to disappointment and frustration, and can have much more serious consequences. Probably more sailors have lost their lives trying to keep schedules than from any other cause.

Because a voyage cannot be scheduled doesn't mean it can't be planned. Recently, Carol and I have been talking about our voyage to New England next summer, where we plan to enter two NEMA regattas, and to have Carol home in time for school in September. We will be sending in entry fees for the regattas, expecting to leave New Jersey a week before the first one, because it usually takes us four or five days to get there. If the weather is unusually bad, we're prepared to miss that regatta, kiss the entry fee good-bye, and concentrate on the second one a week later. Coming home, we will allow twice the time it usually takes, and if need be, I will drop her off at a waypoint, let her come home by bus, and singlehand down later when the weather improves. We will not risk our lives, our boat, or even our nerves on keeping to a schedule.

Although multihulls are almost always faster than monohulls, they are not fast enough to disregard ocean or tidal currents or prevailing wind patterns in planning a voyage. Once, on *Two Rabbits* in Block Island, wanting to leave for Cape May, we found ourselves without that year's almanac of the currents in Block Island Sound. Across the dock was a fellow with a very weighty double-ended sloop. He seemed to have nearly everything aboard, so we asked to borrow his almanac. He obliged, but he did ask, "How much does your boat draw?"

"Sixteen inches," we told him.

"Well then, the current should hardly affect you at all." Buddy, don't we wish it were so!

When you sail up Delaware Bay in the ship channel, the tide can run at two knots. This means that you are going four knots faster with the tide with you than against you. That is probably greater than the difference between your speed and the klunkiest of monohulls'. Cape May is a nice place, why not wait for the tide? If you catch it right, you can cover the whole 96 miles up to Philadelphia in one daylight day, because the tide advances up the bay and river with you, cresting six hours later at Philadelphia. It's an exhilarating passage, with the landscape going by lickety split, even in light air.

Coming downriver, on the other hand, you can't carry the ebb tide long, because the new flood comes about an hour earlier for each 16 miles that you travel south. Even on a multihull, it pays to get out in the channel for the ebb, ducking in toward one coast or the other to avoid the worst of the flood. Almost everywhere you are likely to sail, there are almanacs that will tell you about currents. They are not heavy or expensive, and even a multihull should have one aboard.

Eric Hiscock thought that it sometimes pays to begin a short passage in the evening, to increase the chance of arriving in daylight. We find evening departures gloomy, and if you haven't been sailing the boat for a while, they can be rushed and confusing. But we do often lay over a night, in order to get a morning start. What with bridges and other nuisances, it takes us five hours from home to reach the ocean, and we usually stop just short of it, spending a night on anchor. A morning departure increases our chances of arriving in Block Island, 180 miles away, before dusk the following evening. A morning departure usually is cheerier, and the lighter morning winds make it easier to sort things out and get used to the ocean.

For longer passages, arriving in daylight is a piece of luck, and should not be a part of voyage planning. If it's really important—if the port is new to you, and intricate—it's always possible to reef down on the last night to time your arrival for dawn. Sailing reefed is always dry and restful, and easier than hanging around the harbor mouth waiting for dawn; but it goes against the voyaging psychology of pushing on toward the destination.

The first time he sailed to Bermuda on his 34-foot catamaran *Rhiannon*, Steve Veale arrived off Town Cut about midnight. Through the rest of the night Steve and his crew didn't think they were drifting too far to leeward of the islands. But without a course to follow, they were too tired to pay much attention. When dawn put out the lighthouses and the radio masts, land was nowhere in sight. Against a briskly building head-wind, they were most of the day beating back.

They managed better than Carol and I did. Coming home from a long voyage in March, 1988, we made the stupidest and most dangerous mis-take of our voyaging lives. We had tried to go around the north end of Andros Island in the Bahamas, between it and the Jumento Cays. A lead that we were following across the sandbanks petered out, and we went aground just after high tide. It was midnight before we could get the boat off, and noon the next day before we dared sail again.

By early afternoon we were out into the Gulf Stream. The radio told us that small-craft warnings were up in Nassau and Miami, but there was no place to put in. We were reefed, with the wind 30 knots astern and building, and the current hurrying us along. At 22:00 we took in the main and set the trysail, and at 02:00, an hour after moonset, we took in the reefed working jib and set the storm jib, both to ease the surfing and to delay our arrival. Nevertheless Government Cut came up before dawn.

I don't know why we went in. All the commercial shipping was wait-ing outside for daylight, and though it would have been hard for us to stand still for an hour, with a force 7 and a 3-knot current pushing us northward, we could perfectly well have continued up to Ft. Lauderdale and come in with good visibility. Looking toward Miami, we couldn't see a single navigation light against the glare of the city. The best excuse (which is no excuse) is that neither of us had slept, and we were too tired to think of changing our plans.

Carol steered, and I brought out the handheld radio direction finder. The signal was clear and continuous, and the chart pinpointed the tower on the southern jetty. We were surfing, I was standing on deck, shouting and pointing, and Carol was laboring like a demon to keep the boat head-ed where I pointed. We could see each other clearly in the city's glare, but we couldn't distinguish anything ahead. Probably we were doing 12 to 15 knots, and neither of us saw the huge rocks of the jetties until we were between them.

Let's talk about something more pleasant. On a long voyage, a mul-tihull should follow the prevailing winds and currents of the oceans just as a monohull does, and for best speeds and safest sailing it should go at the same time of year a monohull does. For example, the North Atlantic should be sailed clockwise, the voyage taking nine to fifteen months. Whatever the starting point, the northernmost leg, going east from America to the Azores and Europe, should be sailed in early summer, when gales are fewer and the hurricane season is still in its infancy. Even following that prescription, you have to endure about a gale a week. These are continuations across water of cold fronts that earlier crossed the continent. As you get farther from land, each one is likely to be milder than the last. The first is likely to blow force 8 or 9 for 24 hours or more. The last is likely to blow force 7 for 12 hours—hardly a gale at all. Usually they will be from astern.

To sail these waters in other seasons or in other directions is to invite worse weather, and very frequent headwinds. The long-distance races, now entirely dominated by multihulls, do sometimes sail contrary to winds and currents, sometimes in inappropriate seasons. That does not mean that a multihull can break the long-established voyaging customs with impunity. What the racers do is a feat, and they are incredibly tougher people than you and I are, skilled and motivated beyond our imagining. Do not be fooled by them. They are often small, slight people, and their manner is usually quiet and unpresuming. We can't compete with them, or even start the voyages that they start with any reasonable expectation of completing them.

From Europe, the multihulls along with the monohulls work south toward the Canary Islands. The only difference is that the multihull voyagers make their passages faster and more comfortably, and perhaps as a result they visit more ports or have more time to explore the land. They wait for the hurricane season to be over in the west and the trade winds established in the south, before crossing back to America. Over here, they work north gradually through the winter and early spring, not venturing into colder waters again until the worst gales are past.

Every ocean has its logic of winds, currents, and seasons. Hiscock's wonderful book, *Cruising under Sail*, explains it all in enough detail for long-range planning. Though Hiscock sailed monohulls, what he said applies to us, too. For more detailed planning, other sources may be helpful.

Sometimes it is worth sailing a great-circle course. Ruth Wharram likes to bring along a gnomonic chart on which the surface of the globe is distorted in a curious way, so that a ruler can simply be laid on it, and a straight line drawn that will show the navigator where to steer next to follow the great circle to his destination. It's fun to look at. Great-circle courses can also be found with the logarithm book that we use for our celestial navigation.

Usually there is a compelling reason not to sail a great-circle course. Crossing from New Jersey to the Azores, for example, would take us north into cold and foggy waters where icebergs sometimes drift since our latitude is nearly the same as the Azores. Following that latitude—steering due east—would lengthen the trip, but we make it longer still by steering south of east until we pick up the Gulf Stream. There the current gives us 20 miles a day most of the way across. You'd need a very fast multihull indeed, before it paid you to ignore the lift of that current and steer a more northerly course.

*   *   *

The last job before setting out on a voyage is to bring aboard the supplies not kept aboard: tools and spares, clothing, food, and water. Once again, the weight really matters. The last job when the voyage is over is to take these supplies ashore again. If not, they tend to accumulate, then be duplicated because you forget what you already have aboard. A good multihull practice is to look around the boat every time you go ashore to see if there isn't something you can take ashore with you and leave there.

On longer voyages we probably carry 50 pounds of tools and spares, including a small, but carefully selected, woodpile. That is more than most sailors can use, but as we built all our own boats, we are capable of repairing them on passage. However, we know we can't have a spare for every eventuality, and we rely on foreign ports to have wood, glue, fastenings, rope and anchors, a sailmaker, and the like. Whenever possible we try to avoid thinking, "What if . . . ?" Even a monohull can hardly accommodate a what-if mentality, if taken far enough. The spare might break, so better have a spare spare. There is no end to it, and the boat goes down, down, down into the water.

In Horta two years ago we met the engaging Filipino Tony Wee. He had been writing to me about buying *Hummingbird* plans, but advancing age and a heart attack had convinced him to sail now, rather than build his own boat. With his son, he arrived from Boston on a 26-foot fiberglass monohull. Tony had been reading about multihulls for years and feared that the monohull might sink, so he filled the whole cabin with foam, and the two of them slept in the cockpit the whole way across the Atlantic. "What if, what if . . . ?"

Many people have strong feelings about their clothing so I hope my observations won't grate on anyone. However, I find that the rest of the world is now as informal as America, and I have never been anywhere in a sailboat where I would have felt more comfortable in a coat and tie. Clubs, restaurants, and embassies can comfortably be entered in a sport shirt and slacks. In many ports abroad and especially in ports not used to tourists, Carol feels more comfortable in a skirt than in pants, and always takes a couple of them with her. Raingear is always a problem, and the best of it doesn't last many seasons. We have never found rain pants useful, though we might if we sailed in colder waters. A good rain jacket is a necessity; the best ones have hoods permanently attached. We find sea boots awkward, and prefer to take enough sneakers so that we always have a dry pair.

Food is usually the bulkiest and weightiest item to be brought aboard, and I'm thankful that Carol is so good at organizing it. I wouldn't like to subsist as they did on *Cufflinks*, a Searunner 31 that was taking two Englishmen home after many years' residence in Zimbabwe. When we met them in Bermuda, they were selecting three cans each morning, peeling their labels, boiling them in a big pot, and eating the food right out of the cans. For the rest of the day, they made do with coffee from a big thermos, made from the can-boiling water. "Saves washing up!" they explained; but when they came aboard *Hummingbird* for dinner, they made quick work of the fresh meat and vegetables.

Another three-can multihull was the 40-foot Wharram catamaran *Truganini*, that we met in Barbados. She had six crew, and they took turns preparing three meals a day. The five English crew tried to choose their three cans to blend the flavors; but the sixth, whom they called "the Swede" and treated as a moron, would stir together the three cans nearest to hand. Later we found out that he was a physician.

Both these boats were consuming in one port food that they had bought in another, and needn't have carried on the passage. I suppose they were hoping to save money or not get sick. John Bellinger, a millenarian, left Canada for the South Seas with five years' worth of rice and lentils aboard his 45-foot Wharram, the bulwarks barely awash.

Even on a long passage to strange places, don't take more food than you will need to get there, and another 25 percent to allow for light air or a breakdown. If the place where you're going has people, it's pretty sure to have food, too. In port, Carol and I always eat at least one meal a day in a restaurant, shopping daily for what we consume aboard. It's a way of getting around, seeing things, and meeting people. And the food is better.

When we sail to Bermuda, we do bring enough canned food for the homeward passage, because Bermuda has an import tax instead of an income tax, and whatever you buy there costs double what it does elsewhere. In any other port, we count on restocking the boat, and usually it's

better than what we can get at home, because in foreign places fewer people have refrigerators or freezers, so the markets have a larger variety of
preserved food. Fresh fruit, vegetables, and eggs are not cold-stored
abroad, so the carrots don't turn to rubber in 24 hours, and the eggs will
be fine after a month of tropical sailing. The Canaries are the best place
we've found for stocking a boat. West Africa is the worst, because the
people are too poor to buy much preserved food.

Freeze-dried food does not save weight on a passage, unless you
have a desalinator, because the water to blow it up must be brought along.
It is expensive. Few multihulls we know catch rain, because usually
there's wind along with rain, and sailing becomes a full-time occupation.
Caught rain cannot be counted on, so you must still leave home port with
enough water for a drought-stricken passage.

On a voyage you will be awake at irregular hours, and as a result you
will probably eat more snack food than you do at home. If you smoke,
you'll probably do more of that, too. If you don't smoke, I can't imagine
how you'll put in the time. Whatever you do, don't quit just before an
ocean passage. A New Zealander friend tried it, and wound up smoking
the docking lines. Alcohol is as delightful at sea as on land, but even in
light wind you need to be sharp when your boat is underway. We confine
ourselves to one good belt before dinner each evening, though Ruth
Wharram takes two with no ill effects.

When crossing an ocean we become ravenous for fresh greens, so we
grow alfalfa sprouts in glass bottles. The seed package explains how to do
it. One trip we grew dry cress on dampened paper towels. It was hotter-
tasting than watercress, but very good, too. Out on the ocean it's nice to
have a little horticultural project in the cabin, and I think it controls
scurvy. Sailing in a modern yacht, it may seem ridiculous even to mention
this disease; but once or twice, nearing the end of a passage, both of us
have been listless, and wondered why our teeth felt funny.

Carol, who knows best, has a few miscellaneous observations about
provisioning. Bring spices and herbs aplenty, because preserved food
lacks both taste and variety. Bring more matches than you think you'll
need, and have them in several different, absolutely watertight containers.
Bring one giant pot (your pots should be aluminum for weight, and your
crockery plastic, for several reasons), bigger than the crew needs, so that
you can cook for guests in port. Paper towels in foreign ports are mad-
deningly metric, and will not fit your roller. Underdeveloped places have
staples but not luxuries, like pet food.

One other item, not weighty, that you would do well to bring along if voyaging foreign is a knowledge of foreign languages. Nothing else— not even money—will do so much to ease your business and augment your pleasure. English is today's *lingua franca* (sorry, you Froggies), and you can get by with it most places, but it won't be easy or fun. Because all Scandinavian, German, and Dutch sailors speak English, you only really need French, Spanish, and Portuguese in the North Atlantic, and in much of the formerly colonial world. Because these languages are related to each other and not inflected, they are not difficult compared to Chinese or even to German. Spanish is certainly the easiest because it is pronounced exactly as written, and because it is spoken nearly the same way everywhere. I know of no patois of Spanish to compare with the English of Jamaica, the French of Haiti, or the Portuguese of the Cape Verde Islands. Why not get started on it? Though most of our friends in the Azores speak English, they wouldn't be as good friends if we hadn't made the effort and learned Portuguese.

16

Nice-Weather Sailing

L ET'S GET UNDERWAY from the anchorage. We scan the deck to make sure that nothing extraneous—no Sunday newspaper, no barbeque grill—is lying around that may trip us or foul a line. The winch handles are in their proper places. The jib is hanked on, the sheets are led fair, and the sheet cars are in their proper places on the tracks. No halyard comes around the wrong side of a shroud, and the main sheet is eased enough so that the sail can be fully raised the first time. These preparations are good seamanship aboard any boat, but are doubly important in a multihull, because after the sails go up, things happen faster, and because we are about to give a theatrical performance before a hostile audience. From half the other boats in harbor, at least one hostile eye is turned toward us. They're hoping we'll foul up. Around the yacht club bar this afternoon, they're hoping to tell their cronies: "You should have seen that trimaran go out of here this morning. First they put the jib up upside down, then. . . ." We're not going to give them that satisfaction.

Unhurriedly, we raise the main first, sweat it and cleat it off, and ease the topping lift. The sheet is free to run. Good. If the main should fill while we're raising the jib, it will head the boat up into the wind again. If we raised the jib first and it filled while we were working on the main, it would head us off.

The jib comes next, and we make sure that its sheets also are free, not fouled around a turnbuckle or a hatch. Then I pull the boat up toward the anchor. You move aft, to be near the jib sheets and tiller. When I break the anchor free from the bottom, we'll have a bit of forward momentum, and you'll see to it that as long as we're moving forward, we're heading into the wind. Meanwhile, I'm dipping the anchor to remove as much sewage sludge as I can before putting it down on deck. The boat stops for a moment, then begins to move astern. It happens very slowly, and you can't notice it by looking at the water, unless there happens to be a chewing-gum wrapper floating near the rudder. But you are watching the mast of a nearby boat against the land, and when we start moving astern, you steer in reverse to get us off on the tack that we've already agreed is the best one. If my hands aren't foul with anchor slime I may back the jib to windward to turn us quicker. When we're off the wind enough for the jib to pull well—the main is still luffing—I release it, and you sheet it in to leeward. The boat stops backing up and begins to move forward. I come aft, and when we're making a bit of a wake and there's no danger of coming up into the wind again, I sheet in the main. Watch out for that ferro-cement ketch; she has a lot of scope out. We're underway.

From a mooring it's even easier, because there's nothing noisome to bring aboard. Before raising sails I have arranged the docking line that tied us to the mooring ball so that the middle of it is through the ball eye, and both ends of it are on our deck cleat. By casting off one and pulling in the other, I'll have us free without the uncertainty of untying knots. If the anchorage is crowded, I may have brought in the anchor from one bow or the other, as extra insurance that we will come off on the desired tack. If it is too crowded to give us turning room once we're underway, we may have decided to walk the anchor rode around the boat and cleat it off to a stern. Then the drill is reversed: I get the anchor up first, and you at once raise the jib. There may not be time to get the sludge off the anchor, and we'll have to heave to and raise the main later, when we're in less crowded water.

I suppose there are circumstances when it would be better to leave the anchorage under motor, but I can't think what they would be. Even a dock can usually be left under sail. Some marinas have fairways too intricate for sailing boats, especially for wide sailing boats. There an auxiliary motor is handy; but once out of the maze, I'd rather tie up to the gas dock and get the sails up there. Motors are not dependable, and the more we get used to working with our sails, the more dependable we find them.

If the anchorage is left under motor, at some point the sails must be put up while we're motoring to windward. It's easier to do with the boat on anchor, because the motion and apparent wind are less, and if a hitch develops there's time to straighten it out. We aren't closing the distance between us and that gritty seawall at the head of the harbor. Both of us can be concentrating on the sails, instead of one of us fiddling with the motor controls. The time never comes when the distance is used up and the sails still aren't right, and we must bear away under ill-set sails and racing motor, looking desperately for another place where we can motor to windward again and straighten things out.

Entering port is also better done under sail. When I went to Tabor Academy, we spent many hours coming up to docks in small boats.

"Imagine that the dock fender is an egg," the instructor would say. "You're supposed to crack it, but not break it." In multihulls we still sometimes come up to docks under sail, and of course we always did on *Vireo* and *Rabbits*, which had no motors. But docks are often crowded with other boats coming and going unexpectedly, and maneuvers under sail need advance planning. Certainly an anchor should be put down in a familiar spot, or a familiar mooring should be picked up without resort to a motor. Avoid that awkward transition between motoring and sailing whenever possible. When you're under both sail and motor, perhaps with sails not entirely under control, is when the bad things happen. The way a multihull can suddenly accelerate in a gust makes motorsailing in harbor an especially bad practice.

When we enter a strange port under sail, we often round up and anchor without any thought to the location. We get the sails down and stowed before looking around for a likely anchoring spot. When we have discussed it and agreed, we start the motor. If the motor quits, we can drop the anchor again. We are not rushed with doing too many things at once, nor in danger of running out of space to complete the maneuvers we have begun. Sail whenever you can, motor when you must, but don't sail and motor at the same time.

Our friend Austin found out about it. He left Tuckahoe after work, with three crew and bound for a week of cruising in the Chesapeake on his Alberg 30. Motoring toward Cape May after dusk, he felt a breeze and raised the main. It gave him another knot, he figured, and saved him some gasoline. However, he didn't see the squall because it was dark, and he didn't hear it because the motor was running. The squall knocked them flat, with the mast in the water, and ripped the mainsail to pieces. He telephoned from Cape May, and I drove down and picked them up. "It was just a squall," said Austin, but it ended their sailing for that week. I don't think a multihull would have been knocked down by that squall, but it wouldn't have been fun.

Sometimes we get bored with shifty winds, and wish they'd stay the same speed and direction. Trade winds, at the right season of the year, are the place where they do. One November, Carol, João, and I spent four days drifting south from the Canaries. It was so calm early one afternoon that we inflated the Repimpa, and João and I took turns rowing out ahead of the catamaran to take her picture. One of them is in this book, and you can see that the drifter is barely filling. Before we had finished, Carol was luffing to keep the cat from running away from the inflatable. For the next sixteen days we made good an average of 126 miles a day—never less than 116, and never more than 140.

The wind was about force 6, which is plenty for a 23-foot waterline catamaran, even downwind. Sometimes it rose a bit and we set the jib square across the boat, tacked to the windward bow. Sometimes it moderated and we went back to the drifter, set square across. Those sixteen days the mainsail was never set. Carol liked the predictability of the passage and the steady progress. I found it boring. "Could have come over here in a dustbin," said *Truganini*'s skipper. The skipper of another 40-foot Wharram cat—the oceans were full of Wharram cats in those years—told us that the one sail he had used most of the way across the trades was a boom tent that he set across the boat as a squaresail. He reported a good passage.

Even the trade winds are not entirely reliable. On the seventeenth day, Christmas morning, we had squalls and heavy rain. Before the day was over the wind had boxed the compass. We made the requisite sail changes and altered course as needed. It was more work, and we didn't make as good progress, but I found it a relief to be sailing the boat again.

Sailing a trimaran is quite like sailing a monohull, except that your efforts are better rewarded. Sailing a catamaran is a bit different. For one thing, if you are steering from one hull and aiming at a visible object rather than using the compass, you should aim your own hull at it, not the centerline of the boat. That may sound obvious, but when a new person comes on the helm of one of our catamarans, we have to watch him, and often have to remind him several times. On a monohull or tri, a helmsman gets used to lining up the forestay with a desired buoy or headland, and that can put a catamaran 15 degrees off course.

Some catamarans do not tack too readily. A good trimaran tacks as quickly as a monohull, and a cat with a deep board usually will tack adequately, pivoting around the board. But in tacking, cats have two things against them: Being light they have less momentum than a monohull, and so lose way quicker, especially if there are waves to stop them; and when the helm is put over, one hull must describe a smaller-radius circle than the other, while both hulls are generating extra resistance since their ends are to some extent moving sideways through the water. A cat tends to run straighter than a tri, but it must have nearly twice as much resistance to turning.

Tillers with Ackerman linkage are a great help. The principle is used in all automobile-steering systems, to make the wheel on the inside turn in a smaller radius. On a cat, the rudders will do it, too, if the distance of the pivot points on the tiller bar is shorter than the distance between the rudders. This can be achieved with curved tillers or with blocking on the insides of the tillers. A majority of production catamarans are set up with Ackerman linkage.

To tack a cat that isn't inclined to it, you need first to come off the wind a trifle without easing the sheets, to build up maximum boat speed briefly without worrying about pointing high. If there are waves, you look for the moment when they are relatively less steep. Then the helm is put down very gradually. The higher the speed, the less the helm can be put down without stalling the rudders. Stalled, they act more like brakes than like steering. If the wake gets too noisy when you're tacking, the helm has been put down too far.

Gradually, as the boat comes up into the wind and the speed diminishes, the helm can be put down farther and the boat will be turning tighter without the rudders stalling. The sheets are not touched. The jib will luff, and eventually it will fill on the other side; in other words, it will be backwinded. If this happens and the helmsman is good, you can be sure that you will succeed in tacking. The helmsman watches the water astern. The moment he sees that the boat has stopped moving forward—*before* he sees her start to move astern—he reverses the helm. With the jib pushing the bows toward the new tack and the rudders steering the sterns toward it, only a freak wave can keep the catamaran from tacking. The helmsman will continue to steer backward and not order the jib let go and re-sheeted on the new tack until he sees that the mainsail is full and the boat is moving forward. If, while the jib is being re-sheeted, the cat shows signs of coming up into the wind again and losing way, the main sheet must be let go. Always remember that the jib heads the boat off the wind and the main heads it up. Catamarans are wonderful boats, but tacking isn't their strongest point.

You may ask, how do we tack *Dandy*, with her jibless biplane rig? The answer is that she tacks as quickly as a trimaran, and apart from her deep daggerboard and her high aspect-ratio rigs, I have no explanation for it. There are no sheets to handle, either, so it's dead easy.

On all but downwind courses, even the slowest sailboats show some difference between the angles of true and apparent wind. The faster the boat, the greater the difference. Iceboats are so fast that they sail downwind close-hauled. When they jibe, the sail comes aback and luffs violently. The drawing shows how it works. The easiest example is on the

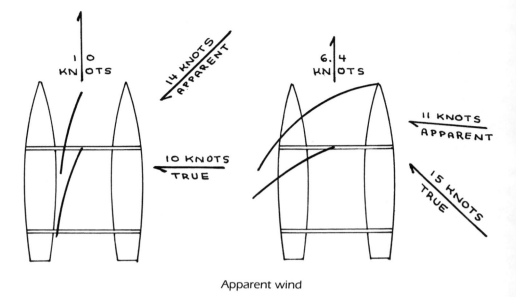

Apparent wind

right, a true beam wind of 10 knots and the boat making a good 10 knots—not impossible for a fast-voyaging multihull. Then it is easy to see why the apparent wind will be 45 degrees off the bow. It will also be a very pleasant 14 knots, which is what makes possible the 10-knot speed. In this beam wind, this boat will be close-hauled, while a slower one would have the apparent wind just forward of the beam. That is why multihulls need flat-cut sails and a rig suited to close-hauled performance. They'll be doing it more often than a slower boat.

Sailing *Vireo* from the Azores to mainland Portugal, we picked up 15 knots wind on the quarter. In 48 hours, we made a good 306 miles toward our destination, though we sailed five or 10 miles farther. We averaged 6.4 knots. The left drawing shows the average condition, with the apparent wind 95 degrees from the bow. Often we were going faster and the apparent wind was forward of the beam. As I remember it, the apparent wind was often about as far forward as the drifter tacked to the windward bow could handle, or about 80 degrees from the bow. Its luff was just breaking and crackling at us from time to time, and that is when any light-weather sail is developing its greatest power. If the wind lightened, we headed up to bring the apparent wind forward and pick up speed. Then we'd try to bring that speed back to the desired compass course. The weather was superb, and it was the nicest two days of voyaging we've ever had.

We were running away from the wind, which decreased its apparent speed. Only when you can bring the apparent wind forward of the beam does its speed increase with your progress. Iceboats can do it on nearly all courses, and multihull racers can usually do it, too. Iceboats set nothing but a mainsail, but multihull racers often set an asymmetrical spinnaker on a bowsprit amidships, because it is closer winded than a conventional spinnaker. You're beginning to see cruising multihulls doing that, too, though I suspect it's an affectation, like a spoiler on the trunk of a family sedan putting down the freeway at 60 mph. The one time we saw asymmetrical spinnakers in action, on F-27s with 25 knots of wind astern, I'm sure they'd have gone faster with symmetrical spinnakers poled out. On the other hand, they were already smothered in foam, and maybe they didn't want to go faster. Though an asymmetrical spinnaker can sail closer to the wind, it has less area and less inherent power than a conventional spinnaker.

We had a spinnaker on *Hummingbird*, but used it very little, except for racing, and I'd never buy another for a voyaging boat. It's the finickiest sail ever invented, taking more attention than we feel like devoting to any one sail while on passage. Every sailor has his horror stories about what happened when the spinnaker collapsed, and in the worst ones a knife is part of the plot. A drifter is a very easy and useful way of adding sail area for downwind courses, especially as it can be tacked to the windward bow of a multihull, without a pole. Of the ones I've tried, the plain cross-cut variety seems best, though sailmakers are eager to show you how they can add area with clever panels running various directions. These drifters are going part way toward being asymmetrical spinnakers. We had a wonderful squaresail on *Two Rabbits* that was more trouble to set than a drifter, but not more trouble to keep full. It was immensely powerful and close-winded. I doubt that a squaresail of useful size can be set with a Bermudan rig, or even with the tall gaff that James Wharram now favors. It's too bad, because a multihull is a wonderful platform for bracing and sheeting a squaresail.

If only working sails were used, any multihull I've sailed reached her downwind destination faster by tacking downwind. In strong winds in a seaway—in the trades, for example—it may be too wet and rough to increase boat speed this way, and better to run off directly toward the destination. In summer weather it is usually better to tack downwind, though it makes navigation tricker. *Dandy* does best tacking about 30 degrees each side of dead downwind, and reaches her destination under 300 square feet of working sail faster than she would with the mains winged out and a square sail set between the masts, giving a total of 600 square feet. Sloops like to head up a bit more than that, and I always thought *Rabbits* got there quickest in light air by sailing 45 degrees off course. This means sailing 41 percent farther to reach the destination, and it sounds radical; but unlike going to windward, there is no leeway down-wind, or if there is, it's in your favor. Without having sisterships or elab-orate measuring devices, it's hard to be sure what's the best downwind angle, but I do believe that unless you don't want to be bothered, tacking works better than just winging her out and letting her wallow. You cer-tainly never will exceed windspeed that way.

Joe Harris claims that with his Pearson Triton he can pass some fast multihulls, upwind and in a dying wind and chop. I'm skeptical, though I haven't shared that with him. It does point out the weakest point of sail-ing for our multihulls: We have little weight, and so we have little momen-tum to punch through the chop. The boat needs to be kept moving, even if it means easing the sheets a few inches. We're better off moving, even if not quite in the right direction.

Phil Bolger says that Dacron sailcloth is the biggest advance in sail-ing in the last 50 years. Nevertheless, Dacron sails don't last as long as people think they do. After 5000 miles, *Hummingbird* needed five more degrees to tack than she did when her sails were new. Coming home with 15,000 miles on her, the sails were rags, and Carol was patching the jib nearly every night. They were American cloth; in our experience, Chinese and British cloth hold up somewhat better. It is unwise to go on even a short voyage without a few spare scraps of sailcloth and some needles and thread. Often, a small tear can be sewn up and prevented from becoming a large tear, until you can get it to a sailmaker.

Kevlar and Mylar sails are now much used among racers, and a friend who races in the Chesapeake has given me impressive arguments for them. They don't last as long as Dacron sails, he admits, but while they last, they hold their shape. The price is still higher than Dacron, but is coming down. That's often the way with new technologies, and it's worth keeping an open mind about these new sails. We had one once on one of our racing prams, and it made a godawful noise when it luffed, but it wasn't new and it did have a good shape. This material likes sunlight even less than Dacron does.

Reefing is an essential part of nice-weather sailing, as well as nasty-weather sailing. On a nice afternoon along the Jersey Coast, the wind often builds to 25 knots, and unless you're going downwind (and straight for the beach) you need to be reefed. In the Caribbean in winter, the wind blows 25 or 30 knots nearly every day, but the sun is out and no front is coming. It's just nice weather. The saying is that monohulls should carry enough sail for the prevailing wind, and be prepared to heel sharply in the gusts. A multihull should be canvassed for the gusts. There is a tendency to reverse this laudable cautionary advice. A monohull has a hull speed that she's locked into—say 7 knots for a 27-foot waterline boat—and once that speed is reached, the skipper is often wise enough to realize that pressing the boat farther just heels her farther and digs a bigger hole in the water, so he'll probably reef. However, a multihull has no such maximum speed, and it's tempting just to leave the sails up and go faster. That's what Dan McCarthy's friends were doing when they bought the farm with the big cat.

The photograph shows *Hummingbird* leaving Cuttyhunk under reefed main and jib. At anchor in the pond we thought there was a lot of wind, and thinking there would be more outside, we reefed as we put up the sails. Outside, we found there wasn't so much wind after all, so half an hour later we unreefed. We don't feel the least bit humiliated about it. There is never harm in reefing, and there may be great harm in not reefing.

Fear of capsize may be the only good reason for reefing a racer, but there are many excellent reasons for reefing a voyager, and the longer the passage, the better the reasons. Who wants a puss full of saltwater? What clothes will you put on after that merry prank, and how many changes of clothes do you have? How about the alarm clock on the bedroom shelf, and that jar of candy? Do we really want them on the floor? This boat is our home, our nest for the duration of the voyage, so why are we rushing to foul her? And she will take only a certain amount of abuse, though most multihulls will take more than we can. Are we really hell-bent to cripple her?

Though multihulls will exceed hull speed readily, on a voyage we rarely find it desirable to do so. We don't have a knotmeter, so high speed won't yield us a number that we can brag about later. What we're looking for is a fast passage, as devoid of incident as possible. We work hard to keep the boat going near hull speed in mild conditions, and in strong winds we'll reef without hesitation.

The force of the wind increases with the square of its speed. This makes a windspeed gauge a poor indicator, because it tells only the square root of what you should be paying attention to. Go out on deck; what you feel is the wind's pressure, not its speed. That's an indication worth having. It's wind pressure, not speed, that will bring the waves on deck, hurl the crockery to the floor, and *in extremis* tip over the boat.

It's hard to make rules about when to reef, because they will vary with the size of the boat, the size of her rig, and many other factors. As a very rough guide, wind force reaches one pound per square foot at 16 mph, or 14 knots. That's when the smallest multihulls with big rigs and the wind forward of the beam should start reefing. Two pounds per square foot is 22 mph or just under 20 knots. At that point almost all multihulls under 40 feet with wind forward of the beam are better off reefed. When the wind reaches 4 pounds per square foot (less than 28 knots), that's the end of nice weather as far as we're concerned, and we try not to be out in it.

*   *   *

Racing is one of our greatest voyaging pleasures. That may sound contradictory, but there are few of us who, seeing another boat nearby, have not given another look at sheet adjustment and checked our progress (perhaps turning just our eyes, not our whole heads) against the other boat. How can we forget bowling into Newport on *Hummingbird* alongside a 45-foot IOR sloop? She had a big genoa, and a half dozen uniformed young men pulling strings. Carol and I sat in our companionway, under our working sailplan, watching the sloop as we gradually came up beside her and then put her astern. Only one of the young men ever looked our way; he was up in the bow and not pulling strings. He had a big grin on his face, and we hope he has a multihull of his own now, because we're sure he wasn't invited back aboard that sloop.

How can we forget departing Newport beside a ragged J-24 with four even raggeder kids running her? Rounding Goat Island, we both popped spinnakers, but they had enough wind to plane, and despite our strenuous efforts, they steadily pulled away. Halfway up Narragansett Bay they dropped their chute. Keeping a monohull on course when planing is a lot of work, and probably they wanted to roll new joints. As we came by, they gave us the rebel yell, and we waved gamely. If you don't call that racing, you don't understand the word.

Formal racing is less cutthroat. The races of Sea Week have been the highlight of all our voyages to Horta, especially in the early years soon after the fall of the Portuguese dictatorship when it was hoped that yachting would be a new road to liberty, equality, and fraternity. As we readied our boats on the moorings, a club launch would come among us, packed with youngsters. "How many can you take?" We took as many as the boat could safely carry. They were all so eager and friendly, and some of them became good sailors and have their own boats today. However, the Azores have now settled down to democracy and the commercial culture that goes with it. A new generation of youngsters sits on the harbor wall during Sea Week, drinking beer and listening to rock music, hardly noticing the sailboats getting ready for the race.

The racing still is fun. Most multihull racing is not done in the clubby, snobbish way that monohull racing is. Typically, the sponsors are associations, not clubs. They are open to everyone, and hoping for new members. To join, you do not have to have a fast boat, or even be a good sailor. We want more racers, especially you! One year in Horta, a 35-foot Aztec catamaran, a bigger and slower sister to the Iroquois, signed up for a race. In addition to living aboard and carrying all the equipment that that implies, the skipper had recently become a ham radio buff with so many batteries that the bridgedeck clearance was half what it was designed to be. Nevertheless, he gamely raced. He finished last among the multihulls, though he did beat a number of monohulls. I forget how he did on handicap. We appreciated having him join us, and he appreciated the party afterwards. Whatever your boat, a multihull association will work out a handicap that will give you a chance to win, on a day when you are sailing especially well. You don't have to have a racer in order to race.

It's the same way in New England, where Carol and I have started racing more recently. Usually there are parties before and after the races, much good talk, and a chance to meet new friends. What's the harm in it? In addition to the social life that goes with racing, it's fun to sail your boat at her maximum potential for a few hours, to make the sail changes and the small adjustments that you might not bother with on passage. Often you will learn something from racing that will be useful later when voyaging.

What in your own voyaging plans is a more attractive destination than the starting line of a race? The only problem with races is that they do start on schedule, so they force a schedule onto a voyaging plan. However, if a few extra days are allowed, and if it is kept in mind that it would be nice, but not essential, to be there for the start, no harm should result.

17

Self-Steering

P EOPLE WANT TO steer your multihull. If friends come out for a day-sail with you, you may have to act like a school teacher and set up a steering schedule to satisfy all of them. On even a short voyage, however, steering can become tedious, especially if only one or two people are aboard. Having a hand constantly on the helm makes it hard to cook, check the chart, or adjust the binoculars, and often while you're doing those things, the boat will wander far off course. Self-steering gets to seem highly desirable, but the danger of it is that if the watch is relieved of steering, he may become inattentive to other things, too.

Some years ago, a big motor yacht with her two paid crew asleep in the cabin, came plowing into an East Coast port and caromed off several other yachts. Parts of the ocean have very little traffic, but in other parts such as the Gulf Stream between North America and Europe, you're likely to be within sight of shipping more often than not; and shipping has the right of way over boats less than 20 meters long. No running lights or radar reflector can substitute for an alert watchkeeper.

Whole books have been written about self-steering. Too many of them assume that the only possible system is a perfect system: You set it when you leave port, and don't touch it again until you reach the next port, or at least until the wind changes direction. It sounds peachy, but like many other systems on a boat, the complications and breakdowns may make it more trouble than manual steering. To keep our self-steering simple and trouble-free, Carol and I have often been willing to settle for less than perfection.

Start with a few lengths of shock cord, each with a rope tail. If you steer with a tiller, you need the shock cords anyway, to tie up the helm in port. If you tie it up with rope, it always works loose sooner or later. It's good to have a couple of different diameters of shock cord to allow for different strengths of helm pressure. We find 1/4-inch and 3/8-inch useful. Tails are 1/4-inch line. There are eyestraps on the deck or connecting beam on each side of the tiller you're using. A shock cord can be stuck through an eyestrap, and the tail led to a cleat on top of the tiller. One of these on each side will keep the helm from swinging around at anchor. One on the windward side will do quite a little self-steering.

The simplest form of self-steering is this: You are underway and the tiller wants to go to leeward because you have a little weather helm. That's exactly as it should be for best performance. But why should you pull against the tiller hour after hour, even if it's only a couple of pounds of pressure? The shock cord will do it for you. By adjusting the tail on the cleat in very small increments—¼-inch can make quite a difference—you will eventually be able to take your hand off the tiller altogether, because the boat is self-steering. Hot dog! You're free! How long she will go on self-steering before wandering off will vary from boat to boat, but any multihull will run straight for long enough to let you go below and light the stove for coffee. Some will steer themselves for many miles at a time. When the boat does wander, she can be brought back to course without uncleating a shock cord, as would have to be done with a rope.

This crude system does not give the perfect straight-line course that a racer usually desires. However, it probably does not result in any worse course than would be steered by hand, if one helmsman was at the tiller for a full three- or four-hour watch. At least when you look at the compass and telltale after not looking for a minute or two, what they say does register on your mind. If you're steering constantly, the compass numbers eventually blur or lose their meaning.

Occasionally a boat is so well balanced that she will go on steering herself this way indefinitely, at least on windward courses. All the boats we've owned have tended to become better self-steerers as the wind grew stronger. Reefed, our two Wharram cats would steer themselves upwind forever. We'd be below, out of the spray. In milder conditions we could always sheet the jib in hard enough and ease the main out enough to achieve windward self-steering with a single shock cord. However, we weren't really sailing to windward. The arrangement cost 10 to 20 degrees in pointing ability, which was terrible if the destination lay dead upwind. It was sometimes acceptable if the destination lay 45 degrees off the true wind. Setting the sails for self-steering rather than maximum drive slows the boat down. We don't often do it, except at nightfall or in steady rain.

We have tried the various arrangements for steering a boat to windward by attaching a shock cord to the leeward side of the tiller, and the main sheet to the windward side—or to a Braine gear, which amounts to the same thing. For most modern multihulls with most of the sail area in the mainsail, this is a crippling thing to do. What's more, to get enough slack in the main sheet to do the job, the boat needs to come off the wind at least as far as she does with the eased main-hardened jib arrangement, and I believe the speed loss is greater. Certainly, it is more complicated. Try it if you like, but I don't recommend it.

Neither can I recommend a simple self-steering system for beam reach courses. Our three sloop-rigged multihulls would all beam reach under jib alone, with the tiller amidships. Once when we were repairing broken rudder hardware on *Hummingbird* between the Canaries and Dakar, we found that she would do it without any rudder in the water. Too bad we wanted to go downwind at the time. Jibs of these three boats were only about a third of total sail area, so jib alone would seldom be a satisfactory rig for them. All the books agree that beam reaching is the hardest point of sail for sheet-to-tiller self-steering. Some drawings show us a cutter rig with the staysail backed and led to the windward side of the tiller. But few of us have cutter rigs, and when I tried it with a storm jib hanked onto an inner forestay, it didn't develop enough power to pull against a shock cord.

For a while James Wharram was experimenting with quite a big sail whose only purpose was to steer. It was a tacking sail, and for 45 degrees of sail angle to the wind, it was luffing and not developing power. For a while I worked on another variety of steering sail, not much bigger than a storm jib, but it jibed instead of tacking, and so developed power quicker. Everything must be very taut for these systems to work, and gravity (the weight of the sail and its requisite boom) can easily be more powerful than wind force. Lines leading to the tiller become complex, and the attendant friction of their blocks adds to the problems.

On a beam reach it is still possible to cleat a shock cord to the tiller and steer less often. We don't find that an enormous amount of voyaging time is spent on beam reaches. On short voyages, the most usual course is to weather, because it takes more time to cover an upwind leg than a reaching or running one. Long voyages are usually planned to take advantage of prevailing weather systems, so the usual course is broad reaching or running. When a beam reach does come, as when *Vireo* was bound for Lisbon, it's usually a whole lot of fun. A multihull can kick up her heels then, and you don't mind steering.

On a broad reach sheet-to-tiller gear has worked well on every boat I've sailed. The jib sheet is led to the windward side of the tiller and a shock cord to the leeward side, as shown in the left drawing. The boat heads up, and the jib develops more power and pulls the helm to wind-

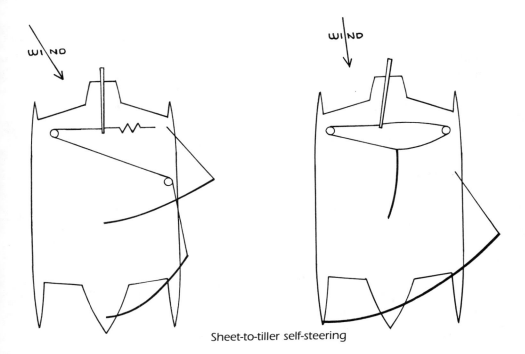

Sheet-to-tiller self-steering

ward, heading her off. The boat heads off, and the main blankets the jib and slackens its sheet, so the shock cord pulls the helm to leeward, heading the boat up again. If the lines are properly tensioned, the boat does not sail a zig-zag course, but reaches on and on uncannily straight. Course made good with this system is better than that from most helmsmen on a three- or four-hour watch.

By sheeting in the jib fairly hard, a course about 160 degrees off the wind can be kept. If the jib is well eased, the course will be more nearly 140 degrees off the wind. On *Hummingbird* it worked with plain sail, with a single reef, and all the way down to storm canvas, though it was less reliable as the sails became smaller and farther apart. The system depends on getting less than maximum power from the jib, and won't give the same broad-reaching performance as will tacking the jib or a bigger headsail to the windward bow. Still, there are times when the mainsail is driving your multihull plenty fast enough, and others when you will sacrifice a little speed to freedom from the helm. We have sailed many thousands of miles with this simple self-steering system.

Dead downwind, John Bellinger uses two jibs to drive his 45-foot Wharram cat. This is an old-fashioned system recommended by Hiscock, but because the jibs must be small, it offers up less sail area to the wind than does a mainsail alone. However, it does work, and John isn't in a hurry. He's been gone 10 years; when last I heard, he had completed a two-year refit in Australia and was headed back out into the Pacific. It looks like he's never coming home. Here's to you, John!

Downwind, we have often used a storm trysail as a jibing steering sail, while driving the boat with headsails. The right drawing shows the setup. There are no shock cords, but the trysail develops power the moment it jibes. We made our trade wind crossing this way, and the only problem we had was that if João or I went forward to take a leak, *Vireo*'s sprit boom projected far forward of the mast, and made a tempting hand-hold. If we hung onto it too long, the boat would round up, provoking curses from the afterguard.

It is weird how straight our boats have run with this system. Even when surfing, with little or no apparent wind across the deck, they never round up. The boom can be swung to port or starboard a bit, and jibing the headsail will alter course about 10 degrees. In the trades, these little adjustments were enough to bring us within spitting distance of Barbados.

If the boat has a steering wheel, it is harder to rig sheets and shock cords to steer her. Even if you could, the friction might be too great to overcome. Once a block with too much friction caused *Hummingbird* to jibe so violently that her boom that had been vanged to the lee rail broke in half. There is a good deal of friction in most wheel-steering gears. However, on *Two Rabbits* we were able to tie shock cord to a wheel, and let go of it for brief spells.

*   *   *

Next in order of complexity comes windvane self-steering. These rigs work on all points of sail, including beam reaches. The consensus is that they don't work as well on multihulls as on monohulls, because they sense apparent wind, and the difference between apparent and true wind is greater on a faster boat. Changes in wind speed—and even in the trades the wind doesn't blow at an absolutely uniform speed—will then change the apparent wind angle greatly, and when the wind speed comes back to normal, the boat may not come back to her desired course. However, a number of multihullers with great experience do favor these rigs.

The simplest one I ever saw was mounted on the outboard rudder of a rusty French ketch that did not look like a speedy vessel. The vane was attached with a rusty C-clamp to a pipe that led down to a trim tab on the trailing edge of the rudder. Wind pressure on one side of the vane would turn the tab, which would turn the rudder in the opposite direction. The tab may seem a complication, but it really isn't, because if the vane turned the whole rudder, it would have to be many times larger, and the direction of its impulse would have to be reversed, perhaps with blocks and lines. I asked the Frenchman whether his boat wandered a bit, and he said, "Perhaps. It matters nothing. I am not steering."

He had the most rudimentary kind of vertical-axis vane gear. These vanes develop little power until there is a considerable change in the wind angle across them. To overcome that, the vane is sometimes made of two panels, so that they look like a V seen from above. This doubles their weight, and whatever the vane weighs must be counterbalanced even in a multihull. But the heavy vane has inertia, so to keep it light, the panels are sometimes fabric. One experienced manipulator of vertical-axis gears told me the fabric panels should be reefable, like sails.

To keep the boat from wandering from one side of the course to the other, as I thought the Frenchman's might, the trim tab should turn a smaller number of degrees than the vane does. To do so, the vane should not be mounted directly on the tab shaft, but on a separate shaft with linkage to connect it to the tab. The vane gear that I've seen most often on multihulls is the one designed by Jim Brown 25 years ago for his Searunner trimarans. It is exactly this kind of vertical-axis gear with differential linkage.

Ian Ebbinge fitted one to his Piver tri and swore by it. His boat was substantially slower than a Searunner, and so it tested everything less severely, but in it he voyaged from Truk to Florida—more than half way around the world—and he did very little steering. Many of the parts of Ian's gear were mild steel, but he lived aboard and kept them greased. Brown's gear has dozens of metal parts that can't be bought off the shelf. If you're planning a long voyage, he recommends that you carry spares for a good number of them. Brown is a bear for spares.

On the second type of vane gear, the vane pivots on a horizontal axis, as shown in the right drawing. This type is counterweighted to stand upright, but if the wind is very slightly to either side of it, considerable pressure will be exerted to push it down. Its rotating axis can then be connected to a trim tab or the rudder, or sometimes to an independent rudder that is connected only to the vane gear and not to the helm. As this type is more powerful than a vertical-axis gear, the vane can be much smaller. Brown put 5 square feet of vane on his 25-foot Searunner, but a 40-foot

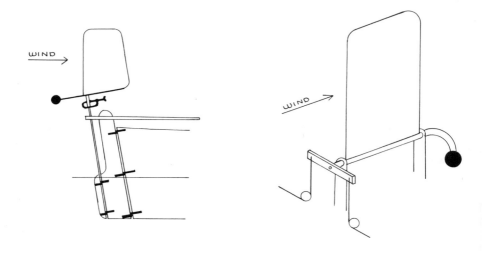

The Frenchman's wind vane (left) and horizontal-axis vane (right)

monohull is often steered by a horizontal-axis gear of less than one square foot. Frequently these horizontal-axis gears are sold as a complete package; you bolt it on the transom and sail away.

They are not often seen on multihulls, because the transoms seldom will accommodate them; and like a leeboard, a rudder doesn't work very well if it isn't under or behind a hull. The skipper who came across the trades under boom tent had a horizontal-axis gear, and said that when the boat surfed and the apparent wind ceased to blow, the vane would come upright. When she stopped surfing and the apparent wind returned, it would slam the vane down hard enough to break the blade that was thin plywood. He had a number of spare blades aboard, but I believe that he went through all of them before he reached Barbados.

Wind vanes are appealing. When they work, they steer more reliably than sheet-to-tiller gears, on a wider variety of courses and without sacrificing as much in sail trim and speed. However, the force that any vane exerts is small, and not enough to overcome a badly balanced sailplan, so sometimes the boat must be reefed or otherwise adjusted to allow the vane to work. Vanes do not use power that must be generated elsewhere. They are entirely mechanical, with their working parts exposed. At least the illusion exists that if something goes wrong, one might be able to fix it.

People say that vane gears don't work at all in winds of gale force and above. They're like a wind pennant spinning around and around its staff. They can tear themselves to pieces, so if you want to have your gear after the gale is past, best take it apart and stow it below.

As long as Carol and I took a third person for crew, we did not find steering on long passages an unbearable chore. We used the three-hours-on, six-hours-off watchkeeping system that means you have a different watch each day and most of a night's sleep each night. Three hours of steering or of playing with shock cords passed pleasantly enough. Only when we started making long passages doublehanded did steering become onerous.

The third possibility is electric self-steering. This has become usual on shorthanded racing boats, and a good many voyaging boats have it, too. Like windvanes, electric pilots require that the sailplan be well balanced, or they will use up electricity in a hurry. They are certainly best suited to motorboats, where there is little helm pressure and the alternator is always running. However, with careful management they can be run for 24 hours on the energy gathered by solar panels during daylight hours.

Autopilots can be hooked into Lorans and other electronic gear and made to steer a great-circle course from any port in the world to any other, provided that land does not intervene. Naturally, the more complex the system, the more likely it is to fail; and as always, electrical systems suffer most from salty surroundings. Even the mechanical parts of these pilots can be troublesome. The kind that move tillers do so with a rod sliding in a cylinder, and we have seen the rod bent into a pretty U-shape when the electrical part demanded more than the mechanical part could perform. If planning an ocean crossing with such a gadget, it is usual to take along several spares. Wheel steering is controlled by an electric motor turning a belt. We have listened to long, but largely unintelligible, accounts of belt slippage and breakage. Like everything else on a boat, autopilots work best if they are part of the original thinking, not added on later. Like everything electrical on board, they give less trouble if they can be mounted belowdecks, away from the worst of the weather.

I would willingly start a voyage with an electric autopilot, but only if it were possible to complete the voyage if the autopilot broke down. There would have to be enough crew to work the ship. That goes for windvanes, too. They are not an extra hand on board, in the same sense that an extra person is. People can break down, too, mentally as well as physically; but there's a better chance of nursing them back to usefulness than there is of finding the fried transistor in the autopilot.

Hydraulic self-steering is seldom mentioned, because it contradicts the cherished image of the he-men out there, pitting their wits and strength against nature. A good many of the biggest ocean-racing multihulls do use it. Olivier de Kersauson, in his unusually honest book, *The Sea Never Changes*, doesn't mind explaining how it shaped the strategy of his record-breaking circumnavigation on *Poulain*, his 75-foot trimaran. After boat weight, weight of fuel was the most important consideration in planning his sailing voyage.

Nearly all long-distance sailboat racers run an engine part of each day to charge batteries. In order to run hydraulic self-steering, a motor must run constantly to power the hydraulic pump. Kersauson made do with electric steering in the Atlantic, going and coming, but used hydraulic steering in the Southern Ocean. Somehow these racers, with motors running constantly, imagine that they are competing with sailing ships of the last century. What is the connection? If you're running a motor, why not run a propeller with it?

None of this is criticism of Kersauson. He's a professional sailor and a good one, and he didn't make the rules for these silly contests. His frank description of what happened, what went on in his mind, and what went wrong with the gear, makes more enlightening reading than most voyaging tales. You and I may not sail so far, but we need to be more self-reliant than he was. No one will fly in a new generator for us, and the technicians to install it. We need to depend less on technology, for our pleasure as well as our success. The sea may not change, but it seems that man's way of dealing with it has changed out of recognition.

18

Emergencies

SOME YEARS AGO, a competitor returning from the Multihull Bermuda Race flagged down a steamer offshore, because the passage was taking longer than he expected. He wanted more fuel to motor in the light air, and he wanted his wife informed that he'd be late. In an article he wrote about it for *Multihulls* magazine, he was annoyed that the steamer captain wouldn't accept payment for the fuel. He did not understand that his "emergency" was imaginary, and that it cost the steamer a great deal to stop.

For real emergencies, there is one accessory that every voyaging boat should carry—an Emergency Position Indicating Radio Beacon, universally known as an EPIRB. It sends a distress signal to airplanes and satellites. It is powered by dry-cell batteries that must periodically be replaced by the factory. Carol and I have had one for 18 years, and although we have never used it, we wouldn't go far from land without it. EPIRBs have saved many hundreds of lives.

Lately it has been possible to buy a fancier personalized EPIRB—something like vanity plates for your automobile. Instead of sending out a simple mayday, it sends a code that identifies the boat in trouble. It is claimed that racer Mike Plant, who was lost in October 1992 when the ballast fell off his monohull, might have been saved if he had registered the code of his personalized EPIRB. He did manage to turn it on briefly, but he hadn't gotten around to registering it. The supposition is that if they had known who was sending, rescuers would have traced his planned route and found him, without having to wait until enough satellites had passed over to make a fix.

Maybe, but I doubt Plant lived long after his 60-footer turned turtle. An upside down monohull—that's how it was found—distinctly is not a survival raft. Two better reasons exist for buying one of these fancier EPIRBs: They broadcast on a different frequency that, because of satellite placement, is more likely to be picked up if you are in the Southern Hemisphere; and because they have a signature, air waves are less clogged with false alarms from them, and their signal is sooner taken seriously. Those two nice lads, having a drink aboard the old man's boat at dockside, are less likely to test out the ole EPIRB if it tells who's making the call. Ninety-five percent of conventional EPIRB signals are false alarms.

For many emergencies—medical, man overboard, fire, gear breakage, bad drinking water—the remedy is not much different in a multihull than in a monohull, except that any remedy is easier to apply on a level platform. I will deal with them briefly. For long voyages, a piece of gear almost as essential as an EPIRB is Dr. P. F. Eastman's book *Advanced First Aid Afloat*. Unlike other books by doctors, it does not unctuously tell you to "consult your physician." Rather, it shows you very clearly how to remove an appendix, amputate a leg, and so forth. We used it once in the trades, when a cross wave dumped a pot of carrots boiling in sea water into Carol's lap. Eastman spelled it out: Butcher-shop-style diagrams allowed us to calculate what percentage of her body was burned, and to calculate the risk. The two dangers, he said, were infection and dehydration, and the cures were antibiotics and forced fluids. João had brought the antibiotics, and I forced the fluids. By the time we reached Barbados, Carol had healed enough to swim. Thank you, Peter Eastman.

We don't like to think about man overboard. Steering, we always sit on a flotation cushion, so we'd never have to go searching for something to throw; and once we bought a floating strobe light, but by the following season its terminals had corroded away to nothing, although it had never been brought on deck. For some years I used a harness when working on deck at night; but its line was perpetually tripping me, and while moving its clip from shroud to forestay and back, I was certainly in as much danger as when handling sails without a harness. I've stopped bothering with it. Carol ties the tail end of the main sheet around her waist, when she's on night watch; and I probably should, too.

There is a saying, only half joking, that half the drowned men ever recovered have had their flies open. This is certainly the easiest and most pointless way to fall overboard. As one who invariably does it himself, I cannot condemn it too much. Lifelines are not likely to stop an adult unless they are 30 inches high, but we did derive great comfort from the one we had across the aft beam of *Vireo*. Nets, as mentioned earlier, are fine while they last. Rob James lost his life after he fell through one, from the big *Colt Cars* trimaran that was supposed to be in apple-pie order.

If someone does fall overboard, current opinion is that the boat should at once be put about, with whatever lack of precision, and kept as near to the swimmer as possible. The old notion that you should sail away on a beam reach, making everything Corinthian-tidy, and then tack and sail back, has now been discredited. Sounds good to me. At sea Carol and I both have a strong feeling that the boat is our safety, and we cling to it. Even in the hottest calms we no longer swim from the boat, out of sight of land. We'd just rather be aboard.

Fire is little danger unless combustibles are kept belowdecks. Eric Hiscock, who once rescued two people from a burning motorcruiser in the English Channel, was understandably interested in fire, and wrote thoroughly about it. Fire at sea is certainly the most awesome of apparitions. Earth and air we survive on, but here the two inimical elements are combined. Nevertheless, fire aboard a multihull at sea is highly unlikely. Should one occur, since someone is on watch at all times, it should be detected in its infancy. Water puts out most kinds of fires. We smoke all the time, and have never had a fire extinguisher aboard. If I had an inboard engine—either gasoline or diesel—or a wet-cell battery with electrical system, I'd have an extinguisher by the companionway and replace it each year. I'm glad I have none of these things, including an extinguisher.

There is not much to be done about lightning: Either it kills you or it doesn't. This gives the *what if* folks a field day to try out their preventives, most of them heavy and expensive. The most bizarre and most common form of lightning prevention is attaching a chain to a turnbuckle and lowering it into the water whenever a cloud appears in the sky. At least chain is cheap. However, most modern boats have large aluminum masts that are excellent conductors and small stainless-steel shrouds that are terrible conductors. The faith that lightning will somehow follow the shroud if the chain somehow completes the circuit is touching but unwarranted.

Kersauson believes that lightning strikes those whose legs are far apart, and that cows in fields are often killed by lightning "because of the large space between their legs." For four or five days of his circumnavigation, in nasty seas and thunderstorms, he steered with his legs carefully together. Poor fellow, I have no absolute proof that he was wrong.

Though Benjamin Franklin was experimenting with lightning 200 years ago, the way it strikes is still not well understood. Some authorities believe that if an aluminum mast is earthed with heavy cable to a square foot of clean copper plate below the waterline, protection will be adequate. Certainly electrical systems are the most likely sufferers in lightning strikes, and anything you really want to save should be disconnected during thunderstorms, especially masthead antennas.

We have been struck once by lightning. We were coming down Delaware Bay on *Two Rabbits*, and I was reefing the main with my arms around the mast. Carol heard the thunder and saw the lightning simultaneously. "I couldn't look at you," she said. "I was sure you were dead." I felt a jolt no stronger than if I had stuck my finger into a 110-volt socket. Apparently lightning strikes are of varying strengths, but still it was unnerving. In a thunderstorm we always know we are safe belowdecks, especially after rain begins, because water is an excellent conductor. But in some parts of the world, and especially in the doldrums, storms are so frequent and wind in them can vary so much that it's often necessary to be doing deck work in the middle of them. We still don't carry any lightning protection, and I don't recommend burdening your boat with protection against something that no one understands. Life is not a sure thing, on the sea or on the freeway.

For other emergencies, we do carry some wood and woodworking tools. We carry some extra rope of various diameters, a small sail-repair kit, spare winch handle, an extra rigging wire the length of the longest wire on the boat, and a few cable clamps. We have needed all these things in the past. On a mass-produced multihull, repairs are likely to be harder to make, and the skipper is less likely to know how to make them. Probably the best solution is to have a yard you trust go over the boat regularly, especially the rigging. The sportier your boat, the more important that is.

We also carry a small bottle of chlorine bleach, if we're starting on a long passage. A few ounces will do, because a few drops will purify a gallon of water. The only time we used it was on our doldrums crossing from the Cape Verdes to Cayenne. We were drinking desalinated water from Tenerife because there was no potable water in the Cape Verdes, nor in the port before that in Senegal. The Tenerife water was not poisonous, but in the weeks that it had lain in the bottles, it had acquired a sickening taste. The Spanish frenzy to get the job over with had infected the desalinating plant. We were putting bleach in the water to improve the taste.

*   *   *

Other emergencies that yachtsmen often worry about—capsize, collision, holing, attacks from whales and other sea monsters—are treated very differently in a multihull, because whatever happens to the boat, it won't sink. A fiberglass or aluminum multihull could conceivably sink, if there were no flotation in it; and even a wood or foam sandwich one would float very low, if every compartment were entirely filled with water. It's hard to think what, beyond being chopped up by the propeller of a steamer, could fill every compartment up. Though I doubt that Dougal Robertson's monohull was in fact attacked by a whale, I do believe something sank her, and I admire the determination, energy, and ingenuity that kept his family alive. In a multihull, none of it would have been necessary.

It's hard to get it straight that a multihull doesn't sink. *Three Legs of Mann II*, the foam-sandwich 53-foot Kelsall tri, eventually fell into French hands, and they found a way to capsize her. They immediately got into an inflatable raft, but stayed tethered to the trimaran during the night. In the morning they cut the tether because they were all convinced that the trimaran was sinking. After their rescue, I interviewed them for *Multihulls* at the Philadelphia airport, and none of them would say that they actually saw her sink, but all agreed that she was sinking. It is likely that in the force 9 then blowing, waves displaced some of the air in the overturned hulls, and she floated lower in the morning than she had the evening before. But how in the world could she sink? Her materials were lighter than water.

Twice Carol and I have crossed the Atlantic in boats with holes in the bows. It was a nuisance, but nothing worse than that. In 1983, after the first gale, *Vireo* was taking water in every seam, from the bad Aerolite glue in her. It came in especially rapidly at the bows, and I think her bow compartments filled to the waterline in an hour, but we only bailed them once a day. The water did not come aft into the accommodation, and we did not feel threatened. The main hull bow was holed in the night by a floating object that we never saw while we were bound for Horta on the *Hummingbird* in 1987. This was a slow leak needing bailing only every other day; but it would have been more troubling if it hadn't been contained by a watertight bulkhead, or if it had had the potential to combine with ballast to sink the boat.

There is no excuse for collision with another boat. Neil Petersen is a young African who has come a long way toward his ambition of making the big time in long-distance singlehanded racing. We met him in Horta in 1991 and again in Newport the following summer, after he had finished the OSTAR. Neil has many interesting things to tell, but the most pertinent is that he and most other sailors who are serious about singlehanded racing do not sleep for more than 15 minutes at a crack. It seems incredible, but they have trained themselves to do it, and if you are not willing to train yourself that rigorously, perhaps you'd better take crew.

In these days of steamers, the routes they are likely to follow are well marked on pilot charts, and other parts of the oceans have precious little commercial shipping. Crossing in the trades, we saw only one ship from the time we turned west away from Africa until we were within two days of Barbados. That ship was in a marked steamer lane from the Cape of Good Hope to New York. There are many yachts in the trades—at this point several thousand may be crossing each winter—but they're all going in the same direction at more or less the same speed, and thus not very dangerous to each other. On our crossing we saw no other yacht from the time we dropped the Canaries until Barbados was in sight. Then a sail—it turned out to be German—appeared on the horizon astern, and we stopped gawking at the land and put up the drifter.

Eight years later we departed São Tiago, Cape Verdes, before dawn, because we couldn't bear to say good-bye to the homeless young men who lived on the beach and had come to depend on us. Before departure we used a flashlight to check in all the hatches to make sure we had no stowaway. We saw no other boat of any sort until two weeks later when we were 200 miles from Cayenne, even though we did cross a marked steamer lane. On that passage, we did not always keep a watch at night, as we had in the trades when João was with us; but when we both did sleep at the same time it was due to exhaustion from sail changes and bad weather, and it was never for the whole night. When Ian Ebbinge and Carolyn Bailey crossed the Indian Ocean, they went to bed like landsmen every evening and slept until dawn. I don't know about steamer traffic in that part of the world.

There are ways of avoiding collisions, and the best one is to be watchful. You are not likely to hurt the steamer, so you can take your own chances, but many steamers don't keep a watch, and in others the watch is not sober. John Letcher, a monohull designer who wrote a book about self-steering, managed to get hit twice, both times in busy coastal waters, and the second time in daylight, when both he and his crew were asleep. Apparently he is a slow learner, though he admits in his book that he took a "foolish risk." If the whole boat isn't reduced to kindling by a steamer collision, the most usual casualty is the rig, and that's nearly as bad in a multihull as in a monohull, except that you do have a better work space to make a jury rig.

Never having done either, I'd prefer capsize to taking a direct hit from a steamer. Yet capsize, the least likely thing to happen to a multihull, is what so many people have been taught to dread. A Toronto sailor built himself a catamaran—about 30 feet she looked in the photos—whose cab-intops were exact replicas of her underwater shapes. There was provision for shifting the mast from one side of the bridgedeck to the other, reversing the rudders and tillers, etc. How her hatches worked I never learned, but presumably it was complicated. I don't think this boat ever capsized, or even ventured out of Lake Ontario. But every aspect of her design was controlled by the fear that she *might* capsize, and every convenience and pleasure was sacrificed to that remote eventuality.

In *The Cruising Multihull*, Chris White tries to assemble statistics on fatal accidents in multihulls and monohulls, and to compare them to the numbers of boats in use. He admits that his results are imperfect, but they seem to suggest a lower fatality rate for multihulls. What's more, of the 28 multihull fatalities in the North Atlantic in a twenty-year period, only 11 were the result of capsize. Seven of these eleven were in racing boats, and as Dick Newick wisely points out: "The price of speed is accidents." I'm sure you'd find that a much larger proportion of monohull fatalities were the result of sinking.

Still, capsize is a possibility, and I know of no accessory you can buy that will forestall it. Masthead floats may have a place on small, narrow, inshore multihulls like the Gougeon 32 and the Rhodes Duet. The only time I ever heard of one working for a voyaging multihull, coming upright again scared the crew worse than going over. Soon thereafter a steamer happened along, and they gladly abandoned their catamaran.

Various methods for righting a capsized multihull have been tried and proven to work in flat-water experiments. I know of no multihull save the above mentioned *Haxted Argo* that has succeeded in righting herself in a seaway without outside help. Perhaps the Australian designer Hedley Nicol was trying to do that. He was bound for California to race against Arthur Piver, but he never arrived and only one float of his trimaran was ever found. It had been sawed off the main hull, and a message had been scratched into the paint of its topsides, but marine growth made it hard to decipher. It may have said, "The sails would fill with water." That was before the days of EPIRBs.

It is also unlikely if your multihull capsizes that the boat will be rescued when you are. Your investment is lost. This gives you freedom to adapt it as a survival platform, without worrying that you may damage it. Some authorities would like your boat to have a special hatch that is above waterline whether the boat is right side up or upside down, to use after capsize. "What if, what if?" This is an extra piece of gear that adds weight and may well leak. In our toolbox we carry a hatchet instead of a hammer. Hatches are not hard to make.

Upside down, a trimaran with a hatch in the bottom will be more habitable than a cat, unless the cat has watertight bulkheads in both ends of the hulls. The trimaran's floats will keep the main hull floating higher. Perhaps on that account the *what if* folks should have tris, not cats. They say it's important after a capsize to secure as much gear belowdecks as possible. Much of it will be on the ceiling (now the floor), and water surging through the hull will want to wash it out. One diabetic trimaran skipper lost his insulin that way, and died of it, though all his crew were rescued. A young Australian with a wingdeck tri cut no hatch in the bottom, but simply went out on deck with the storm that capsized him still raging. He thinks he would soon have washed overboard if he hadn't been rescued, because there was no place to hang onto the smooth underside of his boat. If you anticipate capsize, it certainly pays to paint the underwing of your multihull international orange. That's one safety precaution that doesn't add weight or complication, but we've never bothered with it.

I guess (I really don't know anything about it, never having capsized or known anyone who did) that the scariest time is the first few hours after capsize, when the crew has to be accounted for, the gear secured, and a way found to get in and out of the hull you're inhabiting. New ways to eat, sleep, pass the time, and attract attention have to be worked out. Everyone who's tried it writes that a capsized multihull is even more stable than an upright one, giving a great feeling of confidence. If it happened to me, I wouldn't be in a rush to set off the EPIRB. It could be lost if used too hurriedly. Several satellites must hear it before they have a fix on you, and then it takes the Coast Guard a while to get there. I'd make myself as comfortable as I could, have a bite to eat, and see if any of the cigarettes were still dry. People who have been in one say that an overturned multihull isn't the worst place in the world. People who have spent days in inflatable rafts say they're really the pits. Of course they're still just monohulls, and fragile monohulls at that, with all the nasty motion and poor stability of a monohull.

*   *   *

When your multilhull is secured to land she still isn't immune to emergencies. Theft, piracy, and storms are still a threat to her and to you. Theft and piracy are both best avoided by having a modest vessel. To some extent these threats result from the great and growing inequality in the distribution of the world's wealth, and you are safer if you don't flaunt your own wealth. There are a good many evil people out there and in many parts of the world the ownership of a 20-foot catamaran made of packing crates marks you as a wealthy person.

America is certainly the most thievish place we ever sailed. On our long voyages, Carol and I never lock our boat in foreign ports. Only once did a thief come aboard. In the Cape Verdes we once returned from shore to find that we were missing a $5 pocket calculator. Probably a swimming kid came aboard out of curiosity, and had to leave with a souvenir. From the moment you arrive there, you are besieged by men who want to be your boat's "guardian," often showing you letters of reference from previous yachtsmen. They scull you to the concrete pier, not accessible by dinghy; which is a real service, because the beach is rough, and covered with fish guts and human excrement. The chief value of the transaction is that it redistributes a little wealth where it is badly needed. They asked about a dollar a day, and we paid three.

In Bridgetown, Barbados, the dinghies tie to a pier, thick as flies. In getting his dinghy past ours, some other yachtsman knocked our oars into the water. By the time a couple of local teenagers spotted the oars floating away, they couldn't tell which dinghy the oars belonged to. We were in town at the time. When we returned a couple of hours later, we found the boys sitting patiently on the pier, waiting for the owner to reclaim the oars. This gave us another pleasant opportunity to redistribute a little of the world's wealth. In America, I doubt we'd have seen our oars again.

In recent years, the drug culture has been causing an increasing number of yachting crimes. The tales we used to hear about yachts being pirated in the Bahamas to run drugs to the mainland were all baloney. The Miami River, among other places, has many yards that turn out boats perfectly suited to drug running. As one successful trip more than pays for the boat, yachts were never pirated to do the job less well. More recently, some of the drugs have been filtering out in the transshipment points, for the entertainment of the local poor instead of the mainland rich, and there have been some ugly incidents. In 1988, in French Wells, Crooked Island, we met Mark Carpenter, who had been wintering down there for years. Each fall, he came down with a boatload of books, and distributed them among the (mostly older) local people who still read.

Mark's boat was anchored at Cat Island earlier that season, and was boarded by local thugs obviously strung out on drugs. Mark did have a big expensive ketch, and they had a gun. Mark got out his own gun and suc-

ceeded in bluffing them out of robbing him. Despite his success, two rules
about guns on boats are worth memorizing: Never show a gun unless you
mean to use it; and never shoot except to kill. We don't carry a gun aboard
because, as Carol says: "I'd as soon be shot as do the shooting."

Piracies have occurred in the North Atlantic, but in every case I've
heard where the details have any credibility, the pirate has been a crew-
man picked up in a strange port. Yachtsmen like to think of themselves as
a band of brothers, and most of them are, but there are a few black sheep.
A stranger may be congenial and knowledgeable about boats and even
multihulls, but he may still be a pirate. We have taken on strangers as crew
and have lucked out with them; but it's a risky thing to do.

Tales are occasionally heard of Asian fishermen who turn pirates and
waylay yachts when the opportunity presents itself. There may be something to these tales, but the most notorious one is certainly a fabrication.
Peter Tangvald claimed that his French wife (his third wife, I think she
was) was murdered by piratical fishermen who boarded his boat in the
Sulu Sea. When we met Peter in Horta, he certainly was as rakish and
charming as his writings would have you believe. But he also had an
extraordinary temper, and our Interpol friend intimated to us that the reason the United States would not allow Peter to bring his new Chinese wife
into the country was that it had doubts about what happened to the French
wife.

A couple of years later, on a trade winds crossing, Anne, the Chinese
wife (also charming), hung some clothes to dry where they interfered with
the vane gear. The boom jibed and knocked her overboard, according to
Peter. Some years after that Peter sailed his boat to calculated destruction
on cliffs in the West Indies. Anne's child was killed with him. Thomas, his
teenage son by the French wife, was being towed astern in a smaller boat.
He cut his painter and survived. Thomas, only eight years old when we
knew him, was already sturdy and self-reliant. Peter was a crazy person
and a criminal.

The thing most likely to be stolen from your boat is an outboard
motor. The smaller the motor is, the handier it is to steal. Thieves are not
discriminating, and will steal a British Seagull as readily as a Japanese
motor. Chaining the motor to the boat invites the theft or destruction of the
boat as well as the motor. Once while we were in Nantucket, that happened to another yachtsman, and he was lucky to recover his dinghy (with
the motor chain cut) in a cove not far away. Mac Harris, who lives near
the Inland Waterway in Florida, keeps a dinghy tied to his dock with the

motor chained to the dock, not to the dinghy. From Funchal, the October that we were there, a big French yacht departed for the Antilles (the French Antilles, naturally) with a number of the outboards and inflatables from the public wharf well secured in her hold.

A gale should not pose problems for your anchored multihull, if you are in a genuine harbor, not just a bay, and if you have out the anchor that I have recommended. If you are uneasy, set your second anchor. Look to the chafing gear. However, in a storm even the two of them may not hold. The mushroom anchor that I have recommended for your boat will see her through a storm, but perhaps not a hurricane. The greatest danger in gales and storms at anchor is the other boats around you.

In Cape May we kept *Two Rabbits* on a mushroom, and a big sailing skiff which was our transport to and from the mooring was in a slip. Came a strong gale, force 9, well advertised in advance, and we went out to the cat to double-check everything. Rain came down torrentially, and the skiff, in a very sheltered creek, quickly filled and sank till her sheer was barely awash. She was well tied off and there was no surge in the creek, so she was fine.

In the evening at the height of the gale, Carol and I went down to the dinghy beach at the leeward corner of the harbor. The fetch to the anchorage was only a mile, so the waves were not large. Through the spume we could see that *Rabbits* was riding well; but as we watched, one yacht after another came dragging past her, to right and left, to pile themselves on the beach at our feet. Several production plastic monohulls had been adequately secured, but the factory-installed mooring cleats simply ripped out of the decks. A couple of other boats brought their anchors ashore with them. But one klunky old-timer of many tons' displacement proved to have been attached to the bottom by nothing more than a rusty 1/4-inch chain, and one link parted. Our 50-pound mushroom was fine for *Rabbits*, but would it have held her *and* this klunker, if the klunker hadn't happened to miss her by 10 feet? And if we had put *Rabbits* on a 500-pound mushroom, with heavy chain and line, what would the klunker have ground and battered off her, before it slipped past? I don't know what precautions we can take against the shoddy work of production builders, and the pinchpenny thoughtlessness of other yachtsmen.

In a hurricane—or in a storm, if you have only your seagoing anchors to deploy—you will need to seek greater shelter than most harbors afford. Get the boat inland, as far from the ocean as possible. Cape May, like many harbors, has a noxious creek that empties into it, and we would have taken *Rabbits* up it if that gale had been a hurricane. We would have taken down the mast, even destroying it to do so if need be, because masts are easier to replace than boats. We would have tied to trees, as well as put out all our anchors. Then we would have abandoned the boat.

It may seem heartless to leave a boat without crew when she most needs them. If someone were aboard, a bit of chafing gear might be renewed at a critical moment, or something else might be done that would make the difference between saving the boat and losing her. A number of lives have been lost through this kind of sentimentality, which usually has an economic component. I don't recommend it.

Multihulls survive hurricanes at anchor less well than monohulls. At a certain point they simply become airborne. Hurricanes are now classified from 1 to 5 , and in a category 5 in Hawaii last fall Gary Craft reports that when the 43-foot charter catamaran that he skippered finally broke her mooring, she came "cartwheeling over the breakwater," smashing herself to pieces against the superstructure of a steel Coast Guard cutter. Craft offers a variety of survival strategies: Sink the boat, drag her ashore, hide, run. They all sound good to me.

As described in his *Multihulls* article, Craft flooded his boat's hulls one third of the way up, to make her more like a monohull. After she disintegrated he wasn't sure he'd done the right thing. The extra weight postponed the moment when the cat started flying, but it put a heavier strain on the anchor and rode, which finally did part. My own feeling is that there are certain hurricanes that no boat survives, at sea or on anchor. Winds are always much less a few miles inland because the friction of the land slows them down. Getting the boat inland, whether on water or on land, offers the best chance. And of course, the mast should come down.

Docks are no security in hurricanes, which can easily take pilings out, which means that your boat will be tied to a battering ram. Anyway, most marinas in hurricane-prone areas require that you take your boat away when a hurricane is predicted. The oceans and their shores can be ugly places at times. When we sail along the New Jersey Coast, we are always amazed at the opulent houses we see. Carol says, "In Bangladesh and other sensible countries, the rich live inland, and only the very poorest people have to live on the beach."

19

Entertainment

BEFORE WE PLUNGE from emergencies into nasty-weather sailing, a little discussion of entertainment may be welcome. People who have never gone voyaging often imagine that it is thrilling. The truth is, much of it is boring. "The sea never changes," says Kersauson, and sometimes it's too true to be good. You're looking at the same thing all the time. The days fly by, but the minutes drag, even if you aren't on the helm. In settled weather, not many hours' work are needed to keep the boat shipshape. From the larder of preserved foods, not too many culinary masterpieces can emerge; and whatever you eat tastes marvelous, because your senses are so deprived in most other ways.

Let us be frank. The vision the landsman has of sailing over the sea, with a piña colada in one hand, a fresh, succulent maiden in the other, has no relation to nautical reality. The one drink a day is a gritty belt of grog and tepid water, and the lady is salty and none too fresh. Sex, like inebriation, happens less often on voyages, because both of you are too tired, dirty, and preoccupied much of the time. That does not mean that your feelings about each other suffer. No, you are doing a hard thing together, which knits you together now, and may have other rewards after you reach port, rest, and clean up. For now, what you need are some entertainments requiring not too much concentration. An additional requirement on a multihull is that the apparatus for them not be too heavy.

Naturally, reading comes first. "Reading can be the best part of a man's life," says John Updike. On passage, Carol can bury herself in a prolix Victorian novelist; Trollope and Hardy are two of her favorites. "A good read," one of our voyaging friends calls such novels, and Carol thinks of them as a substitute for socializing. Although I find both authors enjoyable ashore, on a voyage I don't want to be carrying their plots around in my head. The voyage is the plot for me, and when I read I like it to be a piece I can finish at one sitting. O'Hara's short stories suit me best. Often there is a sexual twist, which compensates a little for the sex I'm too tired and dirty to ask for. Too bad I've read them all so many times! The stories of Pritchett and Updike suit me well, too.

They often show such a believable but unexpected side of human nature that during my trick at the helm, I can spend quite a time mulling over a single story. On a voyage, both of us prefer fiction to fact, and we especially do not want to read books about sailing. It is often possible to exchange paperbacks with other sailors, and restaurants in remote ports will sometimes have a shelf or two of books to exchange.

Alexander Pope, characterizing the lives of women, brought forth from his sexist and virgin imagination one of the great lines in English poetry: "A youth of follies, an old age of cards." Whatever your age or sex may be, on a voyage don't overlook the cards. Carol and I are not competitive with each other—and besides, one of us is on watch—so we play solitaire. We carry a book showing hundreds of varieties. Spider, the game with which Napoleon whiled away his years on St. Helena, requires a big table, but next to bridge it is the most cerebral card game that I know. On a multihull, the cards don't go sliding across the table. Often, one of us will play, and the one on watch will keep an eye on the game from the hatch. A hand of Spider can take half an hour, with each move calculated almost like a chess move. Plastic—not plastic-coated—cards are the best choice for marine use.

We play music, but not very well. Carol has no sense of pitch, and I have no sense of rhythm. Nevertheless, the sound of her recorder or my harmonica is welcome on the ocean. When we'll be at sea for Christmas she prepares a concert of carols. I am delighted with the "surprise," and clap for encores. A recorder makes a morning noise, and a harmonica an evening one. We do not attempt duets.

Projects for the improvement of the boat can occupy many idle hours. Nets can be made to suit any space or any cargo. Cunning brackets will hold dividers and protractors. These things do add weight to a multihull, and because your own labor went into them, you aren't likely to remove them, even after the dividers are solid rust. We carry a large rubber stamp with a logo of our boat. We stamp it into other boats' guest books, and Carol stamps it onto T-shirts and embroiders over it. The shirts make wonderful presents for new friends, and the product is gone instead of weighing down our boat.

We write some letters on passage, but Ruth Wharram writes them endlessly. Over our evening drink we like to listen to the BBC news, and Carol sometimes listens to the shortwave through earphones for many hours of a night watch. The sound quality is so bad that I don't enjoy it. BBC will send you a copy of "The Listener" that will help you find your way around the rather complicated shortwave bands, with different frequencies for different oceans. No matter how many hours we listen, one set of AA batteries will get us across an ocean. A French shortwave station broadcasts ocean weather forecasts; but once you're out of range of AM and FM stations, you can't do much about forecasts, anyway. Though the language is foreign and the reception is poor, these French broadcasts are intelligible, because the vocabulary is limited. WWV, an American shortwave station, also broadcasts ocean weather predictions periodically, but we've never been able to catch it.

In the Bahamas, where the forecast does matter to your voyaging plans, it comes each morning from a powerful AM station in Miami, sandwiched between religious programs. Tuning in once, we were startled to hear the evangelist say, "I know all you sinful yachtsmen out there are just waiting for the weather forecast, but you better believe in Jesus!"

Some sailors like to fish. We are not slow to pick up the flying fish that are often on deck in the mornings, wherever the water is warm. They are the sweetest and most delicious fish I know. In deep water they are the feed of larger fish such as dorado that can weigh 50 pounds. There's not much in between. In the trades, we had a small hand line with us and a little spoon. When João saw the dorados surfing down the swell behind us, he couldn't resist putting the line out. A fish took the spoon at once, and the line held just long enough to cut João's finger to the bone before it parted.

Successful ocean fishermen use heavier lines, but not rods. When they get the fish aboard, which can be a considerable task, they cut it up and try to dry in the sun what they aren't eating immediately. Unless the crew is large, some of it has to be thrown away, because sun-drying only preserves it a couple of days. Fishing requires knowledge, and it is unlikely that people who don't practice it at home will be successful at it when they step aboard a boat. Along the coasts, some spots are so hot that even a tyro can succeed. Sailing to New England we sometimes trail a spoon past the Jersey inlets, or bouncing through the tidal rips off Montauk. This will bring us a bluefish about half the time.

Our greatest entertainment in voyaging is celestial navigation. Every offshore sailor should know how to do it, and should have the gear aboard, because electronics are not dependable. We take many more sights than we need, working them with Ageton's logarithm tables that are smaller and lighter than H.O. 249. We use the lightest, cheapest plastic sextant. It has only a sighting hole and no telescope, so we can use it without removing our glasses. We find its results at least as reliable as those of our bigger, heavier sextant that we now leave at home.

After the basics of navigation are learned, there are still enough wrinkles to keep it interesting, like pre-computing meridian passages of stars to get perfect latitudes at dawn or dusk. We like to use the planets and the tricky moon, and as much of the whole sky as we can. I'd like to take a lunar for longitude someday, the way Captain Cook and Joshua Slocum did, but the tables for its computation were removed from *Bowditch* many years ago. On a long voyage we feel that we get to know the individual stars, not just the constellations. We look forward to their rising every night, as you would look forward to a visit from an old friend.

Ocean life is always wonderful to see, and a school of dolphins is often worth being wakened from a nap for. We carry books to help us identify the sea creatures. In the North Atlantic, well offshore, shearwaters and storm petrels are the only birds commonly seen. South of the Gulf Stream, flying fish are everywhere, but north of it only a very occasional billfish breaks the surface, or perhaps a shark. Whales are surprisingly common, and one senses their benevolence at once, just like a dolphin's. However, they are much less in control of their huge bodies, and we don't come too close. Sometimes Carol will bring out an animal book, and try to decide which animal it would be nicest to see next.

Thus we entertain ourselves and pass our days. We murmur to each other about the next port, and what it will feel like to be clean again and to sleep the night through.

20

Nasty-Weather Sailing

T HE ONLY WAY to talk about the winds that make nasty weather in the ocean is with the Beaufort Scale. When the wind is light enough for plain sail, Carol and I find it most convenient to describe it in knots. As soon as we're reefed, we start talking in forces. Though the scale is printed in many books, I give an abbreviation of it on page 184, because so much of what follows depends on it.

Admiral Beaufort devised his scale to "determine wind speed by sea condition." That is to say, you look at the sea, and it will tell you the *average* wind speed and wave height. It won't tell you anything about gusts or squalls, and some phenomena—especially wave height—will not agree with the scale if there is land to windward or if the wind strength has recently increased. The number of knots may look low, but you will remember than when we left off nice-weather sailing, the wind was only 27.5 knots, barely force 7, but wind pressure was already 4 pounds per square foot. Some very speedy and pleasant sailing is possible in winds of less than 1 pound pressure (force 4). In the mildest of hurricanes (force 12), wind pressure is at least 16 pounds per square foot, "that which no canvas could withstand," according to the admiral.

In a multihull at sea, you may survive some hurricanes, but certainly not *every* hurricane. The category 5 that sent Gary Craft's Hawaiian charter cat cartwheeling over the breakwater had sustained winds of 126 knots, and their pressure would have been 84 pounds per square foot. If an Iroquois Mk II had been at sea at the time, fully loaded, that pressure on the aluminum extrusion of her mast would have been enough to capsize her without any help from hull windage or wave action. The five categories of hurricanes are recent upward extensions of the Beaufort Scale. Probably they are useful for meteorological discussion, but less so for voyage planning.

Let us start out in nice weather. As the wind builds, there is often discussion of whether or not to reef. The old saw is that the time to reef is the first time you think of it. However, that makes reefing a matter of temperament, when it should be a matter of judgment. We made a bad judgment once. Coming up the Florida coast, we had the northeasterly force 4 to 5 that often heralds a cold front down there. That's about all the wind *Vireo* was happy handling to windward under plain sail. Brief annoying squalls kept coming through, bopping the wind up another force and forcing me to reef. After about the third one I said, "I'm tired of reefing and unreefing. Next time let's luff through it." But the next one lasted longer.

I was steering from the windward companionway, and Carol was to leeward with the main sheet ready to run. I luffed, but the force 6 kept coming, and eventually we luffed to a standstill. I then had no control with the tiller, and after *Vireo* had thought about it for a moment, she swung away from the wind. My hull came up—we still weren't moving, and the helm was useless—until Carol could see the whole of the windward keel. On a beach cat, it might have been entertaining, but we had been living aboard for eight months by then, and all our precious belongings were with us, right down to our pet mouse. Capsizing would have been like tipping your house over the edge of a dock and shaking all its contents into the drink.

I may have hollered, but at any rate Carol let go of the sheet. My hull came down, and I ran to the mast and dropped the main. We were so scared that we turned and ran back south. We reefed, but it was an hour before we collected our wits enough to realize that we wanted to be going north, so we turned around and started for home again. That evening, still reefed, we came in St. Lucie's Inlet without further incident.

Many books say that although a monohull should luff up for a gust, a multihull should bear away to diminish apparent wind speed and escape the centrifugal force that comes from heading up. It sounds scary to me, and we don't do it. Unless sheet and tiller are well coordinated, there is a possibility of putting wind at a right angle to the sails, where it is sure to generate the most capsizing force. Without doubt, any boat on a voyage should be conservatively canvassed, not canvassed like a racer. She should be able to take at least one force of increase in wind strength without worry about knockdown or capsize.

Because going fast in a multihull is both exhilarating and frightening, in judging when to reef or when to reef further, we look for certain signs to help us reach our decision. Downwind, we know it's sail-reducing time the first time the boat, coming up on a wave, dips her bows until they are flush with the level of the wave. Don't wait until the second time. Don't wait until green water is coming onto the foredecks. Multihulls can do that and survive, but especially if the weather is building, reduce sail the first time the bows come flush with the sea.

Upwind, when a multihull is properly canvassed, it feels like one piece. When overcanvassed, it feels like many different pieces (mast, shrouds, hulls, etc.) working independently or even against each other. That is the time to reduce sail. On *Vireo* we could make progress to weather reefed in a force 6. In a force 7 we really couldn't, though sometimes double reefed we would pretend we were. In a force 8 we could be hove-to under storm canvas. In a force 9 we had to turn and run.

Force 7 is the easiest wind strength to recognize, when foam from the breaking crests aligns itself in strips parallel to the wind, like Sargasso weed in happier times. The force 7 streaks are so easily recognized that they almost seem like friends, except that the waves that come with them aren't friendly at all. Unlike many of the other sea conditions described in the scale, these streaks will form even in small bodies of water. Often we have been driving across the causeway of Great Egg Bay and seen the streaks on the water. "Nice day to be in a car," we tell each other.

Two Rabbits stopped making windward progress earlier than *Vireo*. Her sprit mainsail could only be reefed once, and her Bermudan trysail was small. It controlled the direction the boat was pointing, but only propelled her when the sheet was eased. In bad enough conditions that may be all you want. But on our first trip to Bermuda, we found a southerly force 6 in the Gulf Stream, and we were five days getting across it. By that time we were still north of the islands, but the stream had pushed us a whole degree east of them. In the daytime it may have blown force 7, and calmed down to force 6 at night. Certainly those daytime waves were majestic, with terraces like Asian rice fields. Sometimes they looked higher than our topmast head 27 feet off the water, but estimates of wave heights from the deck of a sailboat are not often accurate.

After you have reefed right down to storm canvas, the next question is when to stop aiming where you want to go, and start aiming to survive. If the wind is from ahead, you may be aiming at your destination, but you probably aren't moving toward it appreciably. If you turn and run, you certainly will be moving away. In a gale you shouldn't need to do it. In a storm you probably do, and in a hurricane you certainly do. Running off is the *only* technique to consider in really bad weather, and the reason for it could easily be grasped by my father-in-law, that intelligent but unnautical man, who immediately grasped that a multihull must be more stable than a monohull. In survival conditions you must keep the longest dimen-

sion of your boat toward the seas, because then the seas will have a harder time turning it over. In the very worst conditions, you should be moving with the seas, because your movement will diminish the impact of the
waves on the boat.

We have not had to face the decision of when to turn and run very
often. Most of the really bad weather we've seen has been on long voyages that followed prevailing wind patterns, and in all the parts of the
oceans where we've been, the strongest winds are even more likely than
the everyday winds to come from the prevailing direction. Hurricane-
strength winds that come from genuine revolving tropical storms are of
course an exception, and we will speak of them later.

The decision of when to turn and run instead of lying hove-to, which
also puts your longest dimension toward the seas, is made simply by your
judgment of wave impact on the boat. The advantage of running will be
to diminish that impact, so you must do it when you think that you or your
boat can't stand the impact as it is. It's a hard decision, because when you
start running, you will be losing some of the miles toward your destination that you made good yesterday. In addition, by the time the decision
needs making, you may well be under the weather. We always are.

Seasickness like many other diseases has a blend of physical and
psychological causes. Carol is usually sick or at least queasy on the first
day of a voyage, and finds it better to eat very little. I am seldom sick then,
but both of us do inevitably get more or less seasick in nasty weather. If it
gets bad enough, we take Valium.

What makes us seasick in nasty weather is not so much the motion,
or any visual problems associated with motion. These may account for
Carol's first-day queasiness, but our sickness in nasty weather is caused
by the fear of death. Valium calms this fear, taking the psychological element out of seasickness, allowing us to cope with whatever physical elements may remain. But Valium makes us dopey, and the fear of death also
makes us dopey, so the decision to turn and run still is not easy. Hove-to,
we are lying perhaps 60 degrees off the wind, perhaps forereaching a little in the troughs and being knocked back by the crests. Most of them pass
under us okay; only the breaking ones are trouble. But Admiral Beaufort
points out that in a storm all the crests are at least overhanging, and in my
experience nearly all are breaking.

What to do? Struggle up through the layers of lassitude and try to
concentrate on it. Take a shot, a really good hit from a breaking crest that
jars the whole boat and knocks her off until she is beam-on to the seas. If

her helm and storm sails are properly set, she will come around until she is 60 degrees off the wind again. But are you ready for another shot like that? Are you ready for a harder one? Have things been building or diminishing lately? Which way is the barometer moving? Concentrate on it: Is it time to turn and run?

Once we are running, everything is easier. If Ruth Wharram is aboard, she will brush out her hair, fix herself a snack, and resume writing letters. In a gale the waves are moving at about 16 knots. While we were hove-to we were gathering a little forward speed in the troughs, and when we came up on the crests we were moving at perhaps 2 knots. Now that we are running off we may only be making 3 knots, so the speed of the wave hitting us is 13 knots instead of 18 knots. It doesn't sound like a big difference, but wind pressure increases with the square of its speed and water pressure increases at least that fast. Waves at 13 knots, then, have half the pressure that they did at 18 knots.

Both of our Wharram cats would run off in a gale or storm with storm jib sheeted flat amidships and the helm lashed. The course would be about 140 degrees off the wind on whichever jibe we chose, and we could be below in the shelter and dryness of a cabin. *Hummingbird* never would do it at all. She would heave-to much like the Wharram cats, needing no more attention then than they did, but if we tried to get her to run off unattended, she insisted on lying ahull beam-on to wind and seas. If we went out on deck (already a very undesirable development) and tried to steer her downwind, even with only a storm jib flying, we took off like a scalded cat, surfing down the waves and rounding up in the troughs. Despite our admiration of the way that trimaran sailed in light and moderate conditions, we do not look back on her with the fondness that we feel for the little cats, because she didn't take care of us when we most needed her.

I have heard that other trimarans do the same thing, and perhaps some cats do, too. It may be some special quality of Jim Wharram's designs that they keep heading slowly downwind like a cow eating its way methodically down a row of tomato plants. For whatever reason, some multihulls need to be restrained, downwind in nasty weather. My guess is that the racier the boat is—cat or tri—the more it needs restraint.

Drogues or sea anchors have been the subject of much design work. Jim Brown once drew one for his Searunner 31 that, with all its tricky components, weighed 125 pounds. From your friendly chandler you can buy various kinds of bags and parachutes. From the look of some of them, when dragged through the water, they might make a noise like a kazoo.

That might be a relief from the pounding of the waves. The truth is, anything can be a drogue. The laundry will work fine if there's enough of it. The problem is to keep it connected to the boat.

In *Yachtsman's Choice*, the swan-song book of the wonderful old *Rudder* magazine, Walter Boudreau describes a lifeboat voyage, after the barquentine he had been sailing on was sunk by a submarine in 1943. The fourth day a gale blew up, and the sea anchor aboard was not big enough to hold the bow up to the seas. They made another out of the spars, and it worked fine until the line parted. "Row for the sea anchor, men," the captain said grimly. "Your lives depend on this." Grimly they rowed, but in the gathering dusk they could not reach it. My guess is that if they had, a new line attached to it would soon have parted also. There were 10 men aboard, but without a sea anchor to hold her long dimension to the seas, the lifeboat capsized over and over again. Only Boudreau and the mate were alive in the morning.

From our few experiments with drogues, I don't think a satisfactory harness can be made with the gear already on board, such as anchor lines. It is tempting because it saves weight, and on many voyages you never need a drogue. But chafe and other forces work much more energetically on a drogue than they do on an anchor attached to the bottom; and once you stream a drogue, it's almost impossible to make adjustments. In fact, even after the storm is over and the seas are down, it's always a fearful job to get the drogue back in again. During the storm, the forces on it seem never to slacken. You can't get any back, and if you try to let more out (perhaps to move the chafe point a foot or so) the whole of it is very likely to slip through your fingers and be gone.

So far we have never carried any special gear for a drogue, but I think that if I were going transatlantic again, I'd make room for some in my hold and on my payload weight list. Aging makes us all more cautious, though with each year that we live it makes less sense. My design attention would be on the harness, not the drogue itself, and the nylon line would be at least 1/2-inch, not the 3/8-inch that is plenty for our working anchors. (For your boat, you may need to scale this up or down in proportion.) It would be a bridle of two ropes exactly the same length, and I'd splice eyes on the inboard ends, to go over big cleats on the sterns. It would have chafe sleeves around any part of it that might touch the boat, made of a slippery material that could yet be inexorably connected to the rope.

Back near the drogue the lines would certainly have thimbles, but I think not swivels. The ocean loves to unlay rope. The drogue itself might be from the chandler, or it might be laundry, as long as it is well attached. Certainly it should be sized to suit the boat. In a force 8, John Kettlewell found that an 8-foot bought parachute kept his 32-foot catamaran *Echo* heading downwind. She certainly would have headed up if left to herself, because she is very streamlined forward, but with much windage aft. Once we found that throwing out nothing more than 150 feet of 3/8-inch anchor line in a big U-shape from *Vireo*'s sterns did as much to keep her heading downwind as a storm jib would have. Remember that the purpose of sizing a drogue is to keep the boat from surfing, but not to stop it dead. If it did that, much of the advantage of turning and running would be lost.

*   *   *

Nasty weather is never so nasty in port as at sea, and sometimes it's possible to get in before the worst. We tried to, coming home from the Bahamas one miserable July. We bailed out of the Gulf Stream about 2 degrees south of Great Egg Inlet, but then the wind left us, and came back the next morning as a northerly force 7. Under storm canvas we were pointing more or less at the Jersey Coast, but we weren't much surprised when, in early afternoon, we came up off Ocean City, Maryland, not New Jersey. We knew the inlet well and could have gone in, but it was smothered in breakers. Wearily, we hove-to on the offshore tack. Two huge grey warships had been following our activities most of the morning. Thanks, fellas!

At midnight we could still see the loom of Ocean City, and with wind now down to force 6, we wore *Hummingbird* and raised the reefed jib and double-reefed main. The sails were small enough for the wind, Carol noted in the log, but big enough for the seas. At first light we were four miles from the jetties. We shook out some of the reefs and had a glass of rum. We cleared the inlet an hour before the rising wind shut it again. We ran her on a sandbar, threw down the anchor, cooked and ate a whole pound of canned bacon, and slept till evening.

Now it is time for hurricanes. We have only seen two, and both were minimal category 1 hurricanes. That is not entirely luck, because hurricanes are to some extent predictable. In the North Atlantic, the strongest ones are likely to be later in the season, in September. Whatever foolish things we may have done at sea, we have never sailed anywhere except in the very safest season of the year. We have insisted that our sailing plans take precedence over our land plans. You better had, too.

Our most recent hurricane was milder for us, because we happened to be farther from the eye, which was purely luck. We were sailing *Hummingbird* to Horta in early July, 1991. Three days out, trying to steer her downwind under storm jib in a force 7, I had broken off the rudder blade. That time we had only lain ahull a few hours before the wind moderated enough to put in the spare blade, allowing us to get moving again. But we had discovered that although slower, it was more pleasant in that boat to lie ahull than to run off at 12 or 15 knots, rounding up periodically to slam into a crest. Five days later when the hurricane came (naturally we did not get the official word that it was a hurricane until much later that summer), we dropped the storm jib as soon as we began surfing too much, and were happy enough to lie ahull. Comfort was one consideration, and not having a further spare blade was another.

However, the storm continued to build, and in the end we lay ahull for 20 hours. The wind peaked at force 10, for we were perhaps a hundred miles north of the eye, and in the navigable sector. Still, some crests hit us hard enough to take cigarettes out of our hands. The boat did take it. At the height of it, the storm jib that I had just lashed down on deck threw off its lashing and began climbing the forestay. It was still sheeted, and it flogged the stay fiercely. We also thought, in our groggy way, that the windage of it might be the little extra that was needed to capsize us. I went out, unhanked it, and brought it below. I don't know how much more wind and sea *Hummingbird* could have taken, lying ahull like that; but at the time, we felt there was a limit.

Some books make much of the distinction between wave capsize and wind capsize. I don't get it. Never having capsized, I don't know much more about it than most other authors; but it seems to me that the wind makes the waves, and they both come from the same direction. Whether you capsize in a monohull or a multihull, there's likely to have been a conspiracy of wind and waves behind it. Certainly when Dan McCarthy's friends turned over their big cat, under plain sail or perhaps main and a big genoa, waves didn't have much to do with it. Probably there are capsizes in the French trench, with no waves at all. But if a boat is well snugged down and well managed, and if she doesn't have a wing mast that is optimistically expected to act as a stormsail, then wind and wave both aim to capsize her, and not much is to be gained by arguing whose aim was better.

We have never seen a rogue wave. Other sailors have made quite a case for them, and it's true that in any wave train some waves are bigger than others. Some waves break where you are, and some have the good taste to break elsewhere. In any sea, even as regular a one as the trade winds, some waves always come from unexpected directions, like the one that dumped the carrots in Carol's lap. When one of these is breaking, and comes upon a wave in the regular train that is also breaking, it can look like an explosion, and can feel like one if it happens under your boat. Many times we've looked out the companionway at what appears to be a volcano erupting behind us. "Shit!" is the only word that comes to mind; but by the time the other can turn and look, the volcano has disappeared. However, this is not the rogue wave that is sometimes described: one in the regular train, but twice the height of any other. Rogue waves would be a handy excuse for poor seamanship, but of course I'm not accusing anyone; and as I've never seen one, I don't know anything about them. They must be rare indeed, for us never to have seen one in 40,000 miles.

Our other hurricane was not so friendly. As I have described the emotional impact of it in another book, I will deal with it here as factually as I can. In the waters between Bermuda and the American East Coast, 1975 was a summer of disasters. When we arrived in St. George's, two boats were overdue after a tropical storm (force 10) that had passed through before we even set sail. One was *Meridian*, a 35-foot Horstman trimaran, bound home with a crew of five. The other was a small Bristol sloop, owned by a college boy on the way to Bermuda with several of his friends. We were hardly through customs when the boy's father, Tom Bolger, asked to come aboard.

He was a very nice man, and an experienced Bermuda-Race skipper. He wanted to hear about the weather we'd seen. When we told him that we were east of Bermuda before we saw the last of the Gulf Stream, he brightened at once. The aerial search for his son had been called off several days ago, but on the basis of our report he was at once convinced that the search planes had been too far west, and should now try again. He invited us to come around to the Royal Hamilton Amateur Dinghy Club, the snottiest venue on the islands, and we did sail around a few days later. Parsimonious *Two Rabbits* looked incongruous tied to the club dock; but we enjoyed the showers, and we had several lunches with Tom. He was in high spirits now. *Meridian* had been found with her skipper dead from diabetes, but the rest of her crew alive in her overturned hulls; and based on that and our information, Tom had the search planes out flying again, farther east. "I'm trying to keep my hopes up," he said to us once. Then looking down at his plate he added, "Or maybe my wife's."

By the time we sailed back to St. George's, the second search was over and Tom had flown home. We met the crew of *Sabrina*, a sturdy molded-plywood sloop designed to be parachuted to downed fliers in the Second World War, and *Banjo*, a new Dutch-built fiberglass sloop. *Sabrina* left Bermuda one afternoon and we the next, and *Banjo* the morning after that. Our various sailing abilities and common destination meant that we were cheek-by-jowl four days later, just south of the Gulf Stream, when Hurricane Blanche closed in.

Rounding Northeast Breaker Buoy, Carol and I had been able to set the squaresail and had flown it for 50 consecutive hours. We didn't know much about self-steering then and we didn't care. We were having fun and were excited at the prospect of a fast passage. Gradually the wind rose, but it was still southerly. We changed to smaller sails and kept her moving. Changing down and changing down, we were finally reduced to storm jib alone, while the force 7 streaks were on the water. Four hours later, just as an unnaturally early dusk was closing in, skipper Robert Benson spotted us from *Banjo*. "I did not want to approach too closely, because of the size of the seas," he wrote us some months later. Benson was under storm jib, too, at the time, but he took it down an hour later for fear that its vibration would cost him his rig. The taller the forestay, the shorter time a storm jib can be used without shaking the boat apart. We couldn't stand the storm jib on *Hummingbird* in a force 10, but on *Rabbits* with her 16-foot stay, the storm jib saw us through a force 11.

Banjo was lying ahull a short time after when she fell off a wave that Benson estimated to be 50 feet high. Maybe that was that elusive rogue wave, after all. Benson wasn't adamant about his estimate. At any rate, the wave was high enough to give the boat a chance to turn as it fell, and when it landed on the port quarter, the strain on the skeg and rudder was enough to split the fiberglass hull. He and his crew got busy with pumps, and with rags and screwdrivers they tried to caulk the seam.

When he saw us, we were heading—as those lighthearted folks that you meet in waterfront gin mills will always tell you—"where the wind blew us." We were below, and *Rabbits* was steering herself, with her helm lashed and her storm jib flat amidships. As the wind increased—and it did increase at least a force, after *Banjo* fell off her wave—we felt that we were lifting the starboard hull, which was to windward. We were both in the port hull and didn't want to jibe, which would have been easy enough to do, because the wind was moving from south to southeast. Our course, which had been northeast, was now north, with the new waves on our quarter and the old waves on our stern. Jibing would have changed the course to west, away from the storm center, but it would have put the new waves on our port quarter and the old waves on our beam. Perhaps we should have jibed, because that would have taken us more directly away from the hurricane's center, but we weren't admitting to each other that it was a hurricane, and we weren't going fast enough to make that much difference. To keep the starboard hull down, I crawled over and got in it.

Sabrina's twin lifting keels were left part way down, and I suspect that she tripped on them more often than she need have; but the keels had considerable lead in their bottoms. How to manage a monohull in a hurricane, I don't want to know. I believe their masthead never did actually touch water, but they took a terrible beating, as they and their gear were flung back and forth across the cabin. "It was sheer hell," her skipper later wrote me, but they did survive. In the four subsequent days, they made little progress, but finally flagged a steamer to get some water and a fix, because the sextant was bent. After that, they limped into Oregon Inlet. Benson and his crew were able to keep *Banjo* afloat until morning. They had good radios, and the Coast Guard diverted a steamer that picked them up the next noon. (They were searching for mariners more than for drugs in those days.)

We had a good view of the hurricane from our two separate hulls. Though it was night and cloudy, lightning was almost continuous. But there wasn't much to see, because the air was so full of water and the water so full of air that distinctions were hard to make. The boat seemed barely afloat in those aerated seas. Even then, hard rain was a blessing; it took the edge off the seas, just as it does in a force 6. When the wind blew hardest—we were about 30 miles from the eye, according to a track of Blanche the weather bureau showed me later—even our 20-square-foot storm jib was surfing us too fast. The boat was so tiny that, standing up in the forward hatch of my hull, I was able to reach the halyard cleat on the mast and lower the jib part way. That was enough to make the difference, and that's how we spent the rest of the night, while the wind gradually moved around us and subsided. Doped with Dramamine (we had no Valium, but Dramamine is a useful-enough drug so that you won't be able to buy it soon) we both finally fell asleep.

I believe that the main reason we survived was luck. Certainly we were lucky to be in the navigable sector of a fast-moving hurricane.

Though NOAA classed Blanche as a hurricane that night, meaning that winds were over 64 knots, she was moving northeast at nearly 15 knots. That means that on our side of the eye, sustained winds probably never exceeded 60 knots (force 11). In the dangerous sector on the other side of the eye, wind may have been 85 knots. Wind pressure there would have been double what we had. That poor little Bristol, stuck in a tropical storm that hardly moved for three days, may have been in who knows what sector, and may have found her end in worse conditions than we ever saw.

Though that trip to Bermuda was our first offshore voyage, I think our seamanship was good. All these thousands of miles later, I can't think what I'd do differently. We reduced sail in good time and kept her moving. "Light-displacement vessels must be sailed continuously," says Tom Colvin. We used what we had on hand, and it worked. Bringing along a lot of *what if* gear would surely have been suicidal. Our boat survived without losing anything, breaking anything, or hurting her crew. Whatever *Two Rabbits'* shortcomings in light air to windward, she ran straight and did not fail us that night. Her designer James Wharram deserves a good deal of the credit.

Abbreviated Beaufort Scale

FORCE	DESCRIPTION	SEA CONDITION	KNOTS	WAVE HEIGHT
4	moderate	frequent crests	11-16	4'
5	fresh	some spray	17-21	6'
6	strong	extensive crests and spray	22-27	10'
7	near gale	spray in streaks	28-33	14'
8	gale	spindrift	34-40	18'
9	strong gale	crests topple	41-47	23'
10	storm	white sea	48-54	29'
11	violent storm	crests in froth	55-63	37'
12	hurricane	air filled with foam	64+	45'+

Conclusion

U NLIKE MOST singlehanded sailors who have lost their lives at sea, Loick Caradec was in touch with the shore until very near the end. Caradec was a small man, as many of those professional sailors are, and he was sailing the 75-foot trimaran *Royale* in a transatlantic race in November. *Royale* had a wing mast that was supposed to be the storm sail, but on his radio Caradec told his shore crew that even with no fabric sail set, *Royale* was out of control and going much too fast. It is pitiful to think of that small but wiry man on his huge boat, knowing so well what was wrong and not being able to do anything about it. When the trimaran was found, it was upside down. Caradec was not aboard. He may have clung on for a time, but the water was very cold. Only a professional or a lunatic would be sailing those waters in November. Nonetheless, Caradec was tough, and he might have survived if he'd had a better boat.

Speed kills, on water as surely as on land. The reason for having a fast boat should be the pleasure of sparkling performance in moderate weather, not the possibility of setting records in gales. It should be possible to snug down the fast boat and be as safe as a slower boat in nasty weather. The current trend in multihull design worries me.

At the 1988 Multihull Symposium in Newport, just weeks before *Stars and Stripes* won her America's Cup, a panel of six respected designers was asked whether a rotating wing mast was appropriate to a cruising multihull. Five of them flatly said no. The sixth, Derek Kelsall, ventured that a stock aluminum extrusion that rotated could give a nice little boost to performance without compromising safety. Today, at least two of the other five have come out with cruising designs that do have rotating wing masts. They give various excuses for them, such as saying that their wing masts are smaller than some, and certainly won't develop too much power. I wonder if those designers know as much about the ocean as Caradec did, and I wish they could talk with him.

For 30 years, the superiority of multihulls has been obvious to all fair-minded people, and yet they have never achieved the popularity they deserve. The day after the America's Cup victory, the designers and manufacturers of multihulls were swamped with inquiries. A small ad for my boatbuilding business appears in each issue of *Multihulls* magazine, and in the months after the victory, my telephone was ringing off the wall. Everyone wanted the same thing: *Stars and Stripes* performance, with accommodation. Some of them didn't even care what it cost. This has to be tempting to designers and builders whose good products have been indifferently received for so long. However, I believe that the preoccupation with the speed of a multihull to the exclusion of all its other excellent qualities is leading to boats that are not safe.

Wing masts may be the easiest danger signal to point out, but in general, tall rigs are dangerous, whatever mast they have. For years multihulls had lower rigs than monohulls their own length, and certainly some of them were too low. The newest designs often have rigs taller than monohulls, and huge roaches as well. So many other factors—beam, weight, and hull shape, to name a few—enter into a safety equation that it's hard to draw a line between safe and unsafe boats; but I would say that if masthead to waterline is more than 150 percent of waterline length, look out! If the mainsail has full battens and a big roach, that ratio had better be reduced to 140 percent.

If you do all your voyaging along the coast, you don't have to have a sailboat that will survive hurricanes. Several years ago Richard Suriani bought a 33-foot trailerable trimaran. It had been designed to compete against the Gougeons' experimental boats, and I believe that sometimes it almost succeeded. Its wing mast was about 25 percent of mainsail area, and the boat was nearly as wide as it was long, and not heavy. Richard kept it on a mooring back of Sandy Hook, and he had some fun dusting off motorboats with it. Once he sailed it in a race as far as the Brooklyn shore, trouncing a whole fleet of Hobie Cats. Originally he thought he'd sail it to Block Island, but after a few daysails even Richard thought better of that. Last December he still hadn't hauled it, and a bad northeaster plucked it from its mooring, smashing it against the Navy pier. He showed me what he'd salvaged, and the whole pile would have fit into a suitcase. The boat was insured, and Richard had just bought a 33-foot Dragonfly, with a mast fifty-some feet off the water. It will be interesting to see what he does with that.

Even coastwise multihulls, never out of range of NOAA forecasts, should be able to stand up to a gale. Winds build quickly sometimes, and forecasters are more interested in temperature than in wind speed. Nearer land or at the beginning of gale-force winds, waves won't be as high as Beaufort predicts, but I wouldn't want to be out in Richard's last boat in anything more than a force 5.

The people who are now offering designs for very fast voyaging multihulls—boats which, in my opinion, are not able to stand up to a storm, let alone a hurricane—will sometimes say that older designs were slower because the technology wasn't available to make them faster. It's

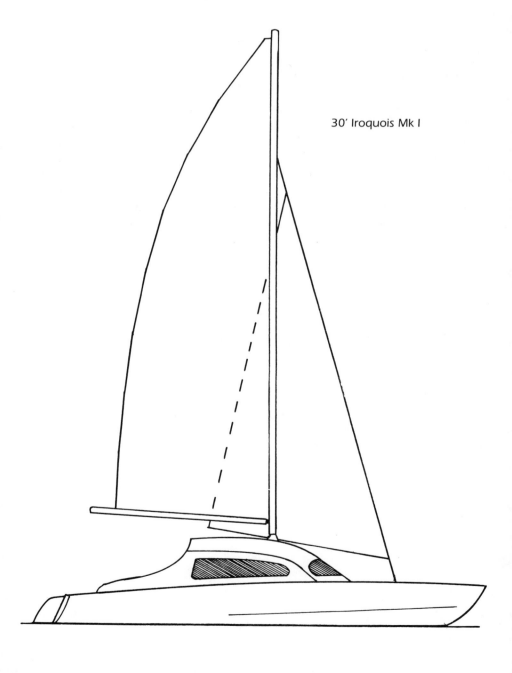

30′ Iroquois Mk I

just evolution, and you can't fight it. That absolutely is not true. The first Iroquois catamaran on the market was a lighter boat with a taller, more efficient rig than the Mk II. You have only to look at the drawing to see that the Mk I, as she came to be called, was a faster boat, but she needed reefing sooner.

Sailcraft built about 100 of them. Mike Ellison entered one in the first Round Britain Race in 1966. Kelsall won with his 42-foot trimaran *Toria*, but Ellison's Iroquois, the shortest of the 10 finishers, came in third over all. For much of the 2000 miles Ellison kept the main sheet in his hand. When the molds were worn out (the heat of curing fiberglass distorts a mold), Sailcraft went back to the designer for a slower, safer boat. The Iroquois Mk II still is no pig, twenty-some years down the road; but it makes you wonder whether a fourth factor—safety—hasn't been added to the old compromise of speed, comfort, and economy. For me, safety has always been an absolute consideration, not a quality to be compromised.

Multihulls certainly have evolved. The wider spacing of catamaran hulls, the better placement of trimaran floats, and the improved shapes of all hulls, especially forward, makes it safe to carry more sail on the newer designs. The question is, how much more?

Appendix 1:
Four Voyaging Multihulls

TWO RABBITS was built one hull at a time in the entire downstairs of a Philadelphia row house. She was named after the bus line (Ometochtli, meaning two rabbits in Nahuatl) that served the Mexican town where I lived several winters, writing novels. She was assembled at the Philadelphia Seaplane Base, and launched in 1974.

She was James Wharram's Hinemoa design, modified by bringing the sheer up to the top of the bulwarks shown on the plans, and eliminating the bulwarks so that the connecting beams were no longer discreetly hidden, like the legs of a Victorian piano. She had the biggest houses I dared put on her, and about twice the interior cubic of a standard Hinemoa. I am sure that in the hurricane the added buoyancy of that interior volume saved our lives. Without it she would have been overwhelmed.

She carried us up and down the Delaware Bay and River innumerable times, to Indian River and Chincoteague, to Fire Island, to New England four times, and of course to Bermuda in 1975. She was capable of astonishing bursts of speed in the right conditions. Once, beating down Delaware Bay into a force 6, she overhauled Reese Palley and his Westsail 32. We were sailing and taking some spray, but he was motoring and puking into the seas that were sweeping his boat from stem to stern. Afterward, he wrote an advertising blurb for Westsail, telling how his boat proved her seaworthiness that day.

Rabbits was a wonderful sea boat, but slow in light air unless the squaresail could be set. Voyaging, she averaged 65 to 70 miles a day. To windward in a seaway, she made good no more than 1-1/2 knots. We sold her after we built *Vireo*, and her fourth owner trucked her to a lake in the Poconos. Last we heard, she was for sale there for $500. She was sheathed with nylon cloth and polyester resin over a good deal of sapwood. Whoever owns her today, I wish him well.

*   *   *

Vireo was built in Cape May in the spring and summer of 1978, and launched in time to shake down to Nantucket. A vireo is a green finch

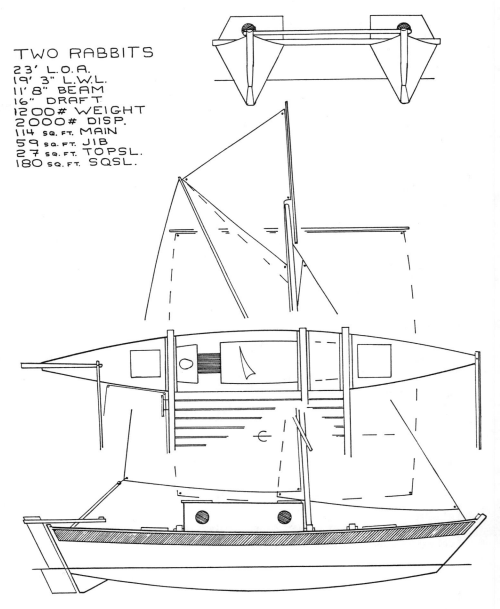

TWO RABBITS
23' L.O.A.
19' 3" L.W.L.
11' 8" BEAM
16" DRAFT
1200# WEIGHT
2000# DISP.
114 SQ. FT. MAIN
59 SQ. FT. JIB
27 SQ. FT. TOPSL.
180 SQ. FT. SQSL.

TWO RABBITS

with a penchant for going to sea. More than once an exhausted vireo came aboard *Two Rabbits* many miles offshore, and spent the night perched on a soup bowl in the galley.

Vireo is a Wharram-inspired design. At the time, Wharram's only designs of this length had his 45-degree racing V-hulls, and we wanted the interior volume of his 60-degree cruising V-hulls. We chopped her off with transom sterns and built her monocoque. All her materials were first class, except the Aerolite glue that gradually washed out of her joins.

She took us on a 10-month voyage to the Azores, Portugal, Gibraltar, Canaries, and Antilles in 1979-80. For the two long passages, we had two indomitable crew: Ruth Wharram going east, and João Fraga coming west. This book is dedicated to them.

Carol and I sailed her doublehanded to Bermuda in 1981. In 1982, she wasn't launched, because we flew to visit my son in Australia. In 1983, we started for the Azores in her, but the first gale revealed that she was leaking at every seam. We nursed her to Horta and sold her water-logged carcass there. Surprisingly, she survived.

She was almost as good a sea boat as *Two Rabbits*, and despite her squat rig, she was very much faster in light air. She averaged 104 miles a day on long passages, and to windward in a seaway she made good 2-1/2 knots. We won a couple of races with her in Horta, and since then her Azorean owners have won a couple more.

She has had so many different owners over there that once, when one of them decided to give a party for all, we could hardly sit down around a 12-foot dining table. Vireo means "I am green" in Latin, but one of her Azorean owners painted her blue.

Cruising and racing among the islands, she takes less green water over her cabins, and that makes her more habitable. However, João reports that she is much neglected in the last year, because the present owners have bought another boat (a monohull!), and her future is in question. When we sold her there 10 years ago, we imagined she had very little future at all.

*   *   *

Our Hummingbird was designed and built in Tuckahoe in 1983-84, and was shaken down to New England that summer. Her name is *Verdelhão*, which is Portuguese for "vireo," and that name made many friends for us among the Portuguese fishermen of New England. However, when I began selling plans for her, *Hummingbird* made discussion easier.

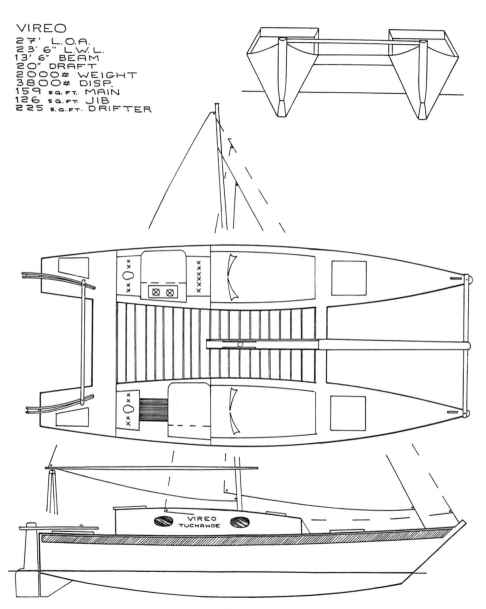

VIREO
27' L.O.A.
23' 6" L.W.L.
13' 6" BEAM
20" DRAFT
2000# WEIGHT
3800# DISP.
159 sq.ft. MAIN
126 sq.ft. JIB
225 s.q.ft. DRIFTER

VIREO
TUCKAHOE

VIREO

Between the building of her floats and her main hull, I had a building commission, and decided to rig her fractional rather than masthead. This required new upper shroud chainplates farther aft on the floats, and as I never removed the first pair, we were often asked why they were there. We'd say, "just in case," and people would nod sagely.

She took us to New England four times; to Norfolk and up the Virginia Inside Passage; to the Bahamas one hot and windless July; to the Azores, Senegal, and Cayenne in 1987-88; and to Horta again in 1991, where we sold her to João's brother José at the top of her form. In our hands and his, she has won nearly every race she has entered. Today, thanks to her skipper as well as her design, she remains the boat to beat in any Azorean race. She regularly crosses the finish line third or fourth in a field of 40 boats, nearly all of them longer than she is; and the skimpy multihull fleet there cannot deal with her handicap at all.

On ocean passages, when her rudder wasn't giving trouble, she averaged 125 miles a day, and in a seaway to windward she made good 4-1/2 knots. Her top speed, limited by her 8-to-1 main hull, was probably no greater than *Vireo*'s or *Two Rabbits*'; but her average speeds were very much higher. In winds of force 9 and more, she could not be left to herself. She would lie ahull under any sail combination, and if steered, she could not be slowed down. She needed a drogue. Nevertheless, she is wonderful fun to sail in light and moderate weather, and the next time we're in Horta we hope José will give us a ride.

*   *   *

Dandy is a nautical term for a traditional two-masted rig, though the two masts are not traditionally side-by-side. We also chose the name because, having time and some money to build her, we aimed for a higher quality of fit and finish than our other voyaging multihulls had had. Her yellow topsides and cabin sides aim to be gaudy. She was built in Tuckahoe, and launched in 1992.

Our other multihulls had been entirely plywood construction, but *Dandy* has molded fiberglass hull bottoms to make her round-bottomed, and plywood from there up. She lacks the payload for ocean crossings, but we lack the ambition too. For coastal voyages, she is the most habitable multihull we've owned. With a plywood-and-foam filler beside the main daggerboard trunk, she will sleep a third crew. However, she is too small—both in payload and in space—to take a third person for more than a few days at a time.

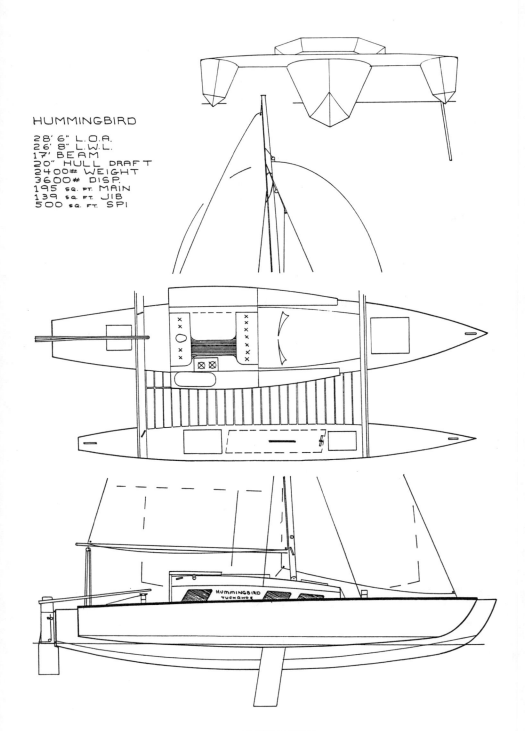

HUMMINGBIRD

28' 6" L.O.A.
26' 8" L.W.L.
17' BEAM
20" HULL DRAFT
2400# WEIGHT
3600# DISP.
195 sq. ft. MAIN
139 sq. ft. JIB
500 sq. ft. SPI

HUMMINGBIRD

Dandy was designed as a test platform for the biplane rig, but her comfort and handiness have endeared her to us. As sailors grow older, the wiser ones move to smaller boats. Age cannot be easy, but it can at least be convenient. If we are still voyaging ten years from now, it is likely to be in a smaller boat than this one.

The forward daggerboard was added to correct the sailplan imbalance of the biplane rig. With it, the center of resistance is far forward of the center of effort, but it gave her a good helm in her second season. Apparently biplanes have very different balancing requirements than sloops. I hope that with her new sloop rig, this second board can be removed.

We've only sailed *Dandy* on two summer voyages to New England, and raced her a bit with NEMA. That may be all we ever do with her. We like the summer weather up there, and the rocky shore, and the distances between ports. The passages up and back give us a night or two out on the ocean, and a chance to practice our old skills. The new rig that I am now drawing will be quite like the *Hummingbird* rig, scaled down. We've had enough experiments for a while. We think she'll make a dandy sloop.

DANDY

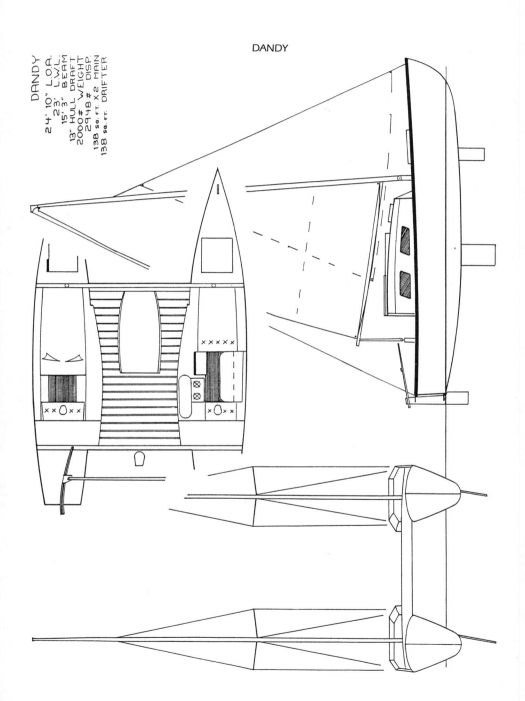

DANDY
24' 10" L.O.A.
23' L.W.L.
15' 3" BEAM
13" HULL DRAFT
2000# WEIGHT
2948# DISP.
138 sq. ft. X2 MAIN
138 sq. ft. DRIFTER

Appendix 2:
Designers and Builders
Mentioned in this Book

Jim Brown
Box 550
North, VA 23128

Russ Brown
no permanent address

Vance Buhler
Buhler Yachts
Calliaqua, St. Vincent
WEST INDIES

Rudy Choy Designs
677 Ala Moana Blvd. #502
Honolulu, HI 96813

Norman Cross
Cross Multihull Designs
4326 Ashton
San Diego, CA 92110

Lock Crowther Designs
P.O. Box 35, Turramurra
Sydney, NSW 2074
AUSTRALIA

Dragonfly Trimarans
Quorning Boats Aps.
Skaerbaek, Frederica,
DK 7000 DENMARK

Ian Farrier
Farrier Marine
P.O. Box 40675
Bellevue, WA 98015

Walter Greene
Greene Marine
RR #1, Box 343
Yarmouth, ME 04096

Gougeon Brothers
P.O. Box 908
Bay City, MI 48707

Edward Horstman
Tri-Star Trimarans and
Catamarans
P.O. Box 286
Venice, CA 90291

Thomas Firth Jones
Jones Boats
Box 391
Tuckahoe, NJ 08250

Derek Kelsall
K-Yacht Designs, Inc.
171 Dover Road
Sandwich, Kent CT13 0DD
UNITED KINGDOM

Greg Ketterman Designs
3215 Hackett St.
Long Beach, CA 90808

Tom LaMers
777 Dayton St.
Yellow Springs, OH 45387

John R. Marples
4530 Firmont Dr. SE
Port Orchard, WA 98366

Prout Catamarans
Kings Close, Charfleet Ind. Est.
Canvey Is., Essex SS8 7TL
UNITED KINGDOM

Dick Newick
5 Sheppards Way
Kittery Point, ME 03905

Bernard Rhodes
voyaging: no permanent address

Seawind Catamarans
287 Ramsey Rd.
Haberfield, NSW 2045
AUSTRALIA

John Shuttleworth Yacht Designs
7 Marina Walk, High Street
Cowes, Isle of Wight PO31 7XJ
UNITED KINGDOM

Tony Smith
Performance Cruising
P.O. Box 381
Mayo, MD 21106

Walker Wingsail Systems PLC
Devonport Royal Dockyard
Plymouth, Devon PL1 4SE
UNITED KINGDOM

James Wharram Designs
Greenbank Road, Devoran
Truro, Cornwall TR3 6PJ
UNITED KINGDOM

Chris White Designs, Inc.
48 Bush St.
S. Dartmouth, MA 02748

Index

Also from Sheridan House

Handbook of Offshore Cruising—The Dream and Reality of Modern Ocean Sailing by Jim Howard
The big new reference book for every cruiser.

The Sailing Dictionary, Second Edition by Joachim Schult
This comprehensive reference work has over 3500 entries and 1500 line drawings.

The Boating Bible—An Essential Handbook for Every Sailor by Jim Murrant
Contains all the information sailors need in one easy-to-use volume.

Marine Electrical and Electronics Bible by John C. Payne
A must for professionals as well as for weekend or long-distance voyagers.

A Cruising Guide to the Caribbean—Including the North Coast of South America, Central America and Yucatan by William T. Stone and Anne M. Hays.
Entertaining and up-to-date volume.

Swan—The Second Voyage by Jim Moore
More adventures of Jim and Molly Moore aboard *Swan*. A delightful tale.

America's favorite sailing books